ASL® 2 – A framework for applicatio

Other publications by Van Haren Publishing

Van Haren Publishing (VHP) specializes in titles on Best Practices, methods and standards within four domains:
- IT management
- Architecture (Enterprise and IT)
- Business management and
- Project management

Van Haren Publishing offers a wide collection of whitepapers, templates, free e-books, trainer material etc. in the **Van Haren Publishing Knowledge Base**: www.vanharen.net for more details.

Van Haren Publishing is also publishing on behalf of leading organizations and companies: ASLBiSL Foundation, CA, Centre Henri Tudor, Gaming Works, Getronics, IACCM, IAOP, IPMA-NL, ITSqc, NAF, Ngi, PMI-NL, PON, Quint, The Open Group, The Sox Institute, Tmforum.

Topics are (per domain):

IT (Service) Management / IT Governance
ABC of ICT
ASL®
BiSL®
CATS CM®
CMMI®
CoBIT
Frameworx
ISO 17799
ISO 27001
ISO 27002
ISO/IEC 20000
ISPL
IT Service CMM
ITIL®
ITSM
MOF
MSF
SABSA

Architecture (Enterprise and IT)
Archimate®
GEA®
SOA
TOGAF®

Business Management
Contract Management
EFQM
eSCM
ISA-95
ISO 9000
ISO 9001:2000
OPBOK
Outsourcing
SAP
SixSigma
SOX
SqEME®

Project/Programme/ Risk Management
A4-Projectmanagement
ICB / NCB
MINCE®
M_o_R®
MSP™
P3O®
PMBOK® Guide
PRINCE2®

For the latest information on VHP publications, visit our website: www.vanharen.net.

APPLICATION SERVICES LIBRARY

ASL® 2
A framework for Application Management

Remko van der Pols

Colophon

Title:	ASL® 2 – A framework for Application Management An ASL BiSL Foundation publication, www.aslbislfoundation.org
Author:	Remko van der Pols
Text editor Dutch edition:	Machteld Meijer
Text editor English edition:	Steve Newton
Review team Dutch edition:	Review board: Lucille van der Hagen, chairman (ASL BiSL Foundation) Reijer de Boer (Capgemini) Frances van Haagen (The Lifecycle Company) Annita Krol (Achmea-GITS) Imro Nanoha (Ministry of Defense/IVENT) Hans Smorenberg (ASR Netherlands) André Smulders (Ordina) Other reviewers: Yvette Backer (Capgemini) Machteld Meijer (VHP/Maise) René Sieders (The Lifecycle Company)
Review team English edition:	René Sieders (The Lifecycle Company) Mark Smalley (ASL BiSL Foundation)
Publisher:	Van Haren Publishing, Zaltbommel, www.vanharen.net
ISBN Hard copy:	978 90 8753 313 7
ISBN eBook:	978 90 8753 822 4
Edition:	Second edition, first impression, June 2012
Layout and DTP:	CO2 Premedia, Amersfoort
Copyright:	© Van Haren Publishing 2012

For further information about Van Haren Publishing, please send an e-mail to: info@vanharen.net

No part of this publication may be reproduced in any form by print, photo print, microfilm or any other means without written permission by the publisher.

Although this edition has been composed with the utmost care, neither the author(s) nor the publisher can accept any responsibility whatsoever for damages caused by possible errors and/or imperfections in this edition.

TRADEMARK NOTICES
ASL® and BiSL® are registered trade marks of the ASL BiSL Foundation.
ITIL® is a registered trade mark of the Cabinet Office.

Foreword

ASL

This book describes ASL, Application Services Library, a framework for application management.

As a public domain framework, ASL is the most significant application management process framework. ASL provides you with support for the implementation of application management in your organization. In addition, ASL's best practices, which can be found on the ASL BiSL Foundation website, help you execute this task more efficiently. ASL is also a knowledge network. This knowledge network, aimed at professionalizing the process of application management, has developed by sharing knowledge and a distribution of best practices.

ASL interfaces with other frameworks such as BiSL® (framework for business information management) and ITIL®.

The implications and goals

Naturally, the implementation of processes should lead to an end result that creates optimum satisfaction for users and employees. Requirements for services, service delivery, and the application management environment can be vastly different. Therefore, according to the ASL approach, processes are pragmatically implemented, based on the specific organizational and environmental needs. During implementation, the following developments and requirements are taken into account, among others:
- External orientation. Processes must link explicitly to the demands and expectations of the external community and must constantly adjust themselves to suit developments in that community.
- Multiple suppliers. IT service delivery is almost always performed by multiple suppliers, so service delivery must fit into a situation involving multiple suppliers, and the processes must take into account the position of the organization in this situation.
- Information chains. Information is, to a large extent, digitally delivered by organizations in the external community, where the various information facilities of various organizations are linked to one another. These information chains are no longer an exception to the rule; however, the external community can rarely be directly managed.
- Anticipation. Processes tend to be reactive and rigid by nature because they are initially implemented for the purpose of control and organization, but predictable results and predictable service delivery are no longer sufficient. The organization and the service delivery are expected to keep up with current and future developments, while anticipating implicit needs and issues.

The changes

This book describes ASL 2, and you are correct in assuming that this is the second version of the framework. We will tell you more about the name later but first we will discuss the changes. ASL has been changed, but not completely.

Because of the future-proof and technology-independent design of ASL, its main structure remains unchanged. There are, however, underlying changes. The growing market dynamics have resulted in far-reaching changes to the managing and strategic processes within ASL. Business processes have also changed, but these changes are less dramatic; this has enabled a pragmatic growth scenario towards ASL 2. This was also taken into account during the design of ASL 2.

Such an evolutionary renewal fits in well with the ASL vision: don't change something that works well. A new framework is not a goal in itself and would not be very useful to organizations that have already invested heavily in the introduction of the previous version.

Despite everything, with regard to content, ASL has become somewhat more complex. The growing need for flexibility in the market has made this inevitable. As a result, the focus has been on suppliers of standard solutions, components, packages, etc., because that is the direction in which the market is heading.

To assist in dealing with this complexity, design and implementation factors have been identified to help address the impact of the market trends on the processes which you are going to implement.

Why call it ASL 2?

The name *ASL 2* emphasizes the fact that the new version is tailor-made for the current situation. However, the framework is upward-compatible to a large degree. Existing ASL users will not experience any limitations, but will discover additional possibilities.

Contributions

Many people have contributed to the development of this new version of ASL. The ASL Review Board has continually followed the development of the framework, kept a critical eye on it, and reviewed the results. My colleagues at The Lifecycle Company and at Getronics PinkRoccade (now Capgemini) have also contributed.

Constructive observations have also come from the issue log, and I would like to thank the people who sent them. However, most thanks should be given to the customers and users who delivered the practical experience leading to the creation of ASL 2 and ASL as a whole.

Remko van der Pols

Review team Dutch edition:
Lucille van der Hagen, chairman (ASL BiSL Foundation)
Reijer de Boer (Capgemini)
Frances van Haagen (The Lifecycle Company)
Annita Krol (Achmea-GITS)
Imro Nanoha (Ministry of Defense/IVENT)
Hans Smorenberg (ASR Netherlands)
André Smulders (Ordina)

VIII

Contents

Foreword V

1 Introduction 1
  1.1 Goal of this book 1
  1.2 Main changes in ASL 2 in relation to ASL 1 1
  1.3 Structure of the book 2

2 Application management in the 21st century 5
  2.1 Introduction and chapter structure 5
  2.2 Developments 6
  2.3 Impact on application management and its design 11
  2.4 Impact and consequences within ASL 18

3 The ASL framework 29
  3.1 The framework for application management 29
  3.2 Structure of the ASL framework 33

4 Application support processes 35
  4.1 Introduction 35
  4.2 Use support 40
  4.3 Configuration management 47
  4.4 IT operation management 51
  4.5 Continuity management 59

5 Application maintenance and renewal processes 65
  5.1 Introduction 65
  5.2 Impact analysis 69
  5.3 Design 75
  5.4 Realization 81
  5.5 Testing 85
  5.6 Implementation 90

6 Connecting processes 97
  6.1 Introduction 97
  6.2 Change management 98
  6.3 Software control and distribution 104

7 Management processes 111
  7.1 Introduction and management topics 111
  7.2 Contract management 116
  7.3 Planning and control 124
  7.4 Quality management 131

7.5	Financial management	136
7.6	Supplier management	141

8 Application strategy 149
8.1	Introduction	149
8.2	IT developments strategy	152
8.3	Customer organizations strategy	155
8.4	Customer environment strategy	158
8.5	Application life cycle management	163
8.6	Application portfolio management	168

9 Application management organization strategy.........................175
9.1	Introduction	175
9.2	Account and market definition	179
9.3	Capabilities definition	184
9.4	Technology definition	188
9.5	Supplier definition	193
9.6	Service delivery definition	197

10 Using ASL...201
10.1	Introduction	201
10.2	Pitfalls	202
10.3	Design and implementation factors and strategies	205
10.4	NEN 3434 and the maturity levels	206
10.5	Additional tools	208
10.6	Integration of services and connection between the models	209

A	Frequently asked questions (FAQs)	215
B	ASL 2 modifications to ASL 1	219
C	Diagram techniques	225
D	Consistency between ASL and BiSL	227
E	Literature and further reading	231

Index...233

1 Introduction

1.1 Goal of this book

This book describes the ASL 2 public domain framework for application management. It describes a framework for application management processes as identified by ASL, together with more detailed descriptions of these processes. The book is used by the ASL BiSL Foundation to determine what ASL is. It is also the core study guide for the official ASL 2 Foundation examination, available via APMG.

This book has been written on the principle that the reader is familiar with application management, with the way in which it is executed, and with the activities concerned. It is not an application management textbook.

It contains tips and suggestions to assist in the implementation of processes, but it is not an implementation instruction manual: that is too complex an aspect to describe here. However, this book does form a starting point from which to set up application management processes.

1.2 Main changes in ASL 2 in relation to ASL 1

ASL 2 is a new version of the old ASL-framework, which we now call ASL 1. The main differences are outlined below, as are the most significant reasons for these differences.

1.2.1 The core changes
The structure of ASL's main features has remained largely unchanged. An in-depth analysis indicated that it was set up in a future-proof and structured manner.

However, this does not mean that little has changed: quite the opposite. Over the past decades, the market has become much more dynamic and complex, and the positions of internal and external suppliers cannot be taken for granted. The most significant changes to ASL 2 are a result of these developments. The most important changes are:
- From internal focus to external focus.
  It has been observed that a uniform model for service delivery and process design does not work. The starting point for designing processes can be found in the external community and in how the organization fits into this external community. This has led to many degrees of freedom, which are all differently interpreted in the design and implementation of processes. Suppliers of standard solutions (such as packages) will be identified easily in ASL 2 as custom suppliers or applications management organizations that focus on integration.

- From single supplier to multiple suppliers.
  Many frameworks, including ASL 1, mostly still assume that an organization has a single (primary) IT-supplier. There is a clear trend towards the componentization of IT services. Nowadays, the presence of multiple suppliers is the standard. In addition, multiple suppliers are often required to take care of IT services for individual parts of the greater application landscape.
- From information processes to chain information processes.
  Over the past decades, the linking of information provisions among organizations has become common practice. Working with information chains has become the standard. This is complicated by the fact that the external community can rarely be directly managed.
- From stabilizing and organizing to anticipating.
  Frameworks appear to be focused on implementing processes in order to create stability and clarity. As a result, management organizations are often considered to be rigid. The future demands constant changes to services and applications, constant adjustment of the scope in which activities are performed, and thus also the constant adaptation of processes.

1.2.2 Impact of these trends on ASL 1

The developments outlined above have changed the content of the ASL-framework to a larger degree than would have initially been expected. They have had a large impact at management- and strategic levels. These processes have undergone fundamental changes and a number of new processes have been added at these levels.

The business processes have also been affected by various changes, but these have been less drastic. Here, the processes have been adjusted to suit the activities performed in a specific environment and to the provision of services in conjunction with other suppliers. This has not created change for the sake of change: change is not an objective in itself. The result was a logical growth trajectory following from ASL 1. Previous investments in process implementation were not wasted because of the introduction of ASL 2 and the change in name. In some cases, extra attention has been paid to upward compatibility. Existing implementations of the majority of business processes will easily comply with ASL 2.

In addition, this book also describes implementation parameters by process cluster. These are parameters that have a major impact on the way in which a process is implemented.

1.3 Structure of the book

Chapter 2 provides an in-depth description of the developments and underlying principles of ASL 2. This chapter is quite detailed to provide insight into the challenges presented by application management, and also substantiates the options within ASL 2. It is a point of departure from which to gain an understanding of ASL 2 and its changes.

The framework is outlined in Chapter 3. In this chapter, the ASL 2 process clusters are described and explained. The next chapters elaborate on the various process clusters. Chapters 4 to 9 describe the various ASL clusters, starting with the operational clusters. These chapters have a consistent structure. The first paragraph describes the structure, the classification, and the implementation parameters of the clusters. Thereafter, individual processes are described in the following paragraphs. From this point in the book, when mentioning ASL, we are referring to the new ASL.

Chapter 10, the final chapter, focuses on the introduction and implementation of ASL. It is not intended to be an actual instruction manual for the introduction of ASL. If that were the case, this book would be twice its size. It is merely meant as a starting point.

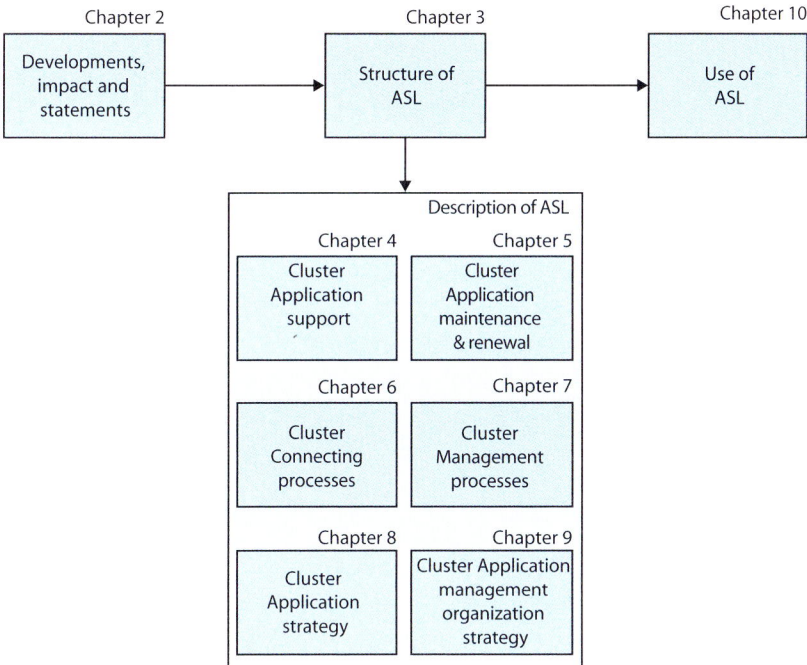

Figure 1.1 Structure of the book

Explicit attention is paid to two appendices. Appendix A contains the FAQs – Frequently Asked Questions. A number of commonly encountered questions or queries are listed here along with their answers. If you have any questions, you are likely to find the answers here.

Appendix B briefly summarizes the most significant changes at cluster- and process level in relation to ASL 1.

Further appendices cover the diagramming techniques for process models, consistency between ASL and BiSL, and a brief bibliography.

2 Application management in the 21st century

> **ASL statements**
>
> - The complexity and diversity of IT services has shown strong growth.
>
> - Specialization and other trends lead to multiple supplier service delivery for customers.
>
> - As a result, the integration of IT services is becoming the issue.
>
> - Integration can only take place if interfacing is clearly defined.
>
> - ASL can act as a framework for service components as well as a tool for service integration.

2.1 Introduction and chapter structure

This chapter deals with the application management environment, the developments that take place in it, its impact on the operation and control of application management and, finally, its interpretation within ASL.

This chapter will also benefit (operational) application managers, since knowledge about the correct goals, preconditions and rules of the game is essential for the execution and implementation of application management and its processes. Knowledge about processes and process steps is no longer sufficient.

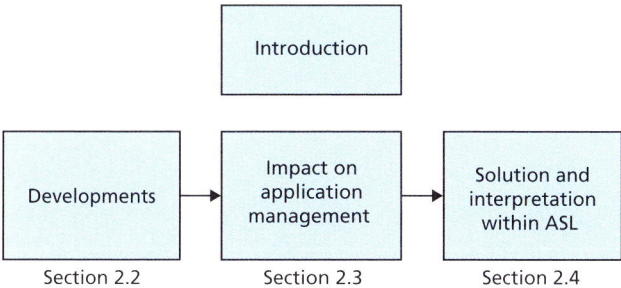

Figure 2.1 Structure of Chapter 2

In section 2.2, a number of developments are discussed, which apply to the past few decades and the next few years. These developments have resulted in multiple supplier service delivery becoming the norm.

The aims of various suppliers with different services and varied angles of approach have led to an increase in the complexity of the control of IT service delivery. The question that needs an answer is how these supplier chains should be controlled.

Two solutions for this problem are described in section 2.3. Should control be maximized and be made uniform, or should the required control be concentrated (minimized) by only focusing on essential matters?

Section 2.4 examines the direction chosen in ASL and this approach is adapted according to its interpretation within ASL.

2.2 Developments

This section discusses a number of developments that have occurred in the past few years and which are expected to happen in future years. These developments have a major impact on the organization of application management and the way in which application management must perform and position itself in the environment.

It concerns the following developments:
- Division into IT management domains.
- Subdivision of the demand organization within the user organization.
- Increasing componentization and specialization of services.
- Growing number of forms of services and differentiation between them.
- Necessity for specialization.

2.2.1 Division into IT management domains

A significant development that has occurred in the past few decades is the division between demand- and supply organizations. The normal position of the internal IT organization as IT service provider for an organization has disappeared. Because of developments such as outsourcing (including offshoring) and the professionalization of the internal IT organization, explicit customer-contractor relationships have come into existence. This has led to the creation of explicit demand organizations.

The division into the management domains has gone a step further. Here we see an even further separation between application management and infrastructure management. Looijen and Delen's model, with its three forms of IT management, has thus become a reality. Looijen and Delen identify three forms of IT management:
- Business information management;
- Application management;
- Infrastructure management.

ASL, as its name suggests, only focuses on application management, the second form of IT management.

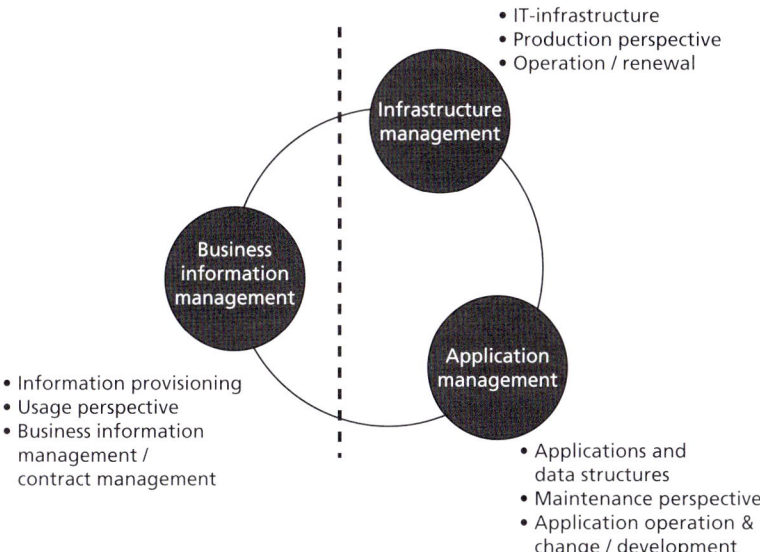

Figure 2.2 Looijen and Delen's model

Application management does not operate on its own. It does so in an environment, also involving other forms of management, such as business information management and infrastructure management. Looijen has identified these forms of IT management in the book *Beheer van Informatiesystemen* (see Figure 2.2). The division is also discussed in lectures and books by Thiadens, but there is an ongoing debate in the Netherlands about the naming of the forms of IT management and the business processes.

Business information management is, on behalf of the user organization, responsible for the management of the functionalities of an IT facility and the support of users. Business information management thus acts as owner and customer of the information system. BiSL is a well-known public domain framework.

Application management is responsible for the management of the application and the databases. This is the party that manages and maintains the information system (application). Requirements for this form of management include knowledge of programming, information system development, design, and impact analysis. Core qualities here are in-depth knowledge of the customer or (at least) in-depth knowledge of the customer's business processes.

Infrastructure management is responsible for managing the operation of the information system, including equipment, programming, and data collection. Another commonly used term describing this is technical infrastructure management. In brief, this is the organization that runs the information systems and ensures that the infrastructure remains in good order. This is also often called the computing center. A well-known framework that is often used in this domain is ITIL.

2.2.2 Growing number of demand organizations: differentiation in demand

The management of information provisioning within user organizations (business information management) is becoming more complex and more differentiated. The central management and coordination of information provisioning within a user organization is no longer something that goes without saying.

The significance of IT has caused the most important stakeholders in business ranks to independently manage certain aspects of information provisioning themselves. Thus, there are often separate customers for e.g. financial information provisioning, personnel information provisioning, various components of primary business processes, generic facilities, and infrastructure. As a result, various separate information domains have been created.

Information chains, in which multiple different organizations have become responsible for the functioning as a whole, have been created. Consequently, customers or co-decision makers can be situated outside the user organization. Each of these organizations experiences a different information chain.

Application management thus deals with a demand organization that is growing ever more complex.

2.2.3 Increasing specialization and componentization

A second development is about specialization and reuse. For decades, IT has been characterized by explosive growth in expansion and effort. To keep costs at manageable levels (similar explosive growth of costs would mean that organizations would have to invest virtually all their resources in IT), organizations employ various strategies:
- Reuse of existing components forming part of the IT landscape. Examples of this include legacy renewal (modernization of existing systems) and the retention and improvement of existing components in future design. The 'legacy is here to stay' idea has broken through.
- Partial use of new components, such as the use of standard objects, packages, shared solutions such as Application Service Provider (ASP), Software-as-a-Service (SaaS) or shared infrastructure. The use of basic components and objects for the construction of applications also has become common practice.
- Transfer of functionality to technology. Functionalities previously programmed into applications, such as document information, workflow control, authorization and the exchange of data are now supported by separate resources and technologies.

Similar developments have also taken place in infrastructure management. A higher degree of freedom than previously experienced now applies to the interface between an application and the infrastructure.

The amount of resources and technologies required to develop, maintain and manage an application has greatly increased. As a consequence the number of suppliers has also grown.

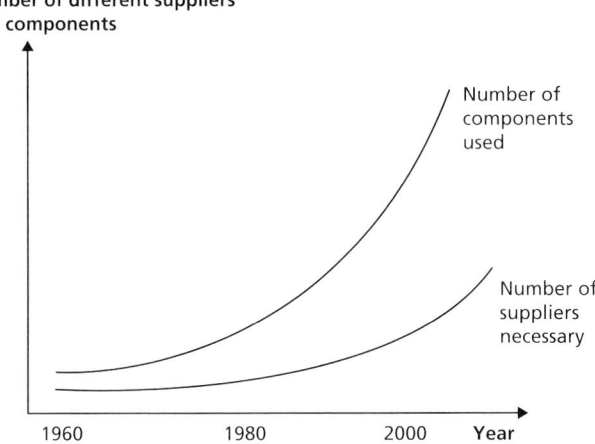

Figure 2.3 Resources and suppliers necessary for information provisioning

2.2.4 Differentiation between forms of service delivery

Forms of service delivery have also become more varied. During the previous century, there were at most two forms of application management service delivery:
- Development, maintenance and management of custom systems.
- Use of standard applications (and therefore the development and maintenance of these packages).

There was also a clear division between development on the one hand, and the usage phase (including support and maintenance) on the other. Over the past few years, the lines between these forms of service delivery have become blurred:
- The division between support and maintenance on the one hand, and initial development on the other, has faded. The systematic renewal of existing systems, the integration of new components into old systems, upgrading and rebuilding are all forms of service provision that divide maintenance and initial development.
- The strict division between packages and custom made has disappeared due to the use of standard components and platforms. Apart from that, both ends of the spectrum simply continue to exist.
- The traditional division of roles between application management and infrastructure management has also become more varied. In practice, numerous hybrid forms exist, such as ASP or SaaS.

Multiple forms of delivery
Many forms of service delivery have developed within application management. Examples of such forms of service delivery include, among others:
- The adjustor/implementer or integrator that amalgamates or combines services to create a functional whole.
- The party that produces a specific component (forming part of this whole), based on specifications provided by the integrator.
- The organization that supplies a standard product or standard component that is used by many organizations.
- The producer of configurable platforms (such as SAP or other packages) that are used and configured by third parties.
- The organization that configures and maintains such platforms for customers, either with or without integration with the underlying infrastructure.
- The organization that supplies custom services to an individual customer, either with or without integration with other systems or the infrastructure.
- The organization that supports a custom application, supports and maintains a custom application, or supports, maintains, and is in charge of the renewal of a custom application.

These forms have a significant impact on how the processes are implemented and operated.

> The application management organization operates together with infrastructure suppliers and other application suppliers. Sometimes an application management organization is responsible for the functioning of the entire service delivery, but this is not always the case.

Multiple forms of control and invoicing
Differentiation has occurred in the various forms of control and invoicing. In the past, job order costing based on time spent and materials used was the dominant model, but currently there is a clear trend towards working with cost units that are more recognizable to customers. Examples of cost units that are defined in more functional terms are function points, subscriptions or costs per service. Units related to the primary process of the customer (such as the number of customers of the customer) are not uncommon anymore.

2.2.5 Specialization of application management
Due to the separation of supply and demand, application management has entered an explicit competitive market. This is a major change for internal IT organizations. Application management organizations must now make conscious decisions about their future services and its core qualities.

They must simultaneously specialize in three areas:
- The market: the customer, type of customer (sector) or type of business process. Knowledge about the business processes, the market and/or the sector is often essential, since applications support or shape the customer's business processes.

- The type of service delivery: the type of application management service delivery (integrator, package supplier, custom supplier) and the way in which financing is set up. Each type varies in design and in the necessary expertise.
- The tools and technology used. Within application management, expertise and experience in the technology used remain a significant factor influencing the quality of services.

This is why application management must make decisions about the market sector (customers), the technology to be used, and the desired type(s) of services. The services that can be supplied only forms a small part of the total possible scope of services, so decisions must be made.

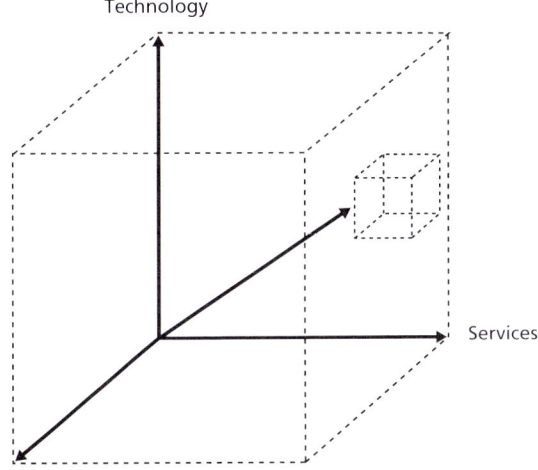

Figure 2.4 Three-way specialization for application management

Even more important than making the correct decisions is the implementation of this innovation strategy into a working scenario. After all, from a customer's point of view, a particular application management organization can be very easily exchanged for another one.

2.3 Impact on application management and its design

2.3.1 Introduction and summary

This section deals with the influence of these developments on application management. We will start with a brief summary. Further elaboration and differentiation will follow in the subsequent sections.

The developments outlined above lead to a situation in which multiple suppliers, as a rule, are necessary for service delivery. This leads to complex supplier constellations.

Two strategies can be used to make the service delivery process as a whole, and the various suppliers, manageable:
- The first strategy is the realization of uniformity and standardization.
- The second strategy is about focusing on managing the essentials and treating the rest as a 'black box'. Here the focus is on controlling the interfaces.

ASL mainly uses the latter strategy. This results in the following consequences:
- The interfaces between application management and the environment influence the design of application management to a large degree.
- Process design and control of the application management processes become primarily an internal matter for the IT service provider.
- The location, role and integration of service delivery into the environment define services and process design. The environment and environmental demands thus become the starting point for the process design.

2.3.2 Management of the whole: the challenge

Due to the developments described in section 2.2, complicated demand and supplier constellations appear. Figure 2.5 describes an example that is extremely simple when compared to the situations of somewhat larger organizations.

IT services consists of services provided by multiple independent parties. Most suppliers provide services to multiple organizations that have nothing to do with one another. It is not unusual for suppliers to provide the same solutions to

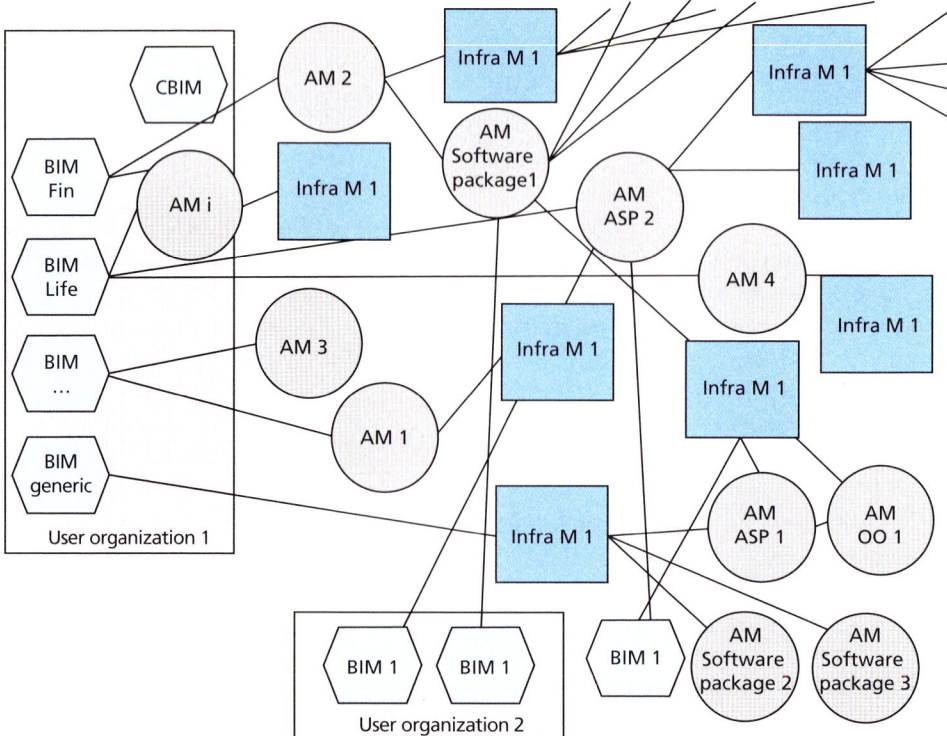

Figure 2.5 Modern supplier constellation

multiple parties (e.g. packages). This is why it is almost impossible to have just one customer organization being the director in this setting.

Unequivocal demands and unequivocal IT orchestration from a single point are (generally) no longer possible.

2.3.3 Solutions to this control problem
This growing operational complexity poses the question of how service delivery can be managed and controlled. Two strategies can be considered:
- The harmonization and standardizing of the service delivery chain. Processes are designed in such a way that they can be controlled or prescribed from a single point. To make this complexity manageable, the processes must be standardized and made uniform. This creates integral process chains on top of the service delivery chain. The essence of this strategy is maximization of control.
- The minimizing of control and focusing control on the components that are essential and well understood.

a. Integral processes and integral service delivery

The first way of solving this control problem is by creating a generically comprehensive IT organization, generically comprehensive processes and a central point from which everything is controlled. In order to keep this manageable, generic process models are needed, which bring everything together as much as possible.

It is plain to see that this approach will often be difficult to implement in practice:
- The first consequence is that suppliers will have to be fitted into a standard customer model. The integration of a supplier into multiple different integral customer processes is impossible, since every customer's demands, agreements, process implementations, and resources will differ.
- A second consequence is that this leads to a strong concentration of control in the area of information provisioning in a single (component of an) organization. A constant trend observed in the past few years is that control of information provisioning is further dispersed throughout the organization: in practice, a movement in the opposite direction is actually observed. Thus, the historically dominant position of the internal IT organization has completely disappeared.
- This has led to a high degree of inflexibility. If a customer changes to a different supplier, processes must be implemented all over again.
- And finally: the accountability and responsibility for results from the supplier are diminishing. After all, the process designer is primarily responsible for the desired result, because they have designed the controls.

b. Restricting control

According to the second strategy, complexity and control are minimized by especially focusing on the issues that are really important to the customer and which are within the field of expertise of the customer (e.g. use in business processes).

> *A comparison*
>
> Hardly anyone knows exactly what takes place when a car is taken in for servicing. Likewise, when buying a car, nobody knows how and with what it is produced. We are not familiar with the underlying processes and we also cannot be bothered with the details. The buyer does not want to control the integration of all the car factory's subcontractors, the car manufacturer, the garage and the garage's subcontractors into a single large process. This is impractical.
>
> On the other hand, the car buyer knows exactly how the car will be used. They know exactly what their demands and requirements are.

However, this control problem is not new and also not unique. Application management in particular has had to deal with the complexity of control, especially in the area of content. It concerns the question "How do we control the complex control structure within applications?".

For many years, the same strategies have been chosen and followed in achieving this. The final step here is SOA, Service Oriented Architecture.

> **SOA**
>
> In the development and maintenance of large-scale applications, a comparable control problem and a consequent development line for solving this control problem have been identified.
>
> The (immediate) solution was SOA or SaaS, but this was simply a step forward towards long term development. This development started with modular programming, in which programs were seen as a black box, and in which no use could be made of previous knowledge of the internal setup and structure of the program.
>
> The next step was object-oriented programming and development and, as a result of this, the identification of components. In this case, the internal data and the internal implementation of the data were invisible to the external community.
>
> In the step towards SOA and SaaS the entire implementation, the database management system in use and the infrastructure in use were, once again, invisible to the external community. Communication only took place via messages. Agreements about what should take place were sent by message and messages were returned containing results or confirmation of action.

The control of service delivery in the IT sphere is starting to behave in similar ways more and more:
- Multiple suppliers work together (whether or not required by a customer/business information management) and create a set of circumstances that provide a working information facility (compare the 'SOA' architecture).
- Here, every supplier has their own process and interpretation, which is not arranged or determined by a third party. This internal process design is seldom essential to the external community. The internal resources are also invisible to the external community (black box component approach).

- Only the interfacing and the guarantees are of importance. While products are exchanged and services employed between the various domains, these are produced, executed or consumed within the domains ("the messaging").

This approach holds various benefits for the customer and the supplier.
- It allows suppliers to be flexible. Because agreements only relate to the interfacing and not to the internal processes and the resources used by the supplier, it becomes easier to change suppliers. There is no dependency on internal processes or internal tooling.
- It offers flexibility in design. As has been indicated, the diversity of operations and processes is only unusually large in the application management sphere. A broad, all-encompassing standardized process will never provide the flexibility necessary for all the various situations, but from a demand point of view, this is not necessary. The supplier is permitted to implement their own process. All that counts is the result.

2.3.4 Consequences of this approach
The black box strategy has the following consequences:
- The interface between customer and supplier is becoming decisive. Because only 'buying' takes place on the exterior, the organizing/designing of the 'interface' is of critical interest to the demand organization as well as the supply organizations.
- The customer will not need to be as active in controlling the way in which a product is produced and the process used to produce it. Process, technology, and resources mainly become internal issues.
- In service delivery, the question is becoming "How is coherence and integration created?". This question applies to the service delivery as well as to the content of the solution (applications).

a. The 'interface' is becoming decisive

Because sales are 'merely' driven by the external appearance, the designing and reasoning processes contributed by customers and suppliers with regard to this interface are essential. This has led to a number of changes to this interface:
- The interfacing is becoming highly functional and output/outcome oriented. The demands on the design of the internal process and on how the solution is internally created have become less important. Whether the solution does what is expected or agreed upon and whether the agreed results or expectations are realized has is becoming important.
- Interfacing is becoming broader and, from an IT point of view, sometimes even immaterial or irrelevant. It does not only concern the functionalities of the solution and the services. The applicable conditions, the underlying intentions, the method of cooperation and the corresponding costs are part of the interfacing agreements. From an IT point of view, this could also include 'less relevant' issues, such as emotions ("Am I being heard", "Do people understand me", "Does it make me feel good").
- The agreed-upon interfacing is not exhaustive and also not rigid. Customers often do not know beforehand what they want or are looking for. Their requirements will

also often change, so it is important to constantly assess and adjust the relationship to take developments and changing requirements into account.

With this approach, the notion of Service Level Agreements (SLAs) and the product-service catalogue have not disappeared. They form part of a broad union of agreements that are summed up under the 'contract' denominator.

> As is the case here, there is an exception to every rule and law.
>
> Despite the interface becoming more functional, there will always be situations in which a customer still attempts to set technical demands or demands related to the supplier's internal process. This can occur when, for example, the customer is a different application management organization. In addition, there is a difference between the design of the supplier's internal process and the demand that this process fulfils certain requirements, such as traceability.
>
> A customer can, for example, also demand – on condition that the agreements allow for this – that an audit on the internal progress of a process or the internal quality is carried out by an expert party. Such an audit can be a useful instrument in giving the customer a good feeling, along with the service provided (or it can sometimes be a denial or an actual confirmation of a negative feeling).

b. The process is becoming internal

The design of processes and the use of process models is thus becoming a predominantly internal matter, important to the internal organization, but seldom of importance to customers. The issue about which process model is used and how it connects to the external community is thus becoming less relevant (to the external community!).

The question about the coherence of different management models has also become less relevant. What is important is that the interfaces are attuned and agreed upon.

> *An example*
> As a rule, in a customized system, the customer prepares a specification at detail level. The goal of the specification process is the specification of the demand. These specifications provide process design input for application management. Based on this, a plan is created and the building process can start. But before building starts, the plan must be approved by the customer.
>
> In the case of a standard application component (standard application), the supplier designs and produces this first. It is not subject to design approval from the customer. From a customer's point of view, the design has been in place before their specifications were created. More than that, the design creates input for the 'specification' process within BiSL. The solution is offered and delivered and the customer can create their specifications based on it.
>
> You will have noticed that in these two examples, the processes between the various control domains take place in different ways. There is no strictly defined, fixed order for these processes.

The agreed upon interface and demands form the starting point of a process (as well as the end point of another process). As a result, the internal process must always be implemented according to what has been agreed, or agreements must be made to suit the existing processes.

If the interpretation deviates too much from what an application supplier can do or is willing to do, another subcontractor (who is able to supply this service) will have to be located or a different service delivery model will have to be implemented.

> A larger application management organization will identify multiple versions of processes to suit various forms of services or the different demands that are set. This means that different processes are identified for e.g. services with low costs as the goal, or services in which high reliability demands are set.

So, now the application management implementation issues have become:
- Which export products have been agreed upon?
- What kind of import has been agreed upon?
- Which (ASL) processes lead to which agreed export product?
- Based on which import products?
- How are the requirements for this monitored?

In this implementation, there are questions like:
- Can I comply with the agreements made: management of the external aspects.
- Am I producing the product using the correct method: management of the internal aspects.
- Are my subcontractors providing me with the right products and quality: management of the back end.
- Is this all well balanced: management of the whole.

This means that processes and process models are not redundant. More to the point, processes are unavoidable in order to internally 'guarantee' that the necessary service delivery is realized. Process models also provide a starting point from which to identify interfaces.

By separating the internal processes from the external processes (internal processes of others), flexibility in supplier relations is created.

c. The place in the service delivery chain and integration are the issues

IT service delivery is structured by customers or suppliers through the design, integration and modification of service provider- and subcontractor (sub-supplier) solutions. The design, fine-tuning and managing of this situation is becoming the third major challenge.

An application management organization can hold a different position in this entity, which can differ depending on the situation, and its role in service delivery can differ by contract. The application management customer is therefore sometimes an actual end-user organization customer, but in other cases it can be a previous service integrator or main customer.

As a result, depictions are created that can be described as service delivery architectural designs, supplier architectural designs or service architectural designs. Figure 2.5 (shown earlier in this chapter) illustrates this.

2.3.5 Generic demands

A number of application management demands remain standard. These demands are:
- *Understandability.* The understandability of service delivery and an understanding of the costs involved are standard demands. The costs of not conforming to the marketplace are simply too high.
- *Controllability* of costs, applications and services. Understandability is pointless if control is not possible. In many organizations, the importance of applications is determined by the immediate business process.
- *Transferability and comparability* of people and application management. Information provisioning is critically essential to many companies; without functioning information systems, organizations would cease to exist. The continuity of information systems is becoming an important precondition for the continuity of an organization. Dependence on individual persons (designers, programmers) is not an option anymore.
- *Flexibility* of applications and an active outlook on the future. Information systems have become so extensive that in most cases, replacement takes a number of years. Applications structurally last longer than expected. Roughly 80 percent of existing applications will still be in place in five years. Because applications are at the heart of the organization, they determine the competitive position of a company, and this will also apply after five years. The time has come for a more forward-looking outlook on these information systems.
- *Reliability.* The inadequate operation of an information system poses direct and drastic continuity risks to an information-intensive organization.
- *Connectivity* of application management and the mutual connectivity of applications form a more critical success factor due to the explosive growth of connectivity between organizations.

2.4 Impact and consequences within ASL

The statements of ASL are a logical consequence of the developments described above. These statements are:
- ASL provides the opportunity for employing the framework and underlying services, for isolated applicationsas well as integral application services.
- The interface between customers and suppliers and the agreements about this is becoming decisive. The external quality has been completely separated from the internal quality.

- In all service delivery, the integration issue is becoming a variable that requires decisive action.
- Pro-activity in service delivery and innovation regarding applications is becoming essential.
- Exchange of knowledge and affiliation with the public domain are becoming more important.

2.4.1 ASL as a component for service delivery and as a total framework

ASL 2 can be used as a framework for a separate service component, but also as a framework for application management that realizes the integration of underlying service delivery. Here are two examples reinforcing these two approaches:
- Sometimes, application management only provides a part (component) of an application and the responsibility for correctly linking to other parts of information provisioning lies with another party. In this way, it acts as a component and is not responsible for other components.
- But sometimes application management acts as an application service provider (ASP) (with agreed or perceived responsibility for the underlying infrastructure). Application management also sometimes acts as a system integrator and has explicit responsibility for the performance of the subcontractors.

There are still more degrees of freedom, e.g. a service is provided for a single customer, or a number of customers are identified for the service. This differentiation also has a great impact. ASL 2 can be used for all these forms.

2.4.2 Separation of the external and internal aspects of service delivery

The developments described with regard to the componentization of service delivery have led to the separation of internal and external aspects of service delivery. Internal quality has been disconnected from external quality. The internal aspect is becoming a black box. The following consequences can be perceived:
- The internal and external quality concepts are completely separate.
- There is a need for a broader interpretation of external quality: contract management is the central process at the front (the side of the customer).
- The controllability of costs in relation to ambition level is becoming important.

a. Difference between external quality and internal quality

Internal quality is what the supplier deems important and what is important in order to provide adequate service. Examples of this are well-structured software, current and comprehensive documentation, clear and well-outlined processes, the right people, etc.

External quality is often a different matter. Examples are an agreable way of communication and managing, agreements and service delivery with regard to time, reliability or costs, flexibility in service delivery (or lack thereof), thinking in conjunction with the customer (or not).

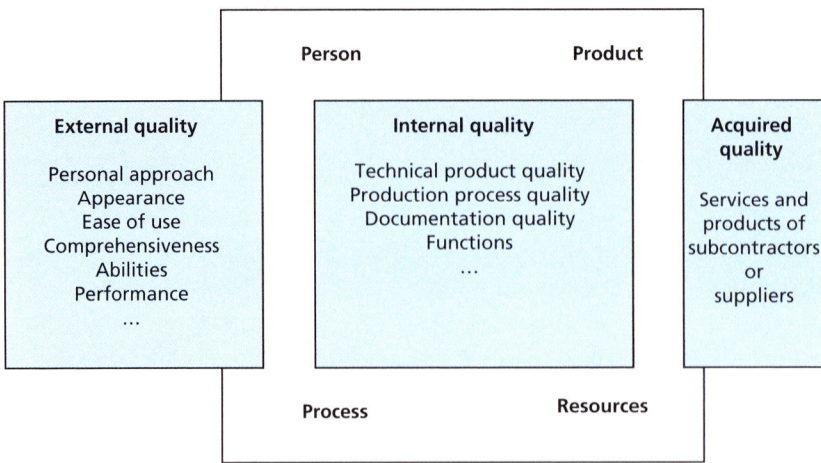

Figure 2.6 Difference between external and internal quality

Differentiation between the concepts of external quality and internal quality is important:
- The supplier's quality is, to a large degree, judged by the customer according to the extent to which the supplier realizes the external quality (and possible explicit expectations).
- Internal quality is generally 'technical' by nature and is strongly aimed at the internal realization process of the solution. The customer is usually not interested in this and, for the most part, does not have the expertise to form an opinion. Besides, they assume that everything should and will go well; even if an agreement is made to the contrary, they will often still expect otherwise. If a customer does have concerns about internal quality, they will have an external expert perform an audit since they do not have the expertise to form an opinion.

Internal quality is thus mainly an internal issue for suppliers. This does not mean that internal quality is not important. On the contrary, the importance of explicitly controlling this quality is now much greater, especially because external control is lacking. And sufficient internal quality is precisely what enables the realization of external quality.

This responsibility is also relevant to the linking of subcontractor processes, services and products to what the organization itself supplies.

b. Contract management as a central process in the foreground

An organization is generally 'judged' by customers according to external quality. Clarifying and describing this external quality is therefore essential. Contract management is the process that manages this.

Broader agreements
External quality can have 'soft' aspects (such as a feeling of commitment felt by the supplier, being treated in a pleasant manner, etc.) and 'hard' aspects. Firmer agreements encompass more than just the functionalities and services provided. Examples here include preconditions and conditions, rules of engagement, the most important interfaces, etc.

These agreements are handled in more detail in section 7.2 (Contract management).

Comprehensiveness
Many agreements are 'hard'. These are definable and unambiguous, for example in case of a confirmation or evaluation. But agreements are not always explicit in their formulation; many hard agreements are often implicit.

> Example: if you take your car to a service center to be serviced, you expect that it will be ready on the same day (unless the service provider says otherwise). The agreement is seldom explicitly made.

It is virtually impossible to establish all aspects of service delivery. Besides, intentions and requirements change in practice and this can even be person-specific (meaning that a new face at the customer's side almost always involves changing requirements). This has two consequences.

First, the set of agreements must be evaluated and adjusted. As a result, contracts will have to become more dynamic and to be adjusted in time in order to keep up with the changing requirements.

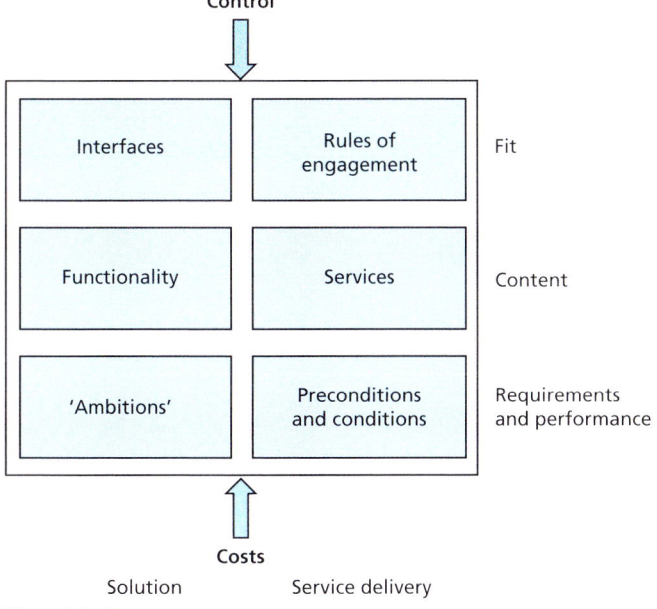

Figure 2.7 Agreements

Reasonableness and respect
Although agreements are becoming broader and more comprehensive, they will never be complete. There is simply too much content involved and parties do not always want records of all agreements. This brings us to the second consequence.

Respect is becoming an essential service delivery condition.

Both customer and supplier must handle mutual interests with respect. Respect oils the gears of service delivery. Among other things, it requires the following actions from customers:
- Providing suppliers with reasonable room for maneuvering and acting maturely with regard to planning and budgeting.
- Acting in a mature manner when faced with errors made by suppliers.

From the suppliers, it requires the following attitude, among other things:
- Not 'milking' customers and not only focusing on the increase of profit.
- Accepting that customers may not always exactly know what they want, and actively assisting in the search process. Investing in the customer and in the relationship.

c. Costs and transparency

Because the internal and external aspects of service delivery are now separated, it is important to have a pricing model that is independent from internal and technical costs.

In addition, customers need to be able to compare various cost scenarios to one another. They do this by considering other options, functionalities, different activity levels, and other services while formulating their query. The aim of this is to attain a sensible balance between the services provided and performance, and between service levels and the relevant costs.

This requires supplier insight into the costs related to the various options and activities, as well as insight into a pricing model that the customer can understand.

This leads to the following underlying demands:
- Insightfulness of service delivery and the relation to the connected costs/prices.
- Prices and types of service that the customer can comprehend.
- Controllable and predictable (internal) costs, costs for application management and possible subcontractors.

This means that application management must have a pricing model that applies to the services to be provided. Application management has to deal with two business cases:
- An external business case, that of the customer. Although this is the customer's responsibility, application management should take it into account.

- An internal business case, the business benefits (for the customer) in relation to the costs actually incurred.

2.4.3 The integration of service delivery and the service team concept

The third consequence and implication of ASL 2 concerns the integration issue. The integration issue applies to both the content of services and process control.

'Content' implies the way in which the application (or applications) communicates and connects to its environment (with other applications or application components), and cooperates with the infrastructure.

The process-oriented integration issue concerns the incorporation into the supplier constellation and the connection to the service delivery processes of the environment.

a. **The service team**

ASL recognizes the *service team* concept as a best practice: this is a single body responsible for the control of the entire information provisioning life cycle. The service team arranges the defining of the desired services and service levels, and monitors compliance and reports on realization.

The service team acts as the contact point and responsible contractor for the customer. It acts as a bridge between the customer and the body of suppliers as a whole and offers the customer a single point of contact.

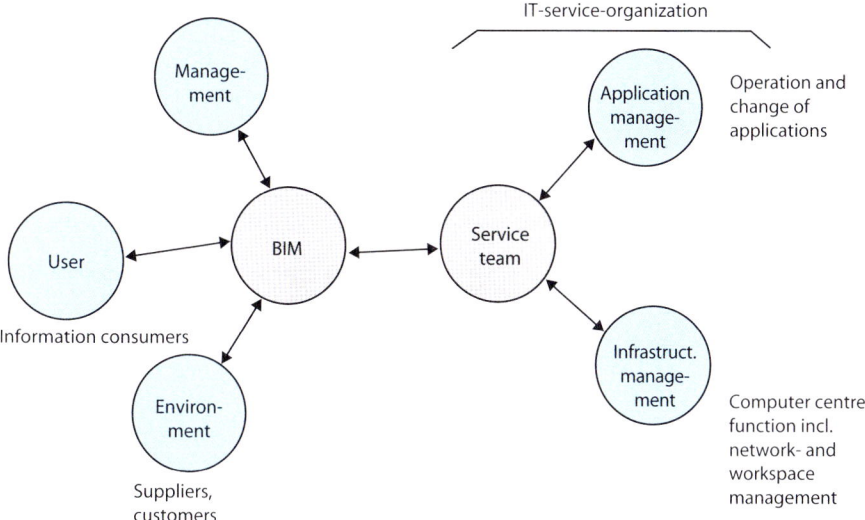

Figure 2.8 The service team

b. Integration as a decision topic

A service team is not a mandatory solution. Customers will have their own ideas about how delivery chains are designed and about their roles and positions in them. Other IT organizations will also have their own perceptions.

The key decision-making topic is the integration issue, the question being "How the integration of service delivery is organized and who is responsible for it". No mandatory standard solution is possible in advance, nor is a standard solution desirable. This is why the integration issue is a crucial topic, about making agreements when defining and establishing service delivery.

2.4.4 Pro-activeness

The fourth implication concerns the pro-activeness of service delivery: the independent recognition and anticipation of evolving developments and situations. Pro-activeness is becoming perhaps the most important precondition for survival as a service provider: the exchangeability of IT organizations in the competitive market has already been discussed at an earlier stage.

Pro-activeness must be considered at all levels of service delivery:
- In application management organization policy and strategy. The aim of the application management organization strategy process cluster is the adjustment of policy and service delivery at an early stage, to suit future demands.
- In the application strategy process cluster, where application scenarios are created, so that migration paths towards the desired situation can be created.
- In the execution of processes and the provisioning of services, for instance in management process quality management (including problem management).
- In use support, including proactive communication and reporting.

These points are expanded upon below. Discussion about pro-activeness will recur elsewhere: it forms an essential part of ASL 2.

a. Application management organization strategy: renewal of services and service delivery

More so than in the past, application management organizations must find their own way – in keeping with future market demand and their own abilities – when supplying services. Customers expect quality services today: the supplier cannot regard service delivery as a learning phase any more.

Practical experience has shown that the implementation of processes often leads to application management that operates highly professionally, but which acts inflexibly.

This means application management organizations must now follow a policy of being able to provide the required services within the medium to the long term. It is important that IT suppliers do not only *do things right* now, but continue to do the *right things*.

Making the right decision is becoming more difficult because it is not possible to provide the complete spectrum of services any more. The Application management organization strategy cluster contains the processes that convert this policy formulation and its execution into actions. It contains the choices that are made, as well as derived choices, such as:
- Which services will not be provided.
- As a derivative of this, which subcontractors could be used to realize the desired services as a whole.

b. Application strategy: renewal of applications

A second form of pro-activeness is the application strategy cluster. A pro-active strategy applied to the future of applications and the application portfolio is a necessity for the customer and the supplier.

Pro-activeness from a customer's point of view
More so than in the past, customers expect controllable innovation from their information facilities. For a number of reasons, a growth scenario is preferred:
- In many organizations, information facilities make up the core of the business process. The majority of organizations have automated the necessary processes long ago. Organizations, users and management have fully focused on this. A complete and drastic initial development demands such a change over from the organization and users that this cannot be controlled from within the organization any longer. And here we have not even considered the scope of the investments made.
- Most organizations are faced with a replacement issue. The desired future functionality in most cases overlaps the existing functionality to a large degree (more than 80 percent). It seldom occurs that existing information facilities are completely redundant, so it is not necessary to redesign and rebuild everything.

With the spreading of risks and investments in mind, customers prefer renewal and innovation to take place in small steps, rather than in 'big bangs'. This has a number of consequences:
- Because of these risks, it is expected that the supplier avoids necessitating drastic and complete initial development. The supplier is expected to foresee the future and define growth trajectories for it.
- This way, in the long term, old and new parts of the IT architecture will work together. An application landscape has been created, in which existing systems work with new components and in which new systems must work with existing data (and its limitations).
- Because the market is dynamic, applications and their components exist for much longer than was originally expected and planned. Many existing applications have been replaced five times in the past during planning, but they still work. The need for future-proof application support, maintenance and renewal has thus become critical.

It occurs more and more that continual improvement – in keeping with the changing business process and new developments – is demanded as part of maintenance.

Pro-activeness from a supplier's point of view
Customers expect a proactive vision about the future of the application from their application service providers. This is also of interest to application management:
- Through the continual and timely anticipation of developments, abrupt changes to applications are avoided. This has led to an increase in the future-proof nature of the solution provided and also to greater continuity in the services concerned. Application management would still like to be 'in business' after five years.
- In addition, return on investment is assured: application changes are in keeping with a future perspective. Through this future-proof maintenance and constant renewal, in the long term, the total costs will decrease.

As a result, ASL describes the application strategy cluster containing processes such as life cycle management and application portfolio management.

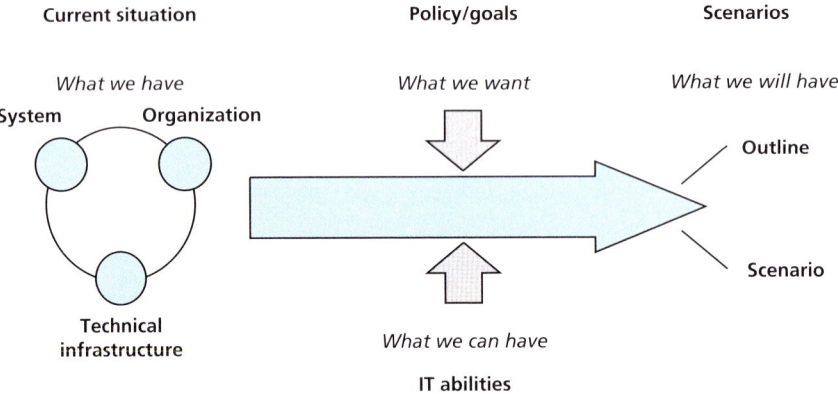

Figure 2.9 Life cycle management

Growth approach
This growth approach starts in the present: determining to what extent the application is aligned to the existing situation, with the expected future situation, and determining what must be done to ensure that it remains aligned.

The output from this exercise is a scenario and an outline that also applies as an application support, maintenance and renewal benchmark. Through this, application management can ensure that applications keep up with customers as they move towards the future.

c. Quality management

External quality is important (because suppliers are primarily judged according to it), and internal quality is no less important. Quality management is the process responsible for this.

The goal of this process is to ensure that process-, product-, organization- and quality system values are adequate to realize the agreed external quality. This requires further measurability of the internal quality and the active solving and prevention of problems/obstacles to service delivery.

> *Problems and the prevention of problems*
> The goal of quality management is not only the solving of problems before they lead to incidents and failures, but also the prevention of problems.
>
> One of the topics within quality management is the management of 'problems'. These problems include shortcomings in the quality system, organization, product, or process.
>
> As a result, no explicit 'problem management' process is linked to 'incident management' in ASL. The philosophy behind this is that an incident should not have to take place before a problem is identified and solved. In other processes, problems can often be thoroughly identified and solved before they lead to an incident.
>
> Problems and incidents must be prevented and this is the responsibility of quality management. Problems must be solved before they become visible to the external community. And if problems do exist, quality management is the process responsible.

Quality management is also responsible for ensuring that future service delivery outlined in Application management organization strategy is applied to the quality system – processes, people and organization – so that the services can be provided. The tactical application and active implementation of this policy is becoming crucial.

d. Active instead of reactive approach to use

ASL describes the *use support* process, which encompasses the incident control or incident management that is found in other processes. But ASL has also recognized proactive communication and now places more emphasis on it. The idea is that issues, complaints and obstacles should not only be correctly dealt with, but that these issues, complaints and obstacles should be prevented through active communication with users or customers (depending on the situation).

2.4.5 Sharing of information

The application support, maintenance and renewal is taking place in an ever-broadening setting:
- Information chain integration occurs more and more. The Internet has made it possible to link the simpler information systems of different organizations together. This has led to interconnected information systems or so-called information chains.
- The integration/linking of multiple forms of IT service delivery. This has been comprehensively dealt with in this chapter.

The application management departments of various organizations will thus acquire many mutual dependencies and relationships. Public domain concepts and the sharing of information will become more important in this more complex setting. There are a number of reasons for this:
- There must be a common basis and common understanding, as well as common definitions, about the forms of management.
- Processes will need to match the specific situation ('custom'), but will also need to be quickly implemented.
- Concrete and adaptable best practices will be needed, which describe how things should be done in certain situations. The practices act as components/building blocks for process implementation.

For these reasons, it is the aim of ASL to be a public domain framework. ASL's range of ideas and best practices are managed by a foundation that incorporates various large organizations.

The goal of this foundation is to update and improve best practices, present new best practices, adapt the framework, and help it keep up with practical developments.

The aim is to not allow ASL to become a static entity from which various dialects arise, but to put the knowledge and experience gained by organizations who work with it back into ASL. In this way, the ASL BiSL Foundation is becoming a knowledge organization.

3 The ASL framework

> **ASL statements**
>
> - To be an accountable, proactive application management organization, operational, management, and strategic processes must be performed.
>
> - The operational and management processes monitor stability, continuity, and alignment with the customer's business process, and agreements with the customer. The strategic processes ensure long-term alignment.
>
> - The pillars on which application management is built are are service focus and domain knowledge (regarding the customer's business process).

3.1 The framework for application management

This chapter explains the ASL framework in general terms. It explains the general structure of ASL and the division in the different process clusters.
The ASL process clusters are described in this section. The following section explains the 'design criteria' behind the ASL framework structure.

The ASL framework consists of six process clusters (see Figure 3.1).
Every process cluster contains a number of processes. The processes within a cluster operate in closely interfaced. In addition, the processes within a process cluster realize a clearly defined goal.

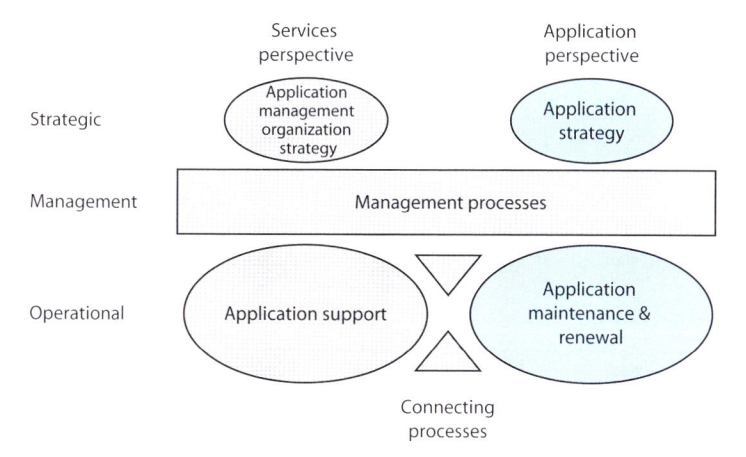

Figure 3.1 An outline of the ASL framework

The six process clusters are:
1. Application support
2. Application maintenance and renewal
3. Connecting processes
4. Management processes
5. Application strategy
6. Application management organization strategy.

The process clusters are described below.

3.1.1 Application support
The operational level has three process clusters. The first cluster of application management is application support. The goal of the application support cluster is to ensure that the applications – in their current state – are optimally applied to support of the business processes using the minimum resources and with the least possible operational disrupting. This is the goal of the applications: they have been developed and are maintained in order that they are use. Therefore the applications must run and work properly.

3.1.2 Application maintenance and renewal
The next cluster is application maintenance and renewal. Organizations change and, as a consequence, the requirements for applications also change. This is why applications need to be modified.

The goal of this cluster is to ensure that the applications are adapted to suit the changing demands and wishes resulting from changes in the environment and business processes. This results in applications that continue to support the business process optimally in the near future. So in these processes the necessary adjustments are made to the software, documentation and data models of the applications.

This 'maintenance' can be small-scale (such as corrective maintenance), but it can also be very large-scale, such as the renewal of a system where large parts of the system are rebuilt.

3.1.3 Connecting processes
The two previously mentioned process clusters do not operate in isolation from each another: they are closely related. For example, they deal with the same application objects. What complicates this matter is that, in different situations, different versions of applications or application components can be used in different locations and possibly also on different platforms. Not all customers use the same version of a particular component or software package.

In addition, users of components generally use packages or components simultaneously from multiple suppliers, and there will be products from different application suppliers on the infrastructure.

This means that synchronization and alignment between the application support cluster and the application maintenance and renewal cluster are important. The connecting processes deploy changed software and data from application maintenance and renewal to application support. Because of the complex relationship between applications and infrastructure, the importance of organizing this synchronization effectively has grown. There are two processes that organize this alignment.

3.1.4 Management processes
The management processes cluster ensures that the previously mentioned process clusters are integrally managed. The management processes address application support, maintenance and renewal. The aim of this cluster is to ensure that existing activities are performed according to goals, agreements and chosen strategies.

3.1.5 Application strategy
Organizations innovate, and likewise, information facilities and applications must innovate and modernize. The increasing need to grow from the existing situation towards a new one has already been explained in section 2.4.4.

Business processes and organizations change and, over longer periods of time, structural changes can occur. Applications are built with a specific structure on the basis of specific technologies and starting-points; these can all go out of date. Often, these starting-points lose their validity over time; technology becomes outdated and is faced with new demands. By observing these structural changes at an early stage, they can be anticipated and acted upon in good time. In this way, potential or future bottlenecks to the information provisioning and information systems can be avoided.

The goal of the application strategy cluster is development of a long-term strategy for the various application objects forming part of the information provisioning as a whole, for one or multiple organizations. By applying application strategy, the suitability of applications and application landscapes for future use is determined in an early stage, so organizations are not forced to abruptly change the information provisioning ('big bang') with major risks involved.

3.1.6 Application management organization strategy
It has also been observed that pro-activeness and innovation in service delivery is becoming a critical characteristic.

In these times of achieving more flexibility, it no longer goes without saying that an IT supplier will provide application management for ever and that existing services will always be continued. The user organization can switch to other suppliers and this also applies to the services of an internal application management organization. Offshoring is an example of this.

In addition, there exist many degrees of freedom in services which application management can supply. For this reason, decisions must be made. Within application management organization strategy, decisions are made regarding what the application management organization's services should be in the long term, and what measures must be taken to ensure that this can be realized by the organization.

The aim of the application management organization strategy cluster is to ensure that the service organization's policy and its future are correctly shaped. In application management organization strategy, the service organization's (i.e. the application management organization's) future services is determined and translated into policy and measures.

> Application strategy and application management organization strategy are two different topics, for which separate policies are created.
>
> Application strategy addresses the objects that are provided. Generally, the market and the customers influence the direction of these objects. Application management organization strategy addresses the services supplied by an application management organization. The organization itself primarily determines the direction.
>
> The separation of both points of view enables an optimal choice of policy for both these fields.
>
> As a result, strategic decisions about the future of the information provisioning, such as SaaS/ASP, ERP, or the technology to be used, are separated from the issue as to what the application management organization can and should provide. What the market demands in an existing application landscape is not always what the application organization can effectively provide. Differences can occur.

Table 3.1 'Process cluster characteristics'

Process cluster	Perspective	Capacity	Time aspect
Operational and connecting processes	Current	High	Continuously
Management processes	Current and next year	Low	Continuously
Strategic processes	Years to come	Low	Periodic

3.1.7 Application management consists of a chain of process clusters

Effectiveness and efficiency in application management can only be realized if these different clusters cooperate, share information, and are aligned with each other. ASL does not consider these clusters to form a chain. It is precisely the adjustment and alignment between the clusters that make application management work and also make it effective and efficient in the long run.

3.2 Structure of the ASL framework

In the ASL framework, two different clustering criteria are identified for the application management processes. This is addressed in the next two sections. They are:
1. Differentiation between the services perspective and the applications perspective. The latter perspective makes it different from other forms of management, such as infrastructure management.
2. Differentiation between strategic (policy-determining) management and business processes.

3.2.1 Service orientation versus application orientation

From an ASL point of view, application management has two important perspectives:
1. Service orientation: providing services to the external community.
2. Application orientation: knowing and anticipating developments in the business processes. This requires knowledge of the business subject matter and is aimed at applications.

Service orientation

The real goal of application management is to ensure that the developed applications are made available to the users of an organization. This is clearly a service oriented aspect.

The future of the application management organization, the services one wants to provide and the demands relating to that service provision, are also aspects that have a clear service oriented perspective. The service oriented perspective focuses on the provision of services to individuals or organizations.

Application orientation

Applications support business processes of organizations, and often form part of these processes. To keep applications up and running in the future, they must change along with the business process of the user organization. This means that there needs to be a lot of expertise within application management, relating to the business process of the user organization, its customers' circumstances, the developments in this field, and the actual applications.

The second perspective of application management is the change of applications in relation to changes in the business process. The processes that follow this approach are, to a large extent, content-based. In order to structurally execute these processes, a large number of methods have been developed that support and shape the content-based nature of the processes.

Examples of these include the steps necessary for creating a design: techniques, phasing, necessary models, types of documentation, etc. These substantive methods are not part of ASL. ASL does not prescribe any standards in this area, and allows various organizations to make their own choices, such as DSDM, Yourdon, Structured Programming, OOS, RUP etc.

3.2.2 Strategic, managing and operational

ASL has three levels of processes:
- Operational;
- Managing;
- Strategic.

Operational
The business processes are, of course, the most important and therefore first in line. Without these processes, nothing will take place, and they are the goal of an application management organization. Operational, from an ASL point of view, does not just mean 'non-managing or non-strategic' In any organization with responsible people and a standard of high training levels a high degree of self-guidance and learning ability should be self-evident.

Managing
Midway between the operational and strategic processes are the management processes. The demands on control have drastically increased and, at precisely this level, the environment requires flexibility and constant change.

Management processes form the dividing line between policy and operation (as in every business). This process cluster ensures that the market dynamics remain in balance with strategic improvement and operational quality. As a result, the significance of these processes has increased enormously during the past decade.

Strategic
A number of processes have a strategic nature. Here, existing structures and working methods are disregarded and the future is fundamentally approached with a fresh outlook, and, based on the various developments, a direction is chosen. The word 'strategy' is used to indicate that this is a direction taken, and not the sole and sacred objective. Adjustments will still be made continually. The word 'direction' can also be used in this context.

From an ASL point of view, these exercises do not continually take place. Generally, they will be executed once or twice a year. They take place by structural observation of the current situation and of developments in the external environment, through the setting of desired goals, through the testing of feasibility and, based on this, devising a strategy.

These process clusters will be more closely examined in the next couple of chapters.

4 Application support processes

> **ASL statements**
>
> - In order to support the use of applications, there are separate application support processes within application management.
>
> - These processes have numerous interfaces with similar processes within infrastructure management and business information management.
>
> - There is no direct one-on-one relationship between these processes, since within the area of interest of infrastructure management, many applications can run and this can often take place in more than one location.

4.1 Introduction

Applications or application objects are meant to be used, operated and managed within an infrastructure.

The goal of the application support cluster is to ensure that the applications in use/operation are optimally employed in support of the business process, using a minimum amount of necessary resources and with the least possible disruptions in operation.

Application support types of processes can also be found in other service management domains, such as business information management and infrastructure management. The content of these processes differs in, among other things, implementation, demands, performance criteria, topics to be managed and characteristics to be controlled.

In the next sections this will become clear. Of course, the processes across the different service management domains have close relationships in communication and information exchange.

4.1.1 Application support topics

Information systems are meant to be used and to be operated within infrastructure management. Internal knowledge of the applications is necessary to consistently and effectively operate applications. The different points of interest related to information systems in the operation phase are:
- The identification of applications and corresponding services (configuration items and service items).

- The operational behavior of applications or application components in an infrastructure, such as the availability, reliability and capacity used by the infrastructure necessary for adequate service delivery.
- The continuity of the information systems/applications running on the infrastructure. Security is also taken into account here.
- Communication about the objects and services and the handling of questions, requests or deviations concerning the objects or services (incidents).

This leads to the following four processes:
- Use support
- Configuration management
- IT operation management
- Continuity management.

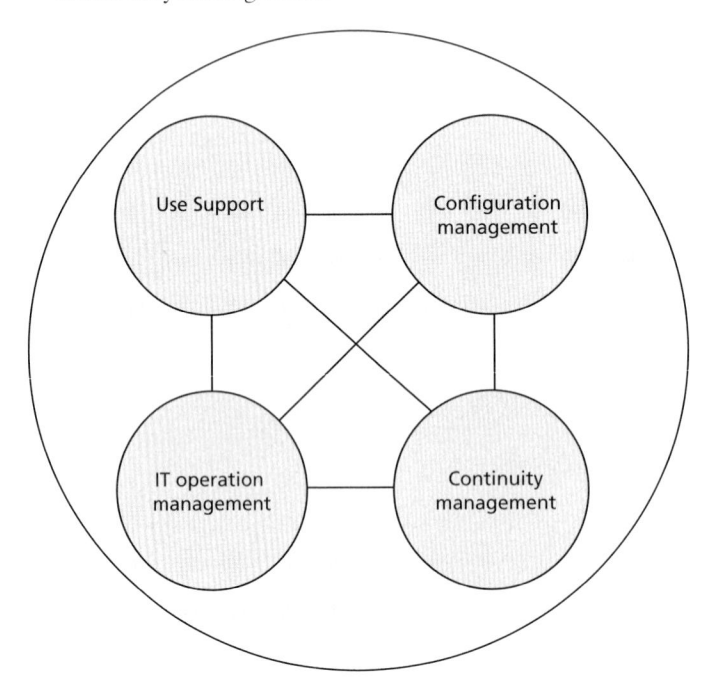

Figure 4.1 Processes within the application support cluster

4.1.2 The relationship between application management and infrastructure management

The processes within the application support cluster are closely related to infrastructure management, among others. In infrastructure management processes occur such as incident management, configuration management and continuity management.

Application management and infrastructure management have a one-to-many (n-to-m) relationship (Figure 4.2). Infrastructure management will generally ensure the production of multiple and varied applications. Support, maintenance and renewal of these applications is mostly performed by multiple application management organizations.

Application management organizations can develop information systems, packages, objects or components that run on multiple sites (platforms or infrastructures). The application versions can, in addition, differ by site.

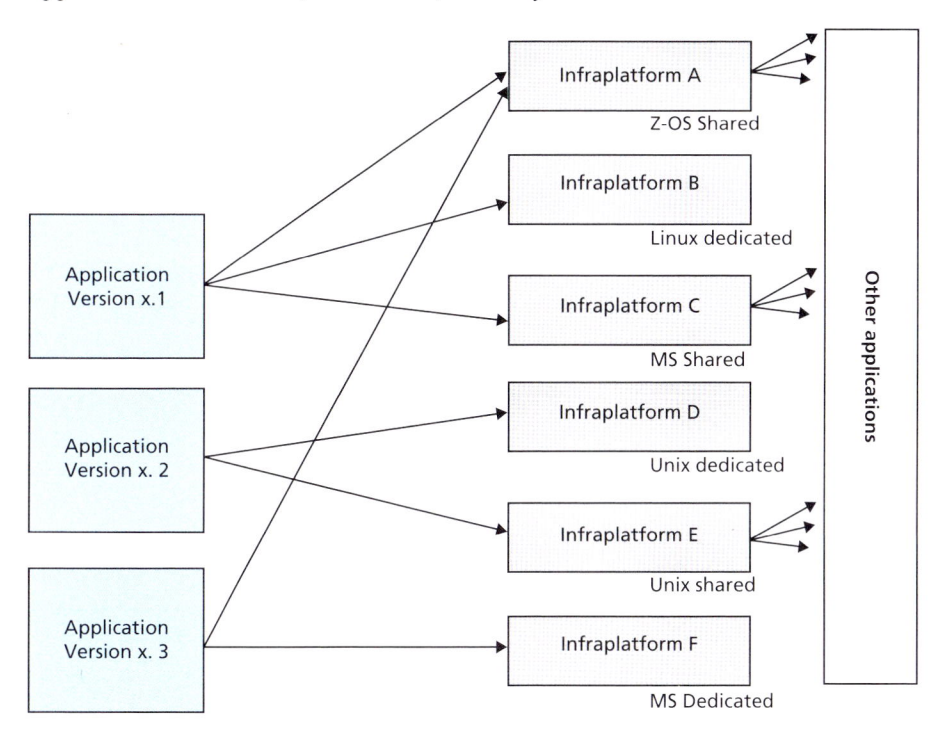

Figure 4.2 The n-to-m relationship between infrastructure management and application management

This n-to-m relationship has various complications:
- Every organization identifies its own application support processes (such as incident and configuration management). Configuration management within application management records all the distributed versions of an application among the different sites. The configuration management of infrastructure management records, among others, various applications or components from different application management organizations. These different processes cannot be 'normalized' to one central uniform process.
- Consequently, the application support processes of the different service management domains have different implementations: the content (what is managed and registered) and the scope (about what). The information required for the different service management domains is different and will also differ within each domain.

4.1.3 Detailing of the processes

The detailing (content and topics) and the demands placed on processes differ by service management domain. Application management converts the business requirements and demands of an information system to a technical solution that can be operated by infrastructure management. Here the conversion of business process and functionality to technology takes place.

For the effective production of somewhat more extensive systems, knowledge about this conversion is often inevitable. The knowledge about, among others, the setup of the application, the behavioral characteristics, the application's internal relationships and the do's and don'ts of them, is derived from knowledge of the business process, knowledge of automation and knowledge of information system development such as programming and design.

> *Some examples*
> Business information administrator A needs an answer to an incidental request for information. The application administrator will indicate which production runs are necessary for this with which preconditions. In addition, he may indicate that these runs cannot take place simultaneously with other runs, since they use the same database and could interfere with one another (thus possibly leading to a deadlock, incorrect data or extremely long runtimes).
>
> Business information administrator B indicates that in the coming year, twice as much type X changes will take place. The application administrator knows that the data access will have to be adjusted for the effective handling of these changes. Extra indexes will be required, or the internal rows in programs will have to be increased.

This knowledge can be found in application management and is not (really) present in infrastructure management. Therefore, the success factors, the expertise, the process descriptions and the Key Performance Indicators (KPIs) are generally different.

Further along in this book, in the closer elaboration of the processes, the various differences will be examined in more detail.

4.1.4 Design and implementation factors and the responsibility of service delivery

The implementation of the application support processes cannot be dissociated from the environment, the service delivery set-up or the agreed responsibilities in relation to services. This leads to the occurrence of different implementations of processes within an application management organization by type of service.

Parameters that influence the implementation of application support processes are, among others:
- *Shared solution* or not. Services can be delivered to multiple customers (e.g. SaaS/ASP packages). But it is also possible to deliver services to a single customer.
- *Direct responsibility* for the operation on an infrastructure. Sometimes, application management (e.g. as part of a service team) has direct responsibility for the

performance on the infrastructure. But there can also be many cases in which this responsibility is absent.
- *Integration responsibility* for the application landscape. Sometimes one service management organization has responsibility for the effective operation of the whole (with possible responsibility for subcontractors). But a service management organization can also be just responsible for its own services.

Besides these three, other parameters are possible. The aim here is to indicate that the various forms have a strong impact on the implementation and execution of processes. Examples are given below.

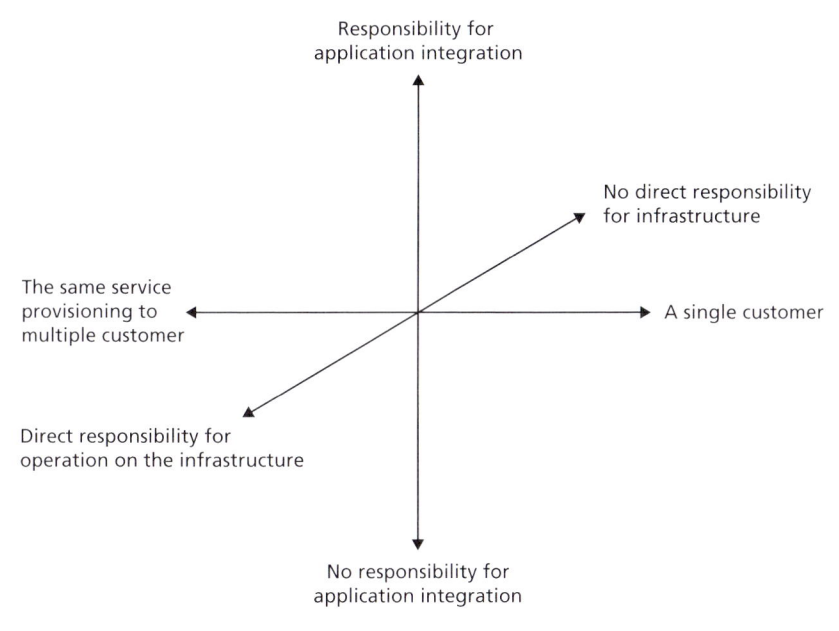

Figure 4.3 Design and implementation factors

Responsibility for the infrastructure
Sometimes, application management is also responsible for the underlying infrastructures used and/or external application objects. ASL is then additionally employed as a service management framework for the overall service delivery.

> *Example*
> In some cases, the application management organization also is the point of contact for the underlying infrastructure services (the service team). In such a case, there will be active and constant monitoring of the service agreements in relation to production. Also application management will control production.

When we are talking about a package or the separation of infrastructure management and application management, controlling and monitoring the infrastructure becomes more difficult. In such a case, application management has no direct control on behavior but is the opposite; application management is guided. In this case, application support becomes more reactive.

> *Example*
> Application management can also act as a supplier of a package and/or an application component that can be used outside the sphere of responsibility. In this situation direct control over the infrastructure environment will not be possible; nor will it be possible to monitor performance continually.
>
> But this does not mean that application support processes are unnecessary. Questions will be asked, issues regarding reliability and continuity will arise, performance might be questioned. However, acting according to a specific situation will mainly be reactive, in response to a call. On the other hand, many measures will have been put in place to avoid such issues.

An application management organization has ample opportunity to anticipate this situation, for example:
- Conducting intensive prior testing during maintenance and testing the various (possible) goal environments including the production characteristics.
- Clearly indicating in advance what the sustainability of the solution is: the conditions under which the application performs well and the conditions under which it does not.
- Striving towards knowing the details of the specific situation, in order to be able to quickly perform a possible defect analysis, or perform it in advance. However, customers will not always be willing to continually provide the necessary details.

4.2 Use support

4.2.1 Goal of use support
The goal of use support is the realization of optimal support in the use of applications by the best possible communication with customers and the best possible handling of calls about the use of – and possible deviations in – services, according to the agreements.

Use support is the process that arranges communication from and to customers. In this communication two aspects occur:
- Primary handling of questions, requests and failures. The keywords here are 'call' or 'incident'. The sub-process 'call handling' (incident handling) deals with the processing of calls
- Proactive communication. This is communication from application management to customers to improve the use of the information provisioning (applications). The communication, you might say, is to reduce questions, requests and failures.

The use support process is critically important for the image of the organization – how it will be perceived. Besides the experience of the end-user or customer in the handling of questions, agreements are also made (service levels) about the speed and handling of (for instance) calls and failures.

4.2.2 Use support topics
The following topics will be discussed:
a. Target groups and environment
b. Proactive communication
c. Call/incident handling.

a. Target groups and integration into the environment

The target group of the process depends on the implementation of service delivery and its place in the environment.

Often, the communication to end users for example, will take place via information management within the user organization(s). The primary customer target group for communication is mostly the business information management. This is not set in stone: it depends on what has been agreed upon. The customer does not always have to be a user organization: it can also be another application management organization, for instance.

Application management operates in an environment along with other organizations and other forms of service management (business information management, application management, infrastructure management). Often these have also implemented incident management processes or use support processes. This is why the implementation and coherence of the various processes must be explicitly determined and agreed upon in advance. There must be clear agreement about the interfaces between the different processes.

b. Proactive communication

The first sub-process in use support is one of proactive communication. Within the proactive communication process, there is communication about relevant announcements such as changes to applications or application services, alterations to their use, changes in services for users ('offline due to ...'), or useful information and experiences regarding skillful use.

Through active and proactive communication, it is possible to reduce the number of calls (incidents) and optimize use. Sources of information include frequently occurring calls/incidents, changes or experiences. The underlying reasoning is that there should not just be reactive response (according to wishes or complaints), but primarily there should be active communication.

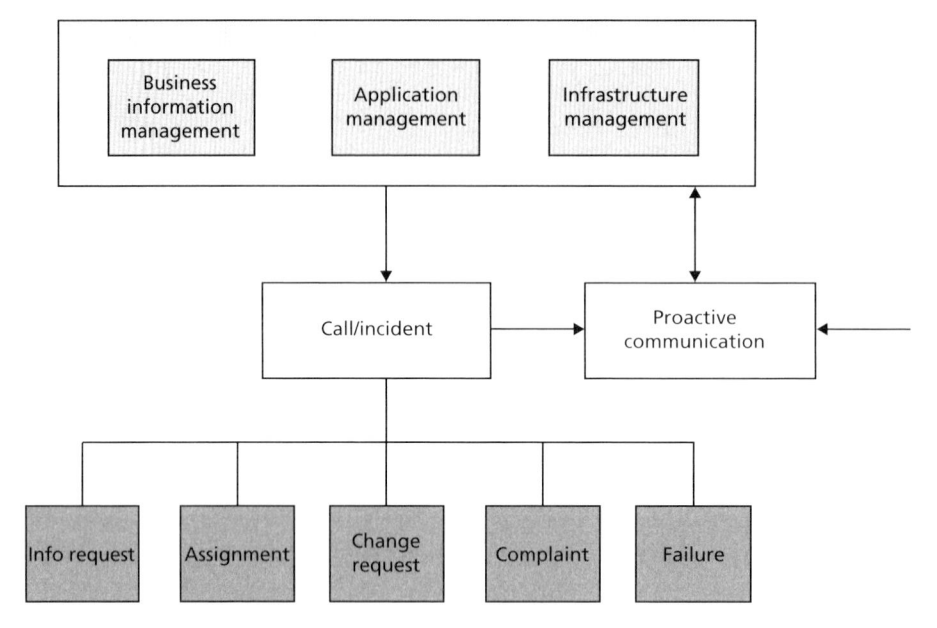

Figure 4.4 Topics of use support

c. Call/incident handling

An incident or call is a question, request, failure, etc. related to the existing application(s) or its functioning. We prefer to use the word 'call', because the concept 'incident' is in many implementation projects often used as a synonym for 'disruption' (a shortcoming in the production).

Calls can originate from infrastructure management, from the customer organization, from the other application management processes and also from other application management organizations (if present). Typical calls within application management are observations of program errors, change requests, requests for incidental runs, or questions about the application.

Call handling
In the call handling sub process calls are received, registered, and actions are taken for dealing with them. The call handling is also monitored. The first action here is the identification of the nature of the call.

Classification of calls
Depending on the nature of the call and the implementation of the process in the organization and the environment, there are various ways in which these are handled. Examples include:
- *Questions,* which must be answered, after which the call is considered dealt with.
- *Disruptions,* a call about a disruption in the processing of the application. Often, something in the infrastructure must be adjusted, after which the call is considered dealt with.

- *Errors* in an application can (although this is highly dependent on the organization and the agreements) lead to rapid adaptation of the application (patches/hot fix procedure), definitely in the case of a custom application. This generally also demands in-depth analysis of the documentation, software and/or data. Consequently, such an improvement also constitutes a change as well. Such (hot fix) changes usually have a separate procedure. Depending on the priority, this change can also be carried over to a forthcoming regular release.
- In addition, there can also be *requests* or *wishes*. Whether these are fulfilled is determined in the change management process. These often involve extremely important changes such as changes to legislation and similar events. Less important wishes can remain unfulfilled for years and they are often used as 'fill up' for a release, so it is not very meaningful to apply handling speed as a performance criterion. In this regard, application management differs from infrastructure management.
- *Assignments*. Instructions for starting incidental production runs can come from business information management, for instance.
- *Complaints* are comments from customers regarding disappointing results or disappointing services.

The Problems theme

Sometimes a call is a manifestation of a shortcoming, a problem. A problem is an undesired situation that requires structural analysis and solution. In the case of a problem, apart from the handling of the incident, it will be necessary to take a more in-depth look at the cause or to have a structural solution developed. If the solution to the incident is adequate, then it is not 'promoted' to a problem within ASL, just for the sake of analysis.

Handling of problems: quality management
The handling of problems is generally ensured/controlled in the quality management process. The reason for this is simple.

Most application management problems (fortunately) do not manifest themselves via use support (making them quickly visible to users). Defective applications, inadequate maintenance or poor (initial) performance are normally not visible to users (except in terms of maintenance costs and changing planning). These defects mostly become visible in planning and control, testing, implementation or acceptance testing. In many organizations, new application releases are generally fairly error-free when released. This means the majority of problems are not visible via use support.

4.2.3 Use support activities
Proactive communication with suppliers and customers in relation to existing services:
- Arrange contact with customers (or customer processes).
- Provide support for the use of resources and information systems.
- Provide information to customers about the implications of (changes to) IT services.

Call handling:
- Accept and register calls (incidents).
- Evaluate call (incident), classify it and possibly assign it to a call handler.
- Analyze the call.
- Possibly escalate it to a problem.
- Possibly forward the call or part of it to suppliers.
- Handle calls.
- Provide feedback about call status.
- Close the call.

Call reporting (report and control):

- Report on open calls and call statuses.
- Distinguish problems and shortcomings.
- Report on time spent etc.
- Report on the realization of possible agreements (service levels) in relation to call handling.

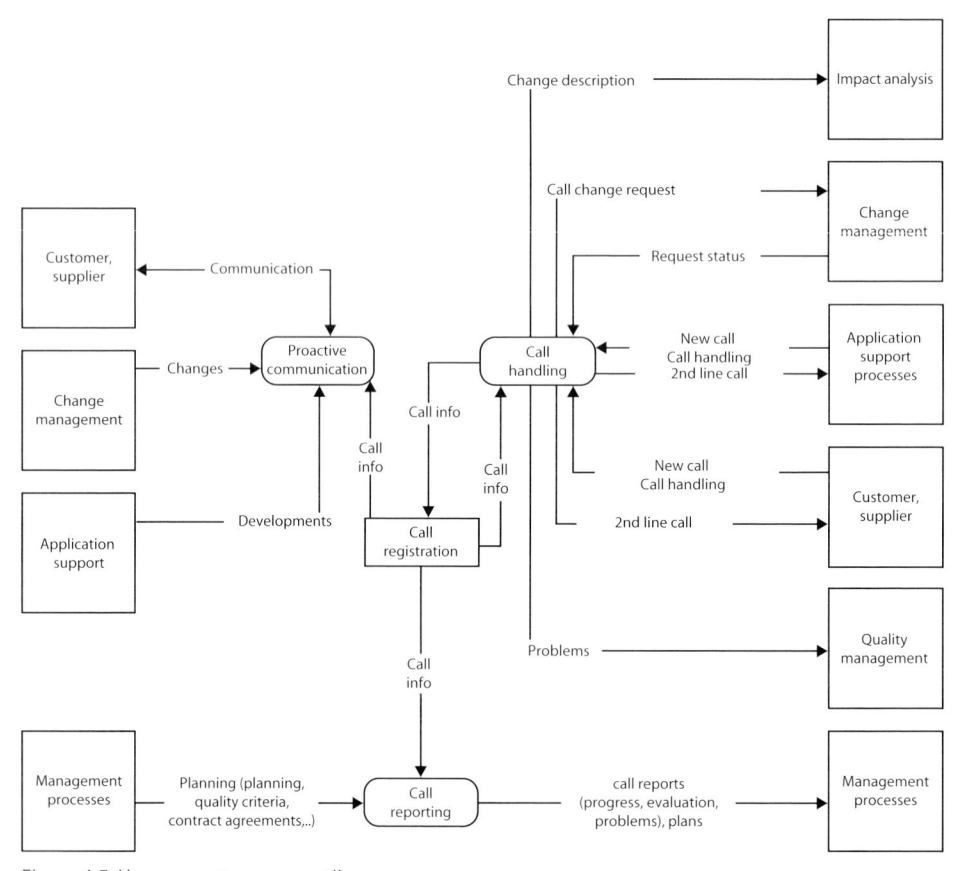

Figure 4.5 Use support process outline

4.2.4 Use support results
Developments and communication:
- Communication about developments in the application and services.
- Proactive information about changes, application status, use of the application, things worth knowing, experiences, behavior, etc.

Call registration:
- Call: subject, content, contact person, etc.
- Status of the calls.
- Calls to other application support processes (second line calls): process that handles the call, handling status, turnaround time, etc.
- Calls to other incident processes within infrastructure management, other application management and business information management (second line calls): handling organization, status, turnaround time, etc.

Problems:
- Cause (call).
- Underlying reasons for escalation to problem.

Call reporting:
- Progress and budget consumption
- Possible service level information, status reports.
- Evaluation of process steps, call reports.
- Problems.

4.2.5 Use support relationships
Customer/supplier
- New call (input): call from customer or supplier.
- Call handling (output): status of call handling or of the reply.
- Second line call (output): call to customer or supplier.
- Finalization of call (input): feedback about the status of an incident to customer or supplier, or the answer.
- Communication (output): information or developments concerning the services or application.
- Communication (input): proactive communication from suppliers.

Application support processes:
- New call (input): call from application support processes.
- Second line call (output): call sent to another application support process for handling or answer.
- Call handling (input) (for second line calls): information about the call handling, or answers to these calls.
- Developments (input): information from application support processes in aid of proactive communication.

Change management:
- Change request (output): a call that leads to a change request.
- Status request (input): status feedback about the request.
- Changes (input): information about changes in aid of proactive communications.

Impact analysis:
- Explanation of change (output): further information about change via use support sent to change management.

Management processes:
- Planning and control
  - Plans (output): expected capacity necessary for the execution of use support.
  - Progress and capacity consumption in call reports (progress) (output): usage (capacity used) in relation to the available capacity, progress.
  - Planning (input): fixed planning and capacity are components of planning. Planning can also be re-planning, adjusted planning and capacity (if necessary).
- Quality management:
  - Planning: (input): planning includes directives, demands made by quality management, the quality system and feedback about problem status.
  - Plans (output): propositions relating to working method and quality.
  - Evaluations, problems in call reports (output): evaluation of procedure and possible problems.
- Contract management:
  - Call reports (output): information on the realization of services of suppliers.
  - Plans (output): initiation of agreements with customers about user communication.
  - Planning (agreements) (input): agreements made about application management's services or products in relation to use support.
- Financial management:
  - Plans and estimates (output): including costs, cost estimates, if applicable, for instance if services are acquired in aid of use support at a price.
  - Planning (input): including for instance financial planning and budgeting.
  - Reports (output): realization of costs and financial entities and the evaluation of the financial structure and the assessments/estimates.
- Supplier management:
  - Reports (output): information about the realization of supplier services, such as the realization of agreements regarding the call handling to second line of suppliers, for example.
  - Planning (input): contains agreements about suppliers' services or products in relation to use support.
  - Plans (output): initiation of the desired agreements with suppliers in relation to use support or incident management.

4.3 Configuration management

4.3.1 Goal of configuration management

Configuration management encompasses the activities for registration and updating of information about the use of (versions of) objects belonging to an information system/application and its corresponding services.

The goal of configuration management is to keep a record of all application objects/configurations and services for which the application management organization has a responsibility, and providing accurate information about this to support other application management processes.

4.3.2 Configuration management topics

Configuration management manages and provides information about the versions of the managed application (objects), the production infrastructure on which they run, the corresponding services and the relationships between these items.

There are two essential objects in configuration management:
- The *configuration items* (CI): the application or application objects (on an infrastructure along with information about this infrastructure).
- The *service items*: the services to be provided.

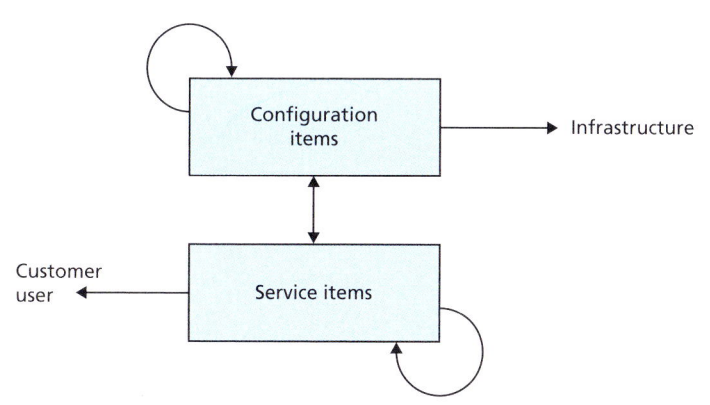

Figure 4.6 Configuration management topics

a. Configuration items

Application management organizations have a responsibility for the use and operation of the application products that they supply or maintain. These applications or application components can run in different locations and even in different versions. Knowing these versions is a priority to provide adequate management and support, especially if versions run in multiple computing centers. In this respect, it is inevitable that information about the nature of the specific infrastructure platform will be recorded.

These applications can consist of underlying components that, in their turn, can each have their own version. These components do not necessarily consist of only software, but can also contain additional objects such as documentation, data definitions, scripts, etc. Such objects are called configuration items.

The management of information about configuration items and the relationships between them is the main goal of configuration management. The administration of this is called the CMDB (Configuration Management Database).

Not the source code or the structure of the sources
More and more often executables (code suitable for running on hardware) are distributed. These are generated using countless underlying sources and components. These sources are stored in the software control and distribution process and the method in which they are structured to form an executable is recorded here. This information, which is often complex and comprehensive, is not recorded within configuration management.

Neither sources and components, nor their structure are stored in a CMDB, but the *identification* of the application version is recorded. So, a CMDB is not a software management system or a software version management system.

In the CMDB, it has been registered as to where which versions of the application run and on which platforms. For every executable on a platform this translation to the sources and or the structure of the executable must however be traceable: with the help of the software control and distribution system, the types of sources, modules, etc., used must be identifiable.

Relationship with the infrastructure management CMDB
Infrastructure management also uses configuration management databases. However, in the case of packages and distributed systems, the application runs on multiple platforms and in multiple infrastructure management organizations. Different versions of the application can be active in these different locations, so infrastructure management's configuration management database cannot be used by application management.

For this reason, there is a separate administration system for application management. The information it contains was discussed in the previous sections. In this section, reference will be made to technical infrastructures.

The management of the objects in this infrastructure takes place in the configuration management process within infrastructure management (machines, system software, networks, etc.) and not within application management. So there is a relationship between these types of configuration management.

b. Service objects

Which application (version) is running and at what location are facts that are registered in the configuration management process. This is an implication of the application(s) assigned in contract management.

The same implication applies to the agreed services, which is especially relevant when multiple customers or multiple service levels are involved.

These services, translated in service items, can be registered in a service delivery database (SDDB). These detailed agreements with customers, the service demands, and all corresponding matters are important for call handling and also for the other application support processes.

4.3.3 Configuration management activities
Registration of configuration items:
- Register and identify the (new) configuration items.
- Monitor, and provide insight into, the current status of configuration items.
- Provide information during impact analysis regarding which objects are used and where.

Registration of services:
- Registration of services and service items.
- Monitoring of the current status of these items.

Providing information:
- Providing information about the versions of application and application objects used.
- Providing information about service items.

Configuration control and reporting:
- Making reports about present objects.
- Drafting time budgets, process evaluations, etc.

4.3.4 Configuration management results
CMDB:
- Application objects (configuration items).
- Location of use, including further information such as contact person, etc.
- Status (version).

SDDB:
- Service items.
- Characteristics of services.
- Possible relevant related documentation.

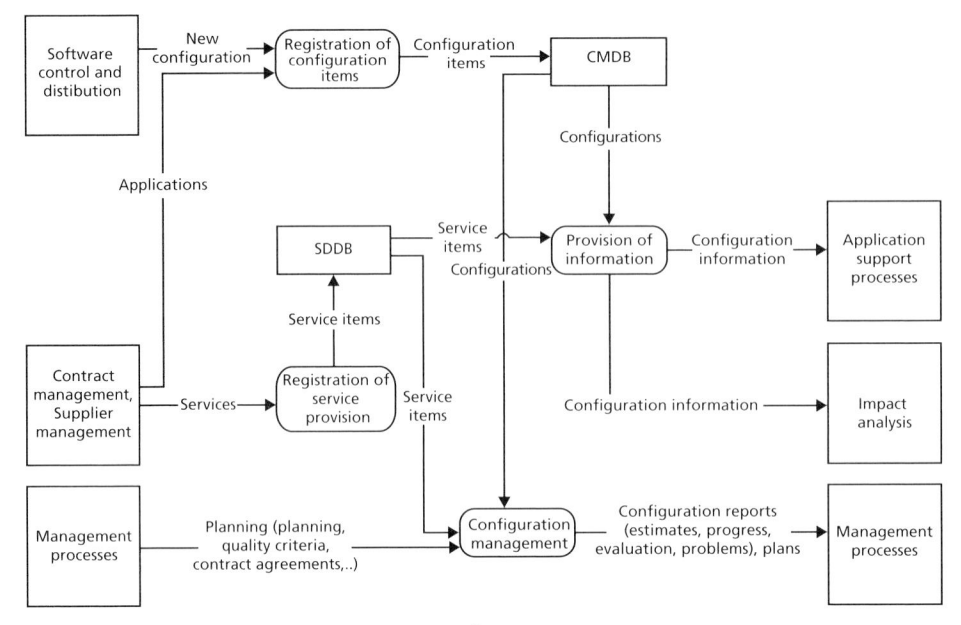

Figure 4.7 Configuration management process outline

Providing information about application configurations and their use:
- To impact analysis.
- To use support.
- Reports about presence of items and changes.

4.3.5 Configuration management relationships

Application support processes:
- Configuration information (output): information about the existing configurations or a specific configuration. This includes information about service items. In the application support processes, information and information requests are not explicitly reflected in the schemes/figures (generic).

Software control and distribution:
- New configuration (input): information about a new identifiable version of an application that has been released.

Impact analysis:
- Configuration information (output): information about the existing configurations or a specific configuration provided to enable impact analysis.

Management processes:
- Planning and control:
  - Plans and estimates (outgoing): expected necessary capacity for the execution of configuration management.

- Reports (output): reports include usage (capacity used) in relation to the available capacity, progress.
  - Planning (input): planning includes established planning and capacity. An input flow can also be re-planning (adjusted planning and capacity, if necessary).
- Contract management:
  - Reports (output): realization of the agreements and service levels (in progress reports).
  - Agreements (input): (service levels) and intentions (in progress reports).
- Financial management:
  - Plans and estimates (output): includes costs, cost estimates, if relevant, for instance when services supporting configuration management are acquired at a price.
  - Planning (input): includes financial planning and budgeting, among others.
  - Reports (output): realization of costs and financial entities and the evaluation of the financial structure employed and the assessments/estimates.
- Quality management:
  - Plans (input): quality section including demands set by quality management regarding the working method, quality of products to be supplied, etc.
  - Feasibility (output): of these demands.
  - Reports (output): evaluations regarding the execution of processes and possible problems.
- Supplier management:
  - Reports (output): information regarding the realization of services by suppliers.
  - Agreements (input): agreements about suppliers' services or products.
- Contract management and supplier management:
  - Services (input): agreements concerning the service/service items to be provided.
  - Applications (input): information about applications (new applications).

4.4 IT operation management

4.4.1 Goal of IT operation management

The goal of the IT operation management process is to ensure, monitor and guarantee that applications (or application components) display the correct and agreed upon behavior in operational situations, and that the services concerned also occur as agreed. The topics that are managed are reliability, availability and operation capacity.

This process aims to:
- Assure that applications and services are designed to comply with operational quality levels (reliability, manageability and efficiency) required by the customer organization (business) or organizations.
- Take care that these applications and services attain these desired levels and continue to do so, identify shortcomings at this point and initiate necessary corrective actions.

- Optimize characteristics in production, such as reduction in the number of failures and incidents in relation to reliability and availability, optimize operational performance, etc.
- Conceive a plan that ensures that the necessary measures are taken in order to realize the set demands in the future.
- Supplying information and reports to clarify that monitoring and evaluation takes place and that service agreements are being met.

The IT operation management process does not just involve execution.

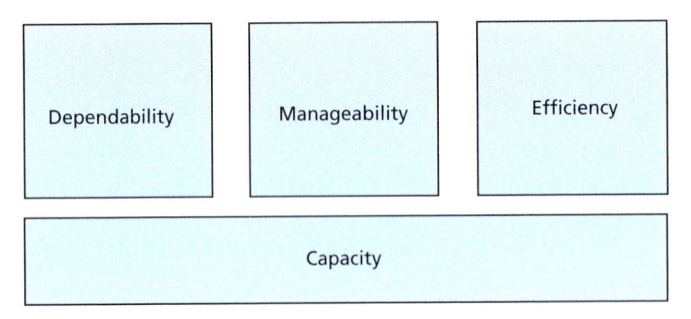

Figure 4.8 IT operation management topics

4.4.2 IT operation management topics

In the IT operation management process various quality aspects of the production of an information system are monitored and managed.

These quality aspects are dependability, manageability and efficiency. The factor capacity plays a major underlying role here.

a. IT operation management types of approach

The following quality aspects are managed in IT operation management:
- Dependability
- Manageability
- Efficiency.

Dependability
Dependability means availability and reliability:
- Availability is the degree to which an application object (configuration item) is able to provide the desired functionality at a specific moment and/or for a determined period. This concerns the start and finish (execution) of the application, processing at the correct times and in the correct order, the execution of incidental processing, opening times of online processing, storage period of files.
- Reliability is the degree to which an object or an object's services provide agreed or expected functionality during a defined time period.

> *Availability and reliability of applications*
> Availability concerns presence, while dependability concerns effective functioning. These quality characteristics apply to the application (objects) and to services.
>
> The availability of an application is the degree to which the application or its underlying objects are present for use in the workspace. This concerns the time periods during which processing can take place, the presence of the application object in the right places (documentation), the execution of the correct processes, the indication of the storage period of the data files in the data center (pay attention to mutual dependencies and consistency).
>
> The reliability of an application involves the way the application operates. Relevant criteria include the number of production failures of the application, the maximum frequency of errors, Mean Time Between Failures (MTBF: the period during which the application operates without failures). This has a relationship with the robustness of the application.
>
> The availability of the services is related to the degree to which the application management organization is available to the user organization or to business information management.
>
> The reliability of the services is related to the degree to which the application management organization operates in compliance with agreements. Criteria here include MTTR (Mean Time To Repair, the average duration of a failure, the time necessary to solve a software error or failure), the speed of feedback in case of incidents, etc. The quality and maintainability of applications play an important role here.

Manageability
Manageability concerns the degree to which infrastructure management can bring and keep an application in its operational state. This involves the transparency and manageability of applications from an infrastructure point of view. Production documentation (including the requirements, control and adjustment abilities of the application in processing, and various other aspects) provides much of the information here.

Efficiency
Efficiency is the degree to which an information system efficiently uses the technical infrastructure and thus becomes useable for the customer. The most important underlying topic here is the capacity of the platform in relation to the demand.

b. Capacity management

One of the IT operation management sub-processes is capacity management. This concerns harmonization of the availability of infrastructure resources with resource demand. The goal of capacity management is the allocation of the correct resources at the right time with the correct capacity to the services concerning the application support, use and production of the system. The aim is to realize and maintain a

cost-effective use of capacity at present and in relation to the future needs of the organization. It is necessary to have knowledge of:
- The numbers, in terms of data processing, the system will be confronted with (number of mutations, etc.) and how applications operate given these numbers.
- Which developments, in terms of data processing or infrastructure, have an impact on capacity usage. Examples include a new release in which calculations have become significantly more complex, requiring longer transaction and runtimes, or a new release of the database management system, improving transaction times to some degree.

Because demand/need can be very dynamic, this process has a strongly continuous nature. The planning and monitoring of capacity takes place by managing three topics and the relationships between them:
- Managing the demand: workload management.
- Managing the correct supply of resources.
- Assessing and monitoring the result: performance management.

Topic	Demand	Production	Resources
Measure	**Workload** • reduce • relocate	**Performance** • optimize	**Resources** • add • relocate

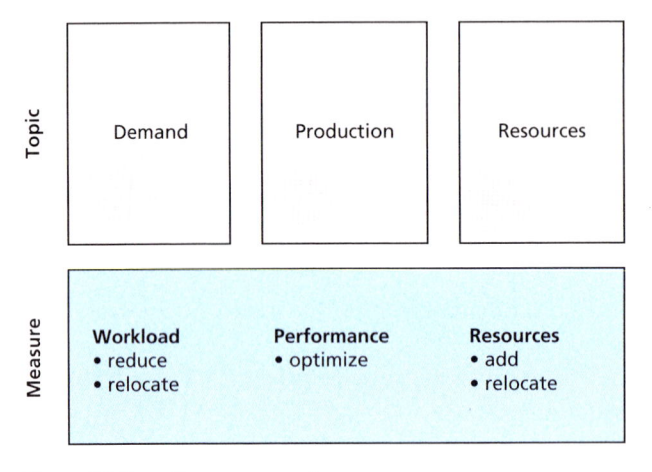

Figure 4.9 Capacity management

Workload management
The goal of workload management is monitoring and giving insight into developments in the use of an application (e.g. numbers of data and users). This provides insight into trends (such as constant growth of application data).

In case of a deficiency, adjustment may be possible by changing the workload, i.e. the changing or displacing of demand. Examples include the shifting of processing (mind mutual coherence), the division of processing, the non-running/executing of incidental processing or other processing tasks.

Resource management
The goal of resource management is to give insight into the capacity resources of infrastructure in relation to the developments and requirements of the application.

Based on resource management and performance management, statements can be made about the minimum requirements for infrastructure set by applications and packages. Resource management measures include the changing of resources, such as:
- Increasing, or, in contrary, reduction (downsizing) of capacity, such as adding extra processors or extending infrastructure (memory expansion).
- Implementing faster infrastructure (processors, storage media, etc.).
- Spreading across multiple servers.

Performance management
Performance management includes following the results of application processing, signaling trends and making recommendations for performance improvement. Performance management provides insight into how applications act handling different amounts of data or after changing functionalities. If this is done properly, it will indicate how applications will act in the future. Based on this, measures can be taken in advance. It also provides insight into application efficiency in relation to resources.

The information necessary, such as response times, duration, CPU load, storage used and network load, is mainly received from infrastructure management.

Adjustment measures include:
- Tuning (optimization of the implementation of resources and program or file production runs and the optimization of programming in relation to resources used).
- Denormalization (regulated redundancy).
- Cleanup of data/files (the transfer of data to archives or the removal of unused data from files/databases).
- Database access analysis (the optimization of data approach by making or changing access paths or indexes for data approach).
- The expansion of rows in program files, using different methods to store data or preserving interim results, etc.

4.4.3 IT operation management activities
Operations planning – the development of an operations plan:
- Determining the general demands (using the contract management and quality management processes) and indicating the regular production runs.
- Making an inventory of developments in operations relating to availability and capacity (in which direction does it develop autonomously).
- Determining specific demands regarding availability (deviations or exceptions in processing, incidental processing, etc.).
- Verifying the feasibility or the impact of changes in applications or services in conjunction with maintenance processes and infrastructure management.
- Predicting the effects of new developments (such as new releases, new technology) on reliability, manageability and efficiency (including capacity).
- Determining and recording demands.

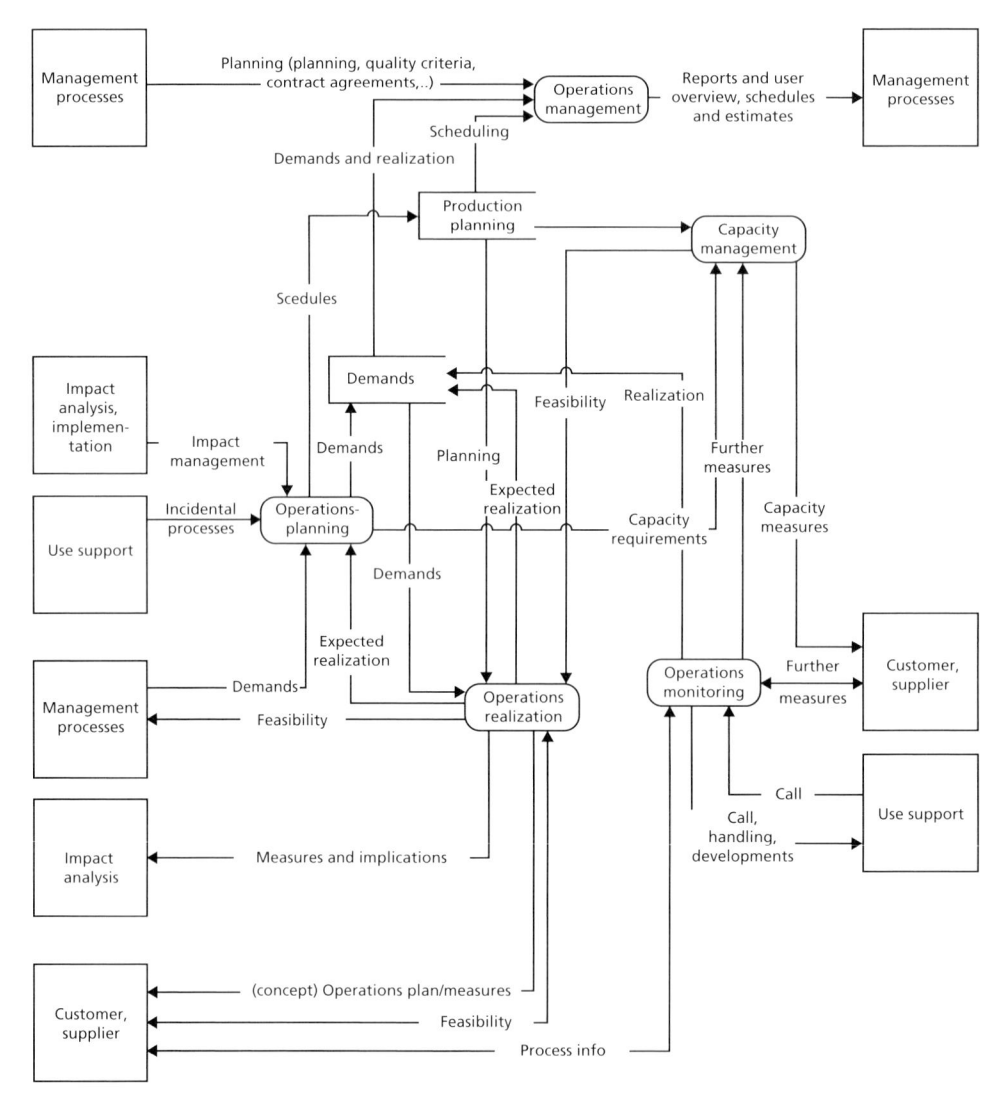

Figure 4.10 IT operation management process outline

Operations realization – determining the specifications and measures necessary to realize the demands mentioned:
- Defining demands and specifications for necessary infrastructure and/or functionality.
- Defining demands (service levels) for subcontractors (such as infrastructure management or network providers).
- Description of points in time at which management operations and improvements to applications and infrastructure can be executed (e.g. backups).

Operations monitoring – the monitoring of the effectiveness of measures and processing results:
- Assessment of the availability, reliability, manageability and efficiency of production runs or the services: determining whether (incidental) production runs have run and been completed without errors, whether applications are (have been) online.
- Comparison with the demands set (for instance based on the production planning).
- Adjustment and determining of additional measures.
- Possibly communication to use support.

Capacity management:
- Workload management;
- Resource management;
- Performance management.

Operations management (reporting and control):
- Drafting various capacity, usage, performance, and workload reports, availability reports and reliability reports.
- Monitoring schedules, progress, time spent, etc.

4.4.4 IT operation management results
Operations plan:
- Details of availability, reliability and capacity demands (for processing etc.).
- Existing operations administrations, such as reliability and availability experiences (failure administration).
- Feasibility of the defined demands.
- Demands and measures for infrastructure management, maintenance and business information management.

Processing planning:
- Application production planning and related information;
- Deviating production runs (incidental production runs);
- Supplementary or incidental production runs (implementation).

Demands:
- Set demands and measures;
- Expected realization;
- Realization.

Capacity and usage overviews:
- Capacity overviews;
- Usage overview (processing, resources used such as CPU, duration, etc.);
- Trends.

Operations reports:
- Progress- and planning reports;
- Availability- and reliability reports (availability percentages, SLA deviations, performance reports, MTBF, etc.).

4.4.5 IT operation management relationships

Customer/supplier:
- Operations plan (output): plans and measures related to processing.
- Measures (output): possible measures for customer or supplier supporting reliability, availability or efficiency of processing.
- Feasibility (input): feedback on these measures.
- Processing info (input): information about production runs.
- Further measures (input and output): measures aimed at achieving the desired results (can also take place via contract management or supplier management).

Use support
- Call (input): call from use support.
- Incidental production runs (input): call/request (for extra, incidental or deviant production runs).
- Call handling (output): feedback on or answer to a call.
- Call (output): call to use support concerning reliability, availability or efficiency of the application(s).
- Developments (output): information regarding supporting proactive communication.

Other application support processes:
- Configuration management: configuration information (generic, not illustrated in process outline).

Impact analysis:
- Impact application support (according to efficiency, reliability, manageability) (input): request for impact on application support.
- Measures and consequences (output): consequences and/or measures to be taken as a result of changes or adjustments as identified in the impact analysis.

Management processes:
- Planning and control:
  - Plans and estimates (output): expected necessary capacity for the execution of operational IT management.
  - Reports (output): reports consist of usage (capacity used) in relation to available capacity, progress.
  - Planning (input): defined planning and capacity make up the planning. Input flow can also be re-planning (adapted planning and capacity if necessary).
- Contract management:
  - Plans and estimates (output): initiation of agreements and possible necessary measures to be taken by customers.

- Reports (output): realization of agreements and service levels (in progress report) and the status of possible measures.
- Planning (input): planning includes contract agreements, service levels, information about developments and expectations regarding production runs, desired or requested intentions applicable to operational IT management.
- Financial management:
  - Plans and estimates (output): includes costs, cost estimates, if relevant.
  - Planning (input): includes financial planning and budgeting among others.
  - Reports (output): realization of costs and financial entities and the evaluation of the financial structure used and the assessments/estimates.
- Quality management:
  - Plans (input): quality section including demands set by quality management regarding the working method, quality of products to be supplied, etc.
  - Feasibility (output): of the demands.
  - Reports (output): evaluations regarding the execution of processes and possible problems.
- Supplier management:
  - Plans and estimates (output): initiation of agreements and possibly necessary measures to be taken by suppliers.
  - Reports (output): information regarding the realization of services by suppliers.
  - Planning (input): planning and agreements about services or products of suppliers.

4.5 Continuity management

4.5.1 Goal of continuity management

Continuity management concerns the range of measures that must be taken to ensure the continuity of execution and support of the information provisioning by means of information systems in the long term. The aim of continuity management is to provide continuity in the business process by ensuring continuity and the presence of adequate measures which will, within a set time period and quality level, ensure adequate functioning even during extraordinary circumstances.

The topic of security forms part of continuity management.

4.5.2 Continuity management topics

Continuity is the degree to which an information system can function in the long term without failures or with acceptable risk levels. Continuity can be threatened in a number of ways:
- Applications are misused by elements in the environment. Outsiders can breach the applications. By employing security measures (data security, physical security, etc.), protection against hackers can be achieved.
- The system is misused from within (fraud). Because people often have access or foreknowledge, this requires different measures, including role separation, measures against improper use, authorizations, hash totals and other forms of monitoring and logging.

- The system may face external threats in the form of unforeseen or unavoidable failures (calamities).
- In addition, the future of a system can be threatened if the technical resources used are not supported by suppliers any more, or because of the internal status of technical resources ("DOS really is history", "the sources have been lost"). System continuity is thus affected from within.

	Use	Resources
External	Security	Calamity
From within	Fraud prevention/ protection	Continuity of resources

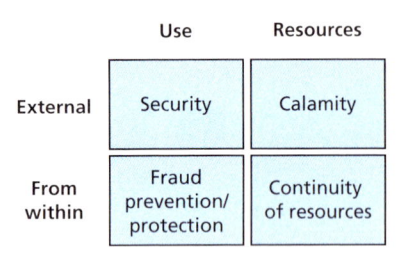

Figure 4.11 Continuity management topics

Measures
There are many continuity measures that can be used against these four threats:

1. Measures against improper external use.
The system and the infrastructure can be secured in many ways. Methods include passwords, firewalls, physical security, etc. Methods for gaining insight into this include dependency analyses and vulnerability studies. These methods are most often made available by infrastructure management.

2. Measures against improper use from within.
Fraud committed by users or management is combated using security, separation of functions and separate authorization within the application, procedures, audit trails, logging of data changes, data collection security. The topics of internal and external security are closely related. Many of these topics are integrated into applications (such as authorization within applications and the logging of data changes).

3. Measures for the protection of resources against external threats.
Protection against calamities can be achieved through emergency fallback (to a second location which can take over data processing), secure backups, fireproof facilities, doubly redundant implementation of infrastructure and production runs, etc. Here as well, infrastructure management mainly provides the necessary resources. In many cases, the use of these resources will be specified and refined by application management (see 'Also application objects must' below).

4. Measures for the protection of resources against internal threats.
To ensure the continuity of infrastructure and application means periodic and structured investigation is an adequate solution. Measures for guaranteeing the continuity of resources include escrow, depot, new releases, migration scenarios.

Also application objects must have fallback facilities
In continuity management, the attention quickly shifts to infrastructure management measures.

In an emergency fallback, the focus is rapidly placed on the hardware. However, application objects are just as essential when it comes to fallback situations. It is important to know which executables or databases must be included.

But it is not sufficient to only include the executables in the emergency fallback procedure. Without sources, there is nothing left to maintain; and this also applies to documentation. Although not in companies that use ASL, of course, documentation is often only available on paper, with comments written alongside. This documentation will get lost, unless alternative measures are in place. This also applies to essential project documentation, such as procedures.

Often, security measures against improper internal use are integrated into applications through separate authorization mechanisms, programmed checks, the saving of changes instead of replacing data, etc.

Not just designing the solution, but testing it as well
Often, good intentions are not put into practice: security measures are not enforced or tested.

Most hacking activity is done by simply guessing passwords. In the initial emergency fallback test, the fallback procedure often does not work because not all the files or their correct versions are present. It is extremely annoying if the first test is enforced by a real live emergency situation.

This means that in practice, a lot of attention should be paid to ensuring execution of the good intentions.

Not everything needs to be secured by fallback
The realization and test of a fallback procedure, for instance, requires much funding and effort. It is often not necessary to have everything secured or ready for immediate fallback. Some production runs (incidental production runs or certain overviews, for instance) are less time critical. Determining priorities and the efficient inventory of which components should or should not be included fallback procedures forms part of this process.

4.5.3 Continuity management activities

Continuity planning – setup of continuity plan based on dependency analysis/vulnerability studies:
- Identify products and services provided.
- Determine threats.
- Determine levels of importance and dependency.
- Perform risk analysis.

- Determine desired ambition level for security, emergency fallback, mirroring.
- Make plan.

Continuity realization – the implementation of measures:
- Execution of the desired continuity measures, including the spheres of security, organizational and technical measures, emergency fallback situations, etc.

Continuity monitoring:
- Test the security.
- Test the backups, rollbacks and fallback procedures.
- Test the continuity plan.

Continuity management: management and monitoring of the continuity management process:
- Manage progress and planning.
- Draft continuity reports.
- Estimate capacity and make plans.

4.5.4 Continuity management results

Continuity plan:
- (Components of a) Dependency- and vulnerability analysis, security demands.
- Continuity and security measures (in a broad sense).

Continuity demands:
- Demands set for security and continuity.
- Expected realization of these demands.
- Realization of demands.
- Continuity reports.

4.5.5 Continuity management relationships

Customer/supplier:
- Concept measures, measures (input): measures desired by suppliers or customers in order to realize the desired continuity measures.
- Complementary measures (input and output): measures to be taken by suppliers, customers, or continuity management to find quick solutions in the case of problems occurring.
- Concept measures, measures, continuity plan (output): suggested measures, whether or not to be taken by suppliers or customers.
- Feasibility (input and output): feasibility of suggested measures.
- Complementary measures (input and output): to realize monitoring.
- (Security) information (input and output): information about the use and securing of applications.

Use support
- Requests (input): requests or calls to be dealt with, concerning continuity management of a more structural nature.

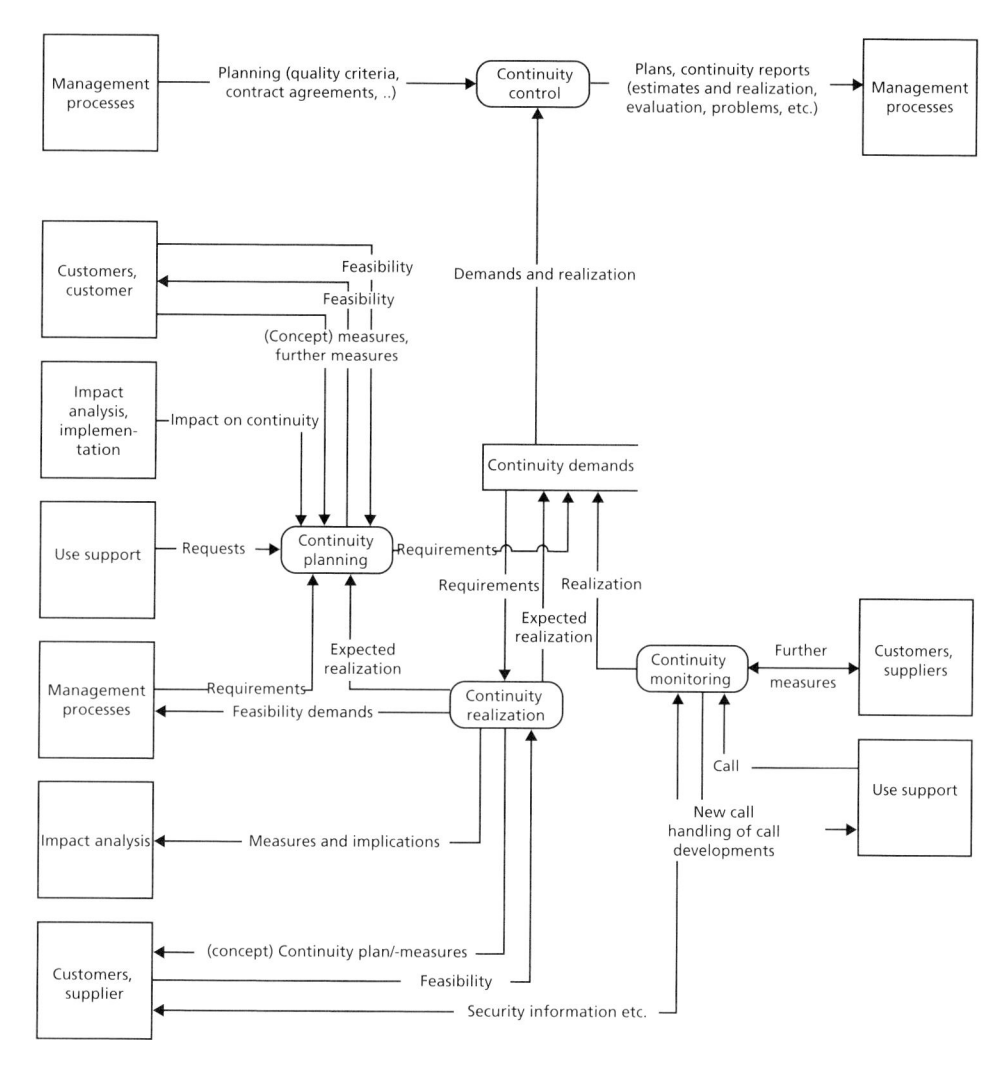

Figure 4.12 Continuity management process outline

- Call (input): call from use support about the continuity or security.
- Call handling (output): feedback or answer to the call.
- New call (output): call to use support.
- Developments (output): information about developments related to continuity relevant to proactive communication.

Impact analysis, implementation:
- Impact application support/continuity (input): request for impact on application support from a continuity point of view.
- Measures and consequences (output): consequences and/or measures to be taken as a result of changes or adjustments as identified in the impact analysis.

Management processes:
- Planning and control:
  - Plans (output): expected necessary capacity for the execution of continuity management.
  - Reports (output): usage (capacity used) with regard to available capacity, progress.
  - Planning (input): defined planning and capacity or re-planning constitute part of planning (if necessary).
- Contract management:
  - Reports (output): realization of agreements and service levels (in progress report).
  - Planning (input): planning includes contract agreements, service levels, desired or requested intentions applicable to continuity.
- Quality management:
  - Plans (input): plans include demands set by quality management regarding the working method, the continuity and securing of the processes and products to be supplied.
  - Plans (output): proposal for demands or feasibility of demands set.
  - Reports (output): evaluations regarding the execution of processes and possible problems.
- Supplier management:
  - Reports (output): information regarding the realization of services by suppliers.
  - Agreements (input): agreements regarding the products or services of suppliers.
- Financial management:
  - Plans and estimates (output): includes costs, cost estimates for use of resources (such as fallback, etc.), if applicable.
  - Planning (input): includes financial planning and budgeting, among others.
  - Reports (output): realization of costs and financial entities and the evaluation of the used financial structure and the assessments/estimates.

5 Application maintenance and renewal processes

> **ASL statements**
>
> - Maintenance and renewal (often abbreviated to 'maintenance' in the book) mainly follows the phasing and processes of application development.
>
> - There is a much smaller degree of freedom in maintenance and the demands are also higher. The main challenge is to find the ideal solution in this tension. Maintainability is extremely important in application maintenance and renewal processes – less optimal solutions always recur. However, in practice, few opportunities arise to improve this.
>
> - More and more, development and maintenance take place in a component-based world. Alignment with the environment is becoming more important.

5.1 Introduction

The second group of processes contains the application maintenance and renewal processes. These include the processes for impact analysis, design, realization, testing and implementation.

In the case of large-scale releases or structural improvements to the application, maintenance can be considerable. Such a renewal takes place in a project-based manner.

5.1.1 The application maintenance and renewal processes

Application maintenance and renewal processes are arranged in a way that is comparable to that of application development. The maintenance/renewal processes are (see Figure 5.1):

- Impact analysis: the activities that take place within the framework of considering and mapping the consequences of a change proposal.
- Design: information analysis and (functional) design.
- Realization: the changing, realizing and assembling of programs (application objects) to form applications.
- Testing: the testing of the changed 'components' (software and service components) with the end result having products that can be accepted and deployed by the customer.
- Implementation: preparing the changed software and other service components for use, while attention is paid to, among others, conversion, acceptance (testing), training, instruction and migration. This is followed by a sign-off.

5.1.2 The method and the quality system

The theoretical and methodical interpretation in the application maintenance and renewal cluster has, to a large extent, been borrowed from application development knowledge and theories. These theories were elaborated years ago. Various development methods have been developed (such as Rational Unified Process – RUP, Dynamic Systems Development Method – DSDM, etc.) They have various differences and similarities in relation to:
- Overall approach (waterfall, incremental, prototyping);
- Phasing (overall, detailed);
- Types of approach (functional, technical);
- Scheme techniques and methodologies used;
- Mode of representation of data, functions and time aspects (orderliness) in a design.

Different approaches can be selected for individual projects or systems, and also at the level of the organization. ASL allows for the use of various methods, because ASL is a process framework.

Moreover, the approach can rarely be considered separate from the environment, since it also describes the interfaces (milestones, input and output) with the outside world. A development method often gives substance to the products that are recognized (such as functional system design, use-cases, software architecture document) and at which point in the process they are used.

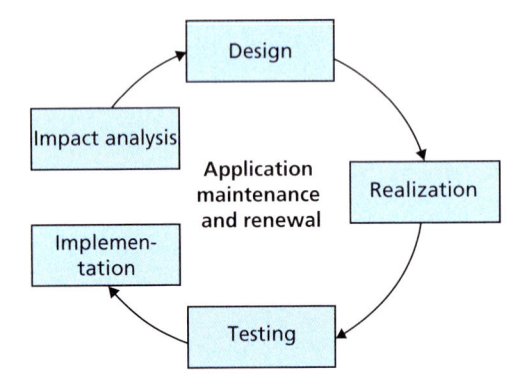

Figure 5.1 Application maintenance and renewal processes

Development methods also often describe the working order. There are waterfall methods, in which designs are clearly layered: a general design is made, after which detailed designs follow. This is hardly the case with a method such as DSDM.

The method used, the techniques, processes, process steps and the manner of integration into the environment and the organization form an essential part of the organization's quality system. The choices can differ by organization and by application. The responsibility for this lies with the process of quality management.

5.1.3 Differences between development and maintenance

In maintenance, methods and techniques are generally adopted from application development, so it is important that application support, maintenance and renewal demands are taken into account at the initial development stage. This is not always done, as a result of which formal acceptance by application management often leads to additional investments and improvements.

This can be avoided by standardizing the implementation of such a test (see deployment theme section 5.6.2).

There are quite fundamental differences between the development and maintenance of applications, although they are less noticeable in the method that is used. This is because, compared to development, application management involves a number of complicating factors:
- The starting point is less favorable: maintenance involves an existing system structure and existing programs. The reasons for choosing a system structure can be superseded by changes in the business process or by more or other technological possibilities. In addition, continuous maintenance also leads to more complex software or structures. Development tools are often not the most modern and generally do not provide the degree of support that can possibly be offered.
- The requirements are higher: a new version must often be taken into production at a specific point in time. Deadlines are often challenging because legislation must be operational and products must reach the market by a specific point in time. In addition, a new release must run properly (in terms of performance and reliability); the new functionality needs to be used. In initial development, there is often still an old situation that can be relied upon.
- The feedback cycle is shorter: a designer/developer will quickly encounter every one of their own less than perfect solutions; the imperfect solution will remain embedded in the application and must be taken into account for a next release.
- Improvement opportunities are fewer: opportunities to improve the application or its management are fewer than during development. This is because there is often a backlog in relation to demand, mainly because of limited financial resources, and a lack of awareness among management that such improvements are actually profitable due to the fact that systems have to be maintained for many years to come.

In maintenance, these conditions constantly play a part in every decision that must be made. Often, concessions must be made due to these reasons; an optimum solution is rarely possible. This means that, in application management, one must compromise creatively between demand, the solutions chosen and ambition level, and the feasibility, taking preconditions and risks into account.

5.1.4 Overlap between support, maintenance and development

The major difference between development and maintenance/renewal has, for the most part, greatly reduced over the past decade. A number of hybrids have developed, such as the renewal of information systems, legacy innovation, unlocking and integration

of legacy, incremental development, prototyping, rapid application development, etc. The drive towards reaching an ideal situation in a single step is rarely seen nowadays. There are numerous degrees of freedom and choices, for instance with regard to:
- Target design. Is there a drive towards the desired ideal architecture or towards an architecture that has been designed from the viewpoint of an existing information provisioning, which leads to smaller steps being taken towards improvement?
- Clarity about interpretation. Was the outline of the final situation drawn in advance (specifications), has it been determined during the various steps of the process, or does it become clear at the end (prototyping)?
- Set up and organization. Is renewal carried out within the maintenance team or in a separate, external organization (or is there a combination of approaches)?

Development, maintenance and support now overlap one another. This has the following impact:
- It has become more necessary to arrange effective application support.
- The need for having the knowledge about applications and application architecture in place has grown: the necessary development capacity fluctuates more than before. After all, maintenance and renewal use the same expertise, i.e. knowledge of the existing applications.
- Software logistics (software control and distribution) is becoming critical, since multiple versions will run in conjunction with one another.
- Greater robustness and more fallback options have become necessary.

5.1.5 Design and implementation factors
The implementation of the Application maintenance and renewal cluster depends on a number of aspects.

Development method used (phasing, export products)
A method influences the way in which maintenance or development is executed. It allows control of phasing, 'export products' (milestones), sequencing, decision times, etc.

The method chosen and used forms a point of departure for the implementation of maintenance processes and also provides tools and preconditions for the organization of the processes. People cannot always decide for themselves what method is to be used. This can be prescribed by the customer or the supplier.

Integration responsibility (or not)
Application development and maintenance takes place more often in an environment where other application management organizations are also responsible for the maintenance of application components, or for other applications with which the application interfaces.

As an application management organization, there may or may not be responsibility for the integration of solutions and services. This, and also the degree to which there must be cooperation with other organizations, has an impact on the organization of processes. In particular, interfacing with possible external application management organizations has an impact on the organization of the impact analysis, design, testing and implementation processes.

Manageability of subcontractors regarding desired functionality
The presence and manageability (in terms of functionality) of subcontractors also has an impact on the organization of processes. If this manageability cannot be achieved (for instance because a standard component or platform is used), functionality becomes a fixed factor. Such changes recur by putting them on the change calendar within the change management process. If subcontractors are manageable, the desired (to be changed) functionality can be defined in the design process.

Responsibility for set up and design
Who is responsible for defining the functionality and how easily this happens are also significant factors. Sometimes services are provided to multiple customers and there may be user groups who also contribute to determining functionality.

Type of product, organization
The nature of an application and its environment also play a part. Organizations in an alternating and dynamic market will make quicker decisions than organizations in which meticulousness, care or preciseness play a major part. In certain situations, specifications will be 'reliable', while in others they will be the first version in the search for the desired specifications.

5.2 Impact analysis

5.2.1 Goal of impact analysis
In an impact analysis the consequences (impact) of proposed changes are recorded and, based on this, the best overall solution direction for the realization of these changes is determined.

The goal of the process is the effective recording of sufficient reliable and accurate consequences of proposed changes in terms of effort, future events, use and operation, so that an ideal solution direction can be chosen.

The changes that are collected and possibly clustered into a release in the change management process are further elaborated in the impact analysis process. In an impact analysis, the consequences of these changes for applications, the subsequent maintenance/renewal process and the environment are determined. The impact can be larger or less than expected – this means that the planning or interpretation of releases can be adjusted in the change management process based on the outcome of the impact analysis. This means that these two processes often work cyclically.

5.2.2 Impact analysis topics

In the impact analysis process, attention is not only focused on the application itself. The majority of the process does indeed involve the application but, in conjunction with other forms of information systems management, attention is also paid to:

- The user organization: which business processes will change and what does this entail for customers/users?
- Infrastructure: what does this change mean for the operation on the infrastructure and the corresponding agreements?

Applications act in an environment in which other components and other information provisioning play a part. An application can also use, or be structured using, components from the environment outside the direct influence of the application management organization. Determining the impact of, and on, this environment also forms part of the impact analysis.

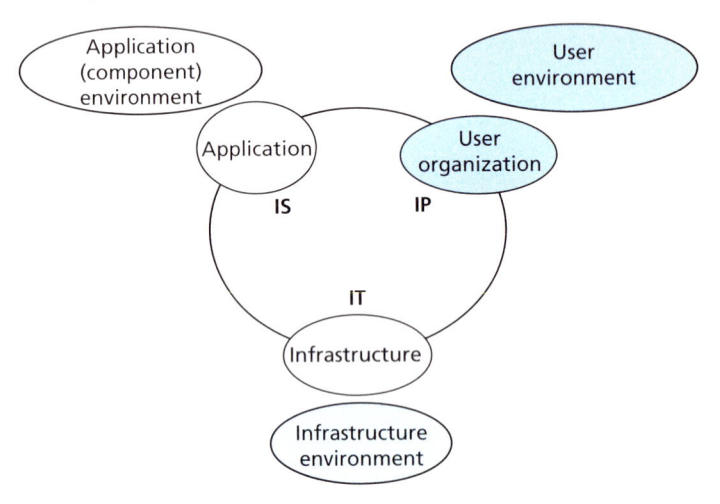

Figure 5.2 Impact analysis topics

Application and application components
To determine the impact, an impact analysis examines which components (functions, sub-systems, data) are primarily affected by changes and what the mutual relationships between these objects are. The impact on the use of external application components is also included.

This means that there is a relationship with the software control and distribution process. This process supplies facilities and necessary information.

One of the results of impact analysis is the change set, the application objects that can be altered due to the changes. A detailed description of this can be found in the software control and distribution process.

Infrastructure and operation
To gain insight into the effects on the infrastructure, it is necessary to know where the application runs and what the possible consequences of the change are. This information is acquired from the application support processes. Configuration management is important here, because this records what is used in which environments. The information does not only come from the application support processes. In the case of large-scale changes, it is necessary to consult (if possible) the infrastructure management organization(s).

Application management is not always able to access the infrastructure environment or infrastructure organization. As to supplying standard applications, for instance, the link with infrastructure management organizations is often complex. The same may apply to the application support processes within application management. This is a point that must be identified and arranged in advance during the implementation of the process.

Users
The impact on the users can be determined in conjunction with the customer (business information management). This means that agreements need to be made about the way in which this is going to be handled.

In maintenance, for the sake of preconditions such as available capacity and available amount of time, concessions are often made that affect the design and completeness of solutions. Often, this will result in various functionalities not (or partly) being automated.

5.2.3 Impact analysis activities
Outlining change:
- Mapping out the changes forming part of a release (acceptance).
- Further elaboration, to respond to questions about the changes.

Assessment of changes:
- Identifying products (configuration items) that are affected by the proposed changes.
- Estimation of the scope of changes to these objects resulting from the proposed change.
- Identifying the relationships between various proposed changes and the relationships with other releases (if any).
- Setting up of a scenario for handling and testing these changes.

Estimating consequences:
- Assessing the consequences for the operation environment, the user environment and for agreements (required capacity, availability, etc.).
- Estimation of the long-term effects (such as maintainability, operability, manageability, continuity and security).
- Assessing of possible additional measures to be taken.

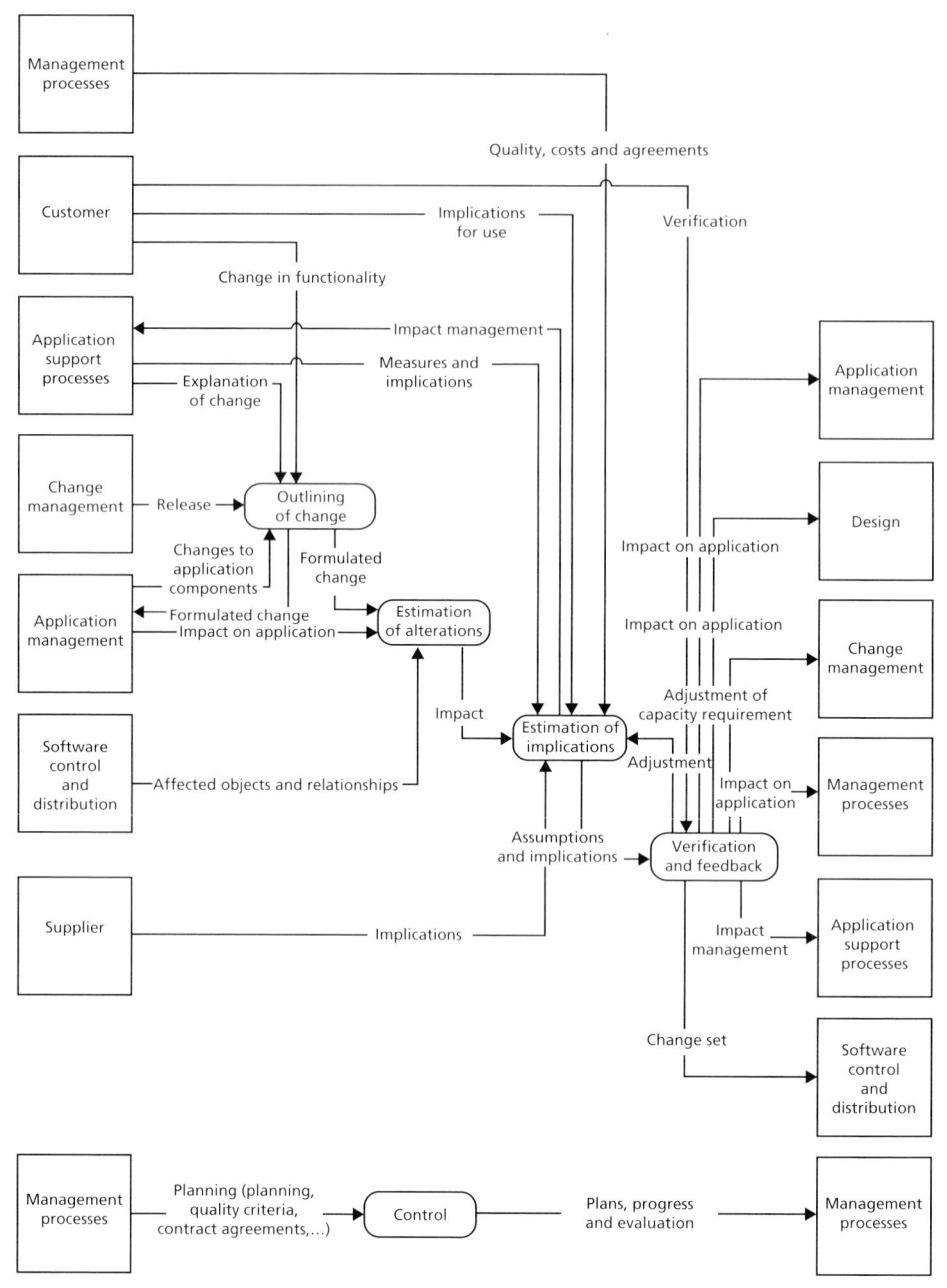

Figure 5.3 Impact analysis process outline

- Assessing the risks involved in making the changes.
- Estimation of the scope of activities resulting from the changes and assessing time aspects.

Verification and feedback:
- Verification for business information management, application support processes and infrastructure management.
- Feedback to the change management process.

Management:
- Estimation of necessary resources and working method.
- Monitoring of progress, agreements and process.
- Evaluation of progress and process.

5.2.4 Impact analysis results
Impact application (impact analysis report):
- Assumptions and departure points for the impact analysis.
- Description of changes and release.
- Impact on objects: affected objects (change set) and impact on various of their characteristics.
- Alternative solution (or selection of alternatives).
- Activities to be executed.
- Scope/estimation of human resources capacity for the release.
- Possible risks and measures to be taken.
- Consequences for user environment, application management and operation environment.
- Long-term impact.
- Scope of change (required capacity).
- Proposed adjustments to release.

Change set:
- Affected objects.
- Possible interference with other releases.

Progress reports:
- Planning, progress.
- Possible problems, evaluations.

5.2.5 Impact analysis relationships
Application management (other organizations):
- Changes application components (input): changes and information about these changes to application components or to components related to applications that are maintained by other application management organizations.
- Impact application (input and output): impact of changes to the application (or component) on other application management organizations that use the application or have relationships with it. Impact of changes to other applications on the application itself.

Customer:
- Functionality change (input): information about changes in functionality or new functionality desired by the customer.
- Consequences to the user (output): impact of the changes on the end-user.
- Verifications (input): verification of the impact analysis.

Supplier:
- Consequences (input): impact of the proposed changes on services or supplier solutions (if requested).

Note: the impact on the infrastructure used is determined via the application support processes.

Change management:
- Release (input): a series of combined changes that must be implemented during the release, with a rough estimate of the expected development capacity.
- Adjustment of capacity requirement (output): feedback about the estimated development capacity necessary for a release, compared to the initial estimate from the perspective of the change management process.

Application support processes:
- Explanation change (input): information about the changes indicated by the application support processes.
- Impact operation (output): assessment of the impact of the release and its changes on the performance of the managed application and the corresponding services (capacity, reliability, etc.).
- Measures and consequences (input): consequences of the new release and measures that must be taken along with their impact.
- Configuration information (input): information about versions used and corresponding services that can be requested via configuration management (not explicitly presented in the figure).

Software control and distribution:
- Affected objects and relationships (input): impact of changes on components (software, design, documentation, data, etc.) and structure of applications, which must change as a result of the release.
- Change set (output): determining the group of application objects so that multiple changes to them can be identified.

Design:
- Application impact (output): outline of the proposed solution direction, including impact, intended solution, etc.

Management processes:
- All management processes:

- Application impact (output): impact of release or development such as estimated development capacity, impact of release on quality, agreements and service levels, investments and additional investments, operability, long-term maintainability, impact on suppliers.
- Planning and control:
  - Planning (input): the planning and capacity of the impact analysis (possible re-planning if necessary).
  - Progress and evaluations (output): realization of impact analysis.
  - Plans (output): estimates for the execution of impact analysis.
- Quality management:
  - Planning (input): includes quality criteria, working method, indicators, among others.
  - Progress and evaluations (output): evaluations, possible problems, realization of quality demands.
  - Plans (output): if necessary, possible deviating additional demands or changes in working method, quality criteria.
- Contract management:
  - Planning (input): agreements made with customers about working method or exchange of information.
  - Progress and evaluations (output): results.
  - Plans (output): proposal for agreements with customer.
- Supplier management:
  - Planning (input): agreements about involvement of suppliers.
  - Progress and evaluations (output): realization of agreements made.
  - Plans (output): possible additional demands or agreements about the involvement of suppliers in the impact analysis.
- Financial management.
  - Planning (input): possible financial agreements/budget.
  - Progress and evaluations (output): realization of these agreements.
  - Plans (output): possible financial consequences.

5.3 Design

5.3.1 Goal of design

The goal of the design process is to set up and record the information system (user) specifications or changes in such a way that they can be easily realized and tested. The primary result of this is functional or logical system design, a non-technical description of the desired functioning.

5.3.2 Design topics

a. Specifications

A design starts with a specification, which indicates what the desired functionality must be (alongside additional directives about security, reliability, performance, availability, maintainability, etc.). Specifications generally derive from the customer.

A specification is not always explicit, and sometimes there is no environment in which to make it really explicit. A supplier, for example, produces components and develops them based on expectations that market developments will move in a certain direction.

There are many methods for clarifying specifications. Sometimes short descriptions (specifications) are adequate, other times functional system design is used, and sometimes even technical solutions are used (prototyping). The result of the design process is a simple and recorded design of the new situation or a design in which the changes are recorded.

b. The design process

The design process has a setup that is similar to the layout of the design cycle.; it consists broadly of four steps:

- The determining of the solution and route to be taken: determining the desired direction of the functionality or the change.
- Designing: the elaboration of this route, drawing the outlines of the solution and designing the detailed structures.
- Producing: drawing up, recording and documenting the functionality to be created or changed.
- Validating: checking the correctness of the work done.

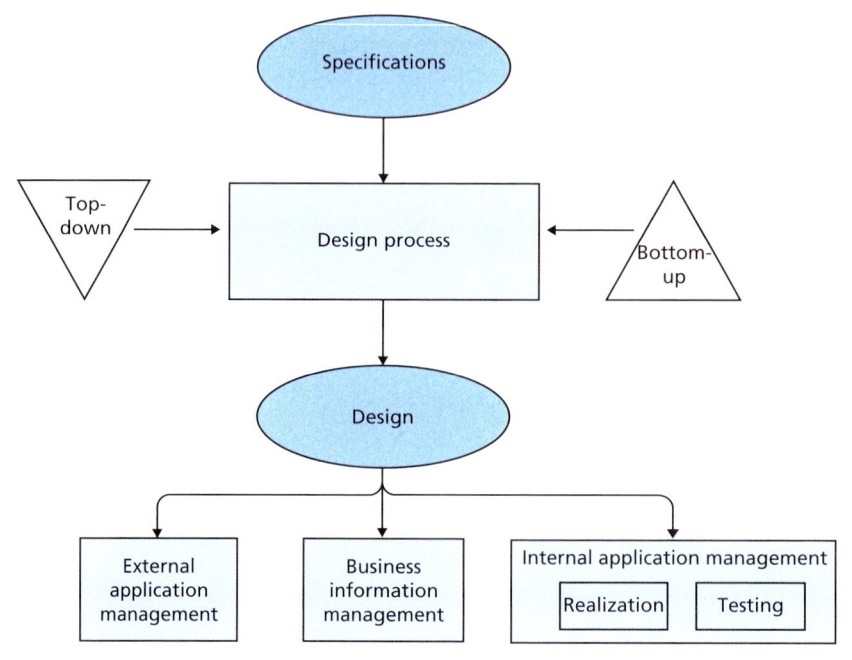

Figure 5.4 Design topics

In maintenance, a bottom-up approach dominates – the smallest possible alteration to the application in order to realize changes is determined. If it turns out that the change does not in any way fit into an application component, the scope is enlarged.

So, in a bottom-up approach, one looks for the easiest and quickest way of realizing or changing functionality within an application or structure.

In creating new functionalities, a top-down approach is generally taken. First, the outlines are drawn up and then refinements are made.

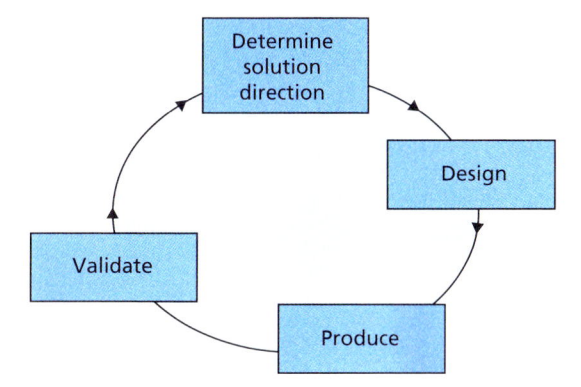

Figure 5.5 Steps within design and realization

In a development environment, designs can be developed using only the top-down approach; in a pure application management situation, the design of a change will generally follow a bottom-up approach.

This is why maintenance must simultaneously deal with both approaches.

c. Setup and content of a design

The setup of a design is mostly described by means of the development-/maintenance method that is employed. The design of an application (and a change) is complete if the data, the functions (data queries and processes) and the time aspects (coherence and order of functions) are all described. The time aspect is covered in use-cases. In the case of older systems, this type of approach is often not documented.
In larger applications, there is often a dividing line between overall design and detailed design.

5.3.3 Design activities
Design activities are generally prescribed by the selected development method and methodology. The following steps recur in almost all development methods.

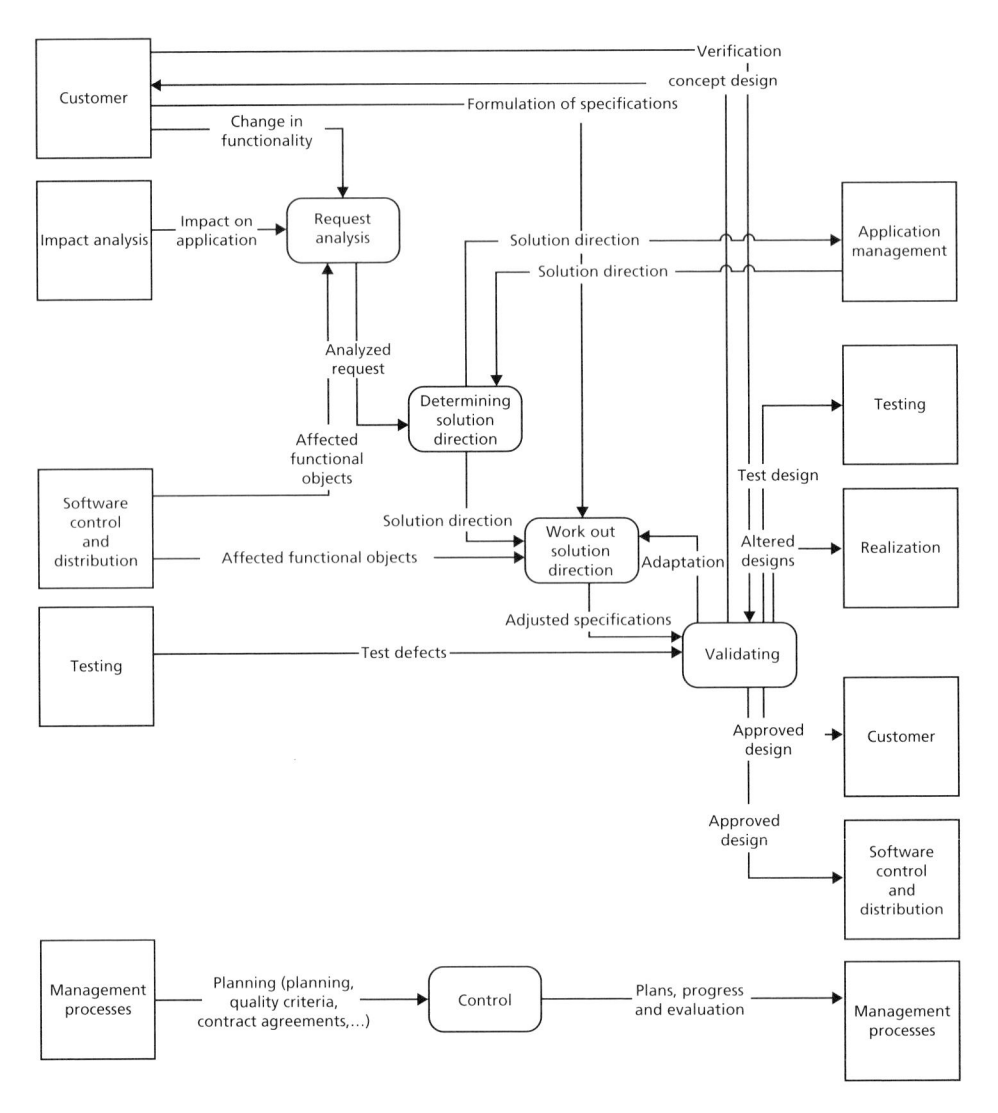

Figure 5.6 Outline of design process

Elaboration of request:
- In-depth analysis of the specified request or indicated change.
- Translation of that information into data requirements and requests, or into changes of data requests.
- Recording the relevant parts of the system.

Determining of solution direction(s):
- Determining the possible solution directions.
- Drawing up advantages and disadvantages, weighing up according to preconditions.
- Selection of a solution direction.

Elaboration of solution direction:
- Determining and translating specifications to design.
- Setup of functional test specifications.
- Documenting (of the changes) in the design.

Validating:
- Internal quality management.
- Feedback to customer.
- Agreement by customer.

Managing:
- Monitoring progress.
- Evaluating progress, results and process.

5.3.4 Design results
Design documentation: application objects (affected functional objects), such as:
- System documentation (recording of the elaborated and agreed upon design specifications into a design): a description of functions of the (changed) application, data model, process flows.
- Possible changes to the design as a result of the specifications.
- Test specifications/test design: a description of the way in which tests must be performed and the test cases that should be used.

Progress data (planning and control, etc.):
- Planning and progress
- Evaluations and possible problems.

5.3.5 Design relationships
Customer:
- Functionality change (input): outline of the specifications and/or desired functionality and requirements.
- Clarification of specifications (input): additional information regarding earlier communicated specifications or detailed specifications.
- Provisional design (output): concept version of the design.
- Verification (input): improvements or additions to the design and/or approval of the design.
- Agreed design (output): approved design.

Application management (other organizations):
- Solution direction (input): specifications or designs.
- Solution direction (output): specifications or designs.

The way in which other application management organizations are controlled can be compared to the process steps of the customer communicating with application management, depending on the structure (see the interfaces under customer). This also applies to the solution directions delivered by other organizations. For the sake of legibility, these interfaces are summed up under the heading of 'solution direction'.

Impact analysis:
- Application impact (input): outline of the ideas on solution direction, including impact, ideas on elaboration, etc. This is primary design input.

Realization:
- Changed designs (output): primary input for realization. The changes, as recorded in the designs/specifications, will be created during realization. This flow can physically take place via software control and distribution.

Testing:
- Test design (output): guidelines and points of concern based on the design for the test process.
- Errors (input): errors, requests or shortcomings that must be solved or answered in the design.

Software control and distribution:
- Affected functional objects: functional objects (designs, etc.) that must be adjusted.
- Agreed upon design: approved changed or new designs that are stored and registered within software control and distribution.

Management processes:
- Planning (input) (possible re-planning):
  - Planning and control: budgeted effort and duration.
  - Contract management: agreements made with customers.
  - Quality management: quality criteria, working methods, indicators.
  - Supplier management: agreements about suppliers and parties involved (such as application management).
- Progress and evaluations (output):
  - Planning and control: realization of planning or re-planning.
  - Quality management: problems, evaluations, realization of quality criteria.
  - Contract management: realization of agreements with the customer, customers' perception.
  - Supplier management: realization of supplier agreements.
- Plans (output):
  - Planning and control: rough estimates of duration.
  - Quality management: possible proposed deviations in quality system, working method, quality criteria, etc.
  - Contract management: suggested relationship and communication with customers.
  - Supplier management: possible deviations in dealing with suppliers.

5.4 Realization

5.4.1 Goal of realization
The goal of realization (also called 'build') is to convert the supplied designs or changes in designs, forming part of the design process, into concrete and correct changes to the automated information system.

5.4.2 Realization topics

Dividing into steps
The process steps within realization are based on the same classification that goes for almost every process in this Application maintenance and renewal cluster.

In the first place, the requirements are made clear (through functional system design or based on a prototype, among others). Based on this, a general outline is determined – the manner in which the change is technically performed (technical system design). Then this outline is developed in more detail. After that, the changes are realized and, finally, tested.

To realize concrete and correct changes to the automated information system, it is necessary to convert logical specifications to a technical solution structure. This is often an explicit step taken in a development method by having a technical system design phase.

Design and documentation
A technical system design is a description of the technical setup of an information system or the change to be made. In a technical system design, the translation from the functional requirements to the chosen technical solution, and the technical decisions are explained. A technical system design cannot always be found in the system documentation.

Sometimes, technical setup and solution are integrated into the functional system design. In such a case, there is always a risk of discussing the wrong aspects with business information management, for instance (that is: technical decisions).

A change is realized by creating or changing software. The structure and chosen solution within the software can be complex in nature. In such cases, additional application documentation is necessary, which can be achieved by incorporating adequate commentary in the source code. Another method is the setup or updating of a software description, or explicitly including it in a detailed technical system design. The quality system must provide guidelines for these decisions.

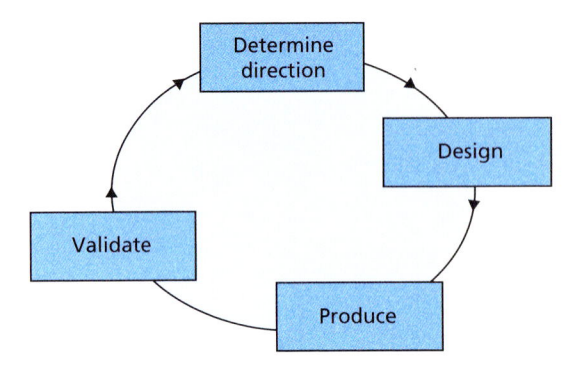

Figure 5.7 Steps within design and realization

Relationship with software control
In the first step within the realization process, a further assessment will be made as to which software is affected, based on the detailed designs. This inventory can differ from the previously identified change set.

Software can be immune to a change, meaning that it is set up in such a generic way that it is not affected by the change. It is also possible that the desired change is of such a nature that underlying software or modules must be adapted, but not this particular item. And then it is possible that additional software must be altered. Such a situation is undesirable because new checks must then be carried out to make sure that these objects or software have not been changed in the meantime, by another release or as a result of corrective maintenance.

The result of the realization step is the change package – the collection of software or data items that have actually changed. This changed or new software must be placed in the production environment by software control and distribution, once the test phase has been completed successfully. More information about change packages and change sets can be found in section 6.3 in the software control and distribution process.

Relationship with operation
In the realization process the functional requirement is translated in a technical solution. The operation of this technical solution takes place within infrastructure management. To execute this task, infrastructure management often requires information, such as which files are used by which software, what the requirements are to run these systems or software, and which dependencies exist between components in the production environment.

This information, the operation documentation, can be recorded in an operation manual (production manual). In any case, agreements will have to be made with the infrastructure management organization about how this information will be communicated and/or recorded.

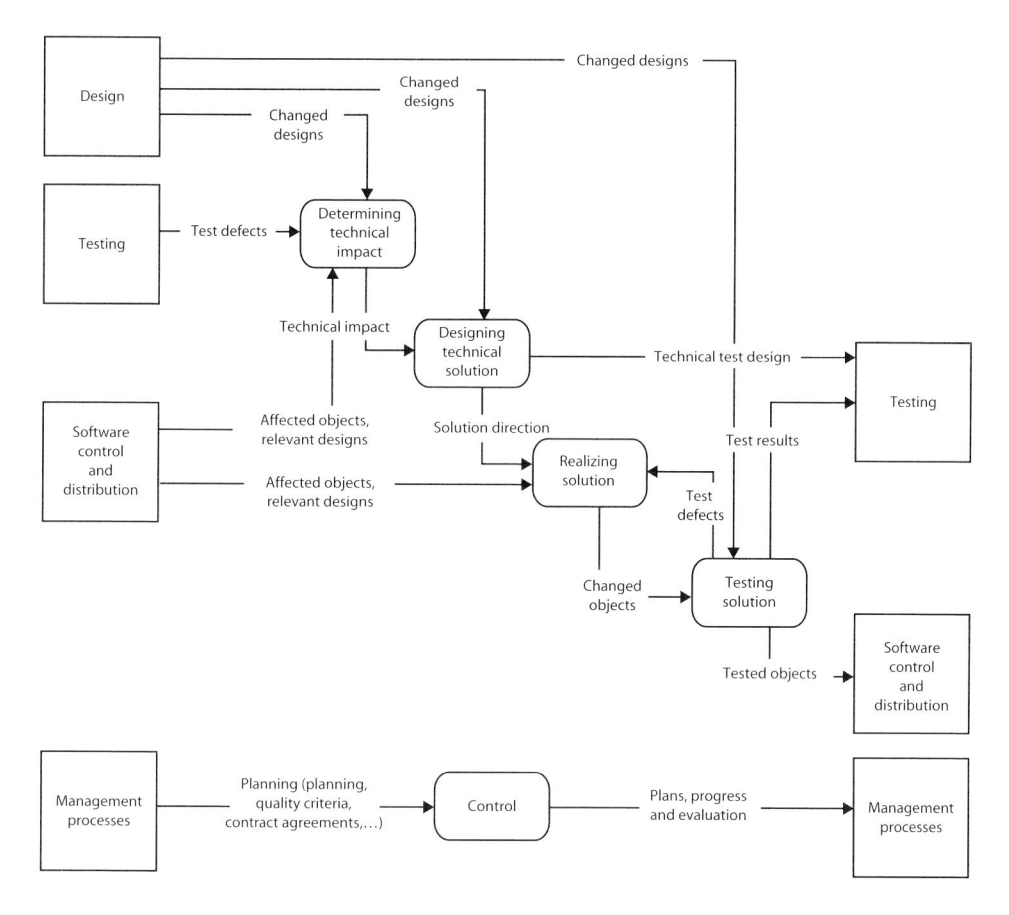

Figure 5.8 Realization process outline

5.4.3 Realization activities

Determining technical impact:
- Examining the current situation, desired functional requirements and design.
- Detailed identification of the affected components.

Designing the technical solution:
- Determining the overall solution direction.
- Determining the subdivision of more detailed changes.
- Determining the desired setup.
- Discussing/checking setup.
- Developing test specifications.
- Documenting the technical solution.

Realizing the solution:
- Changing the software.
- Changing the data objects.

- Changing possible additional objects (such as operation documentation).
- Documenting the software.

Testing the solution:
- Testing the different applications or programs in order to be able to correct software defects (white box).
- Testing the change: the complete entity of changed software and files.

Management:
- Planning the realization.
- Monitoring progress and realization and producing progress reports.
- Evaluating and determining of improvement suggestions or problems.

5.4.4 Realization results
The objects created in the realization process consist of new or changed documentation, a new or changed system, and test results.

New or changed documentation:
- Technical designs: description of the chosen technical solution and setup (preferably with additional motivation).
- Application documentation: description of the functioning of the software.
- Technical test specifications (test design).
- Production documentation: information for infrastructure management (how to run the system in the operational phase and applicable preconditions).

New or changed system:
- The new or changed software (provisional change packages).
- New or changed data definitions (including possible necessary conversions).

Test results:
- Unit test results.
- Possible test data/scripts.

Management information:
- Progress reports.
- Evaluation of process and result.

5.4.5 Realization relationships
Design:
- (Changed) designs (input): the designs or changed designs that must be realized (whether or not distributed via software management).

Testing:
- Test defects (input): defects or shortcomings that must be solved in realization.

Software control and distribution:
- Affected objects, relevant designs (input): software, technical documentation (and perhaps functional designs).
- Tested objects (output): changed software and documentation are stored once again.

Management processes:
- Planning (input):
  - Planning and control: expected effort and duration (or re-planning if the activities run out of schedule).
  - Contract management: agreements made with customers.
  - Quality management: quality criteria, working method, indicators.
  - Supplier management: agreements with suppliers and parties involved (such as application management).
- Progress and evaluations (output):
  - Planning and control: planning and estimations, realization.
  - Quality management: problems, evaluations, possible audit results, peer testing, random checks.
  - Contract management: realization of agreements with customers, customer perception.
  - Supplier management: realization of supplier agreements.
- Plans (input):
  - Planning and control: estimated capacity necessary for realization.
  - Quality management: possible deviations in quality system, working method, quality criteria, etc.
  - Contract management: proposed relationship and communication with customers.
  - Supplier management: possible deviations in the interaction with suppliers.

5.5　Testing

5.5.1　Goal of testing
Tests contain the activities necessary to determine whether the objects that have been designed have actually been realized. Testing will also determine whether applications are manageable and operable once realized.

The goal of the test process is to guarantee that the desired changes are realized according to specifications, and that applications show the correct behavior (after changes).

5.5.2　Testing topics
Testing is an important step towards preventing systems from failing to work in practice. In order to do this in a structural manner, many methodologies and tools have been developed. ASL does not prescribe any methods or methodologies, since these are generally always well adapted.

	Environment	Type of test
Implementation	User environment	Acceptance test
Testing	Production environment	Production test
	Functional system design	Functional system test
	Technical environment	Technical integration test
Realization	Program	Unit test

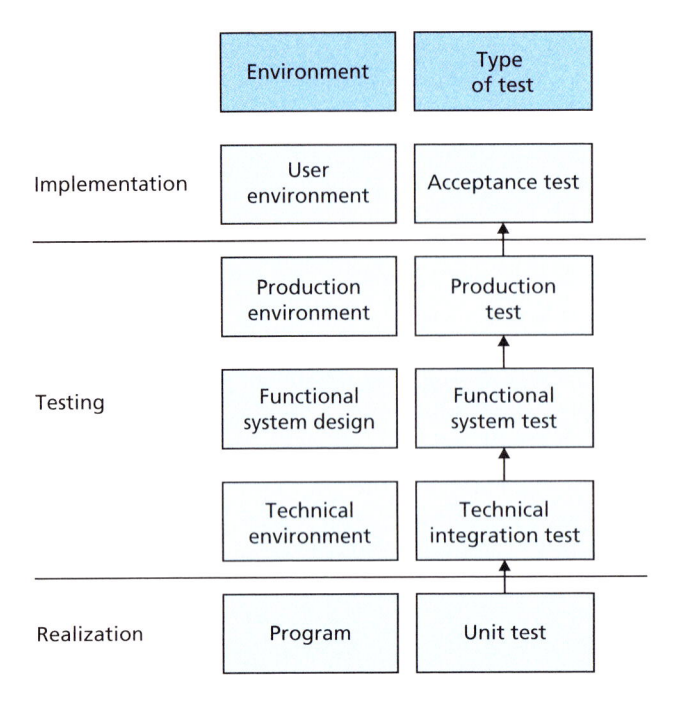

Figure 5.9 Testing in the environment

In the ideal situation, attention is focused on testing from the start of the change process. In ASL, this can be found in process design and realization activities, among others. In the design process, test designs – among other items – can be found (what should be tested and how changes should be tested). This is where the design process and the development of test cases (test data, test scripts) start. It is often a good idea to save these test cases and adapt or extend them in the case of new releases.

Running the tests takes place in reverse order to the change process. First, the realized software is tested, then the whole and, finally, all of it in its environment.
- Unit test. This test assesses whether the realized or changed software meets the requirements. This activity is still part of realization, because this is where it is determined, in a short cycle assessment, whether the realized product in this step complies with the design.

- Technical integration test or technical system test. This test examines:
  - Whether the realized entity conforms to the drawn design.
  - Whether the change operates within the whole system (so not just the changed parts are tested).
  - Whether the whole system is still maintainable after realization and meets the quality criteria that have been agreed upon from an information system management point of view.
- Functional system test. This test determines:
  - Whether the changes are correct.

- Whether the information system as a whole conforms to the agreed functionality.
- Whether the system still works as a whole from a functional point of view.
- Whether the functional documents comply with the agreed quality criteria.
• Production test (also called exploitation test). This test determines (mainly by the operation organization/infrastructure management):
  - Whether the changed or renewed system in operation conforms to the (for instance, in contract management) desired or required primary criteria (for example, in respect to runtimes, transaction times, etc.).
  - Whether the system conforms to the required secondary requirements (such as necessary production documentation, capability for adjustment, etc.).
• Acceptance test. Here, the customer/business information management tests:
  - Whether what was agreed upon has been realized (as a part of assignment discharge).
  - Whether the system is useful to the user organization. So, in this case, the customer organization also tests its own quality.

The first test step (unit test) belongs to the realization process – it constitutes the checking (step) of this process. The final step, the acceptance test, is not part of application management but is part of business information management. The acceptance test is performed during implementation. However, handling the results of an acceptance test follows the regular procedure within testing.

Testing in a chain environment is usually more difficult. There is no separate test for this. If this is not explicitly agreed upon and organized, the test takes place in the actual production situation.

5.5.3 Testing activities
Functional (logical) system test:
• Prepare testing.
• Perform test.
• Determine impact of test defects.
• Evaluate and determine solution direction.
• Have test defects handled.

Technical system test:
• Prepare tests (create test cases or adjust test sets).
• Perform tests.
• Determine impact of test defects.
• Evaluate and determine solution direction.
• Have test defects handled.

Production test support:
• Provide support during performing of tests.
• Determine impact of test defects.
• Evaluate and determine solution direction.
• Have test defects handled.

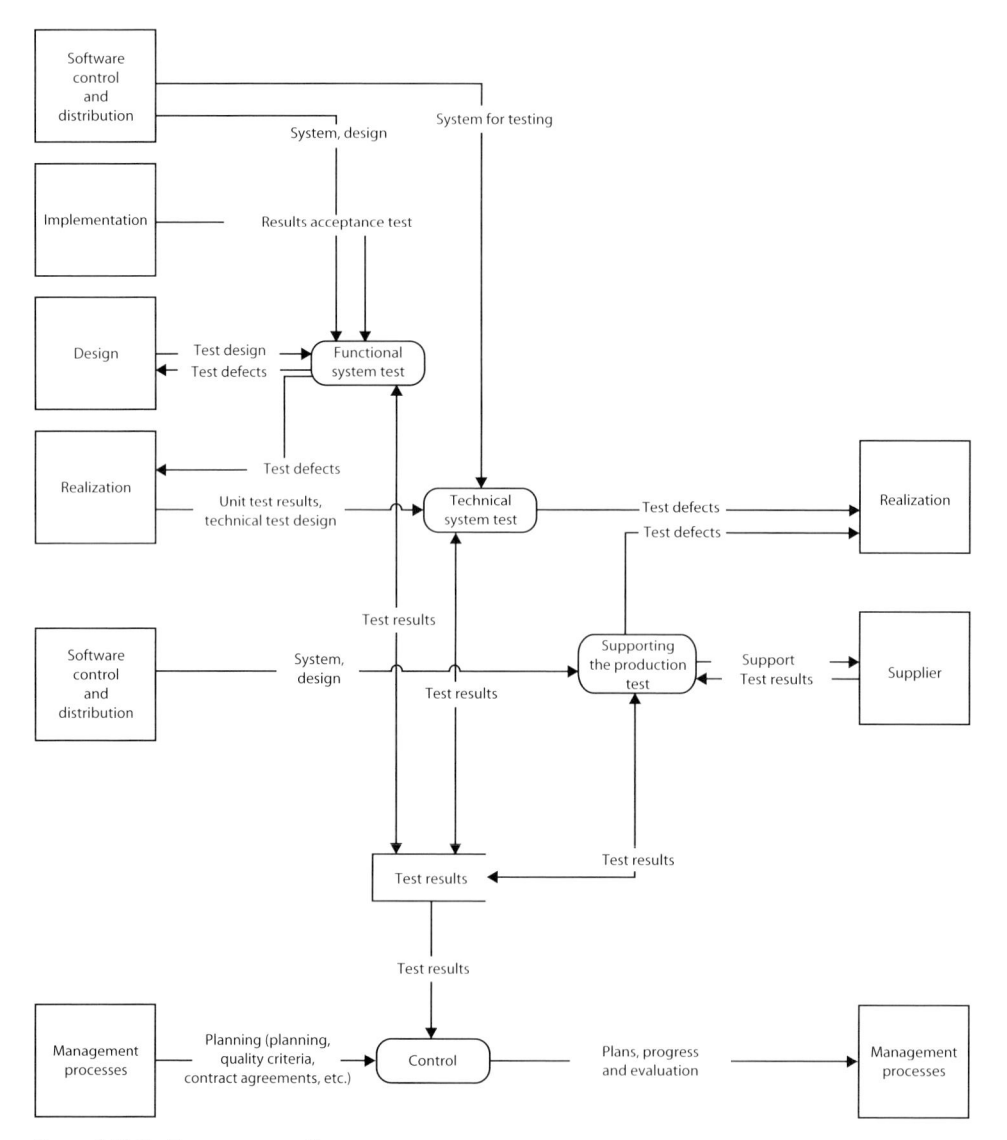

Figure 5.10 Testing process outline

Management:
- Make progress report.
- Make error reports.
- Evaluate process and result.

5.5.4 Testing results
Test products:
- Test results (expected outcome, outcome).
- Test records (number of test defects, status, to be finalized by).
- Test defects/requests.

Management reports:
- Progress reports.
- Evaluation.

Test support:
- Test cases/test sets.
- Test software/test scripts.

5.5.5 Testing relationships

Supplier:
- Support (output): support is provided for possible tests performed by suppliers (such as infrastructure management in the case of a production test).
- Test results (input): results of the tests.

Design:
- Test defects (output): tests result in defects and questions. These must be solved or answered in the realization or design processes.
- Test design (input): a functional test design is created in the design process.

Realization:
- Test defects (output): tests result in test defects or questions. These must be solved or answered in the realization or design processes.
- Technical test design and unit test results (input): in the realization process, a technical test design is created which includes an indication of how technical testing can or must take place. Unit test results are also communicated.

Implementation:
- Calls acceptance test (input): the results of the acceptance test are sent to the test process via the implementation process.

Software control and distribution:
- System, design (input): different versions of the system or parts of the system and/or the designs.

The various system versions to be tested are made available by software control and distribution. Also, test sets (test cases) and possible specific software can be saved and reused by storing them, using software control and distribution. Software control and distribution places the correct versions of the application objects to be tested in the right environments, such as system test environment, functional system test, acceptance test, etc.

Management processes:
Planning and control:
- Planning (input): the test planning and test capacity (possible re-planning if necessary).
- Progress and evaluations (output): realization of the planning.
- Plans (output): estimates concerning the execution of tests.

Quality management:
- Planning (input): includes, among others, quality criteria, working method, indicators.
- Progress and evaluations (output): evaluations and possible problems and realization quality requirements. The test system (including, among others, test strategy, test techniques, test quality attributes as described in test plans,) forms part of the quality system.
- Plans (output): if necessary, possible deviating additional requirements or changes in working method, quality criteria.

Contract management:
- Planning (input): agreements made with customers.
- Progress and evaluations (output): test results and possible impact on contract agreements with customers.
- Plans (output): proposal for agreements.

Supplier management:
- Planning (input): agreements about suppliers' or subcontractors' products and quality.
- Progress and evaluations (output): realization of agreements made.
- Plans (output): possible additional requirements or agreements with suppliers.

Financial management:
- Planning: (input): possible financial agreements/budget.
- Progress and evaluations (output): realization of these agreements.
- Plans (output): possible financial consequences.

5.6 Implementation

5.6.1 Goal of implementation
The implementation process encompasses all activities that must be performed in order to effect the change proposals from change management, for actual use and data processing. The goal of implementation is to satisfy the necessary preconditions to enable error-free use of a new version of the application and completion of the maintenance process.

5.6.2 Implementation topics
The implementation of an application should, in principle, not require much effort from application management – the application has been produced, tested and found to be correct. This requires more effort from the external parties – users must be prepared, software must be installed in the infrastructure, and possibly the infrastructure needs to be adapted.

It can be necessary for application management to provide support here:
- Support during deployment for use by the user organization.

- Support when putting the system into production by infrastructure management.
- Support for the use or integration of changed functionality and software by other application management organizations.
- The completion of the change and the securing of application- and project documentation for the organization's own processes.

This means that these last activities are for the internal organization.

For the application management party that will be managing the software, implementation forms the first concrete step towards application management.

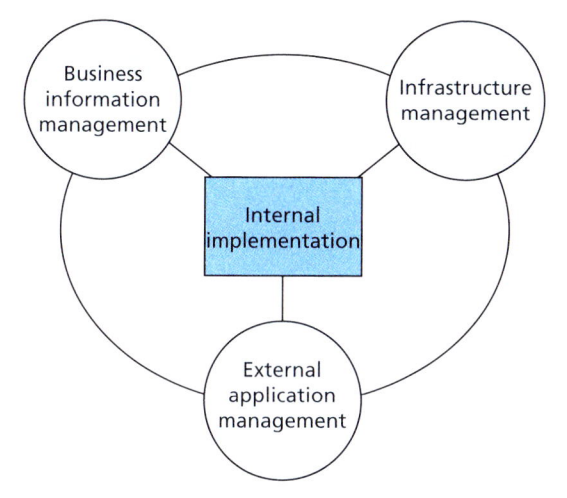

Figure 5.11 Implementation topics

Another important step is the acceptance test. With this test, the business information administrator will investigate whether all changes have been built in the correct manner, from a user's perspective. Based on this, a declaration of agreement is drawn up.

It is also validated here whether the application conforms to the requirements set by application management.

b. Execution and organizational aspects

The activities to be performed depend on a number of factors:
- The agreed services.
- The nature of the application and its abilities.
- The nature of the change, the manner in which this change is carried out, and its impact (some changes require complex data migration while others do not).

> *Examples*
> Release 12-01 is complex. The data model in this release has undergone some in-depth changes and, for this reason, extensive programs have been built to convert data to the new structure. This complex single-use software required some significant support from application management. Release 12-01 also entailed that data quality checks were set at a significantly higher level.
>
> This has had quite an impact on business information administrators and users. Data had to be checked and corrected. During preparation for implementation, application management
>
> developed and used monitoring software to locate possible errors. Supplementary queries were also requested by the user organization to pinpoint inconsistencies. The impact on the production environment was substantial and it required much support.
>
> The 12-02 maintenance release is simple – no conversions, no migrations.

> **Topic: Deployment**
>
> *Operation and acceptance criteria*
> In implementation, it is important to validate whether a new application or new version can be deployed. By testing whether an application is operable or maintainable, obstacles to application support, maintenance and renewal are perceived in advance and are hopefully solved. The testing of support, maintenance and renewal criteria is usually conducted among others in testing.
>
> If development is performed by organizations outside support, maintenance and renewal, additional steps and tests are necessary, because the responsibility for the objects is transferred. In that case a separate test also becomes necessary to make sure that the other parties have also created actual applications and/or software that meet the support, maintenance and renewal criteria. The test can be performed by, or on assignment of, the receiving party. Usually, such an organization requires guarantees that the criteria have been taken into account earlier in the process.

5.6.3 Implementation activities

Support the transfer to production:
- Supporting the preparation of the exploitation process and installation.
- Supporting, or executing, the changing of data definitions in the production environment, support of technical conversions.
- Preparing and supporting the scheduling of data processing (see also the IT operation management process).
- Preparing the actual assignment for transferring into production (production assignment).

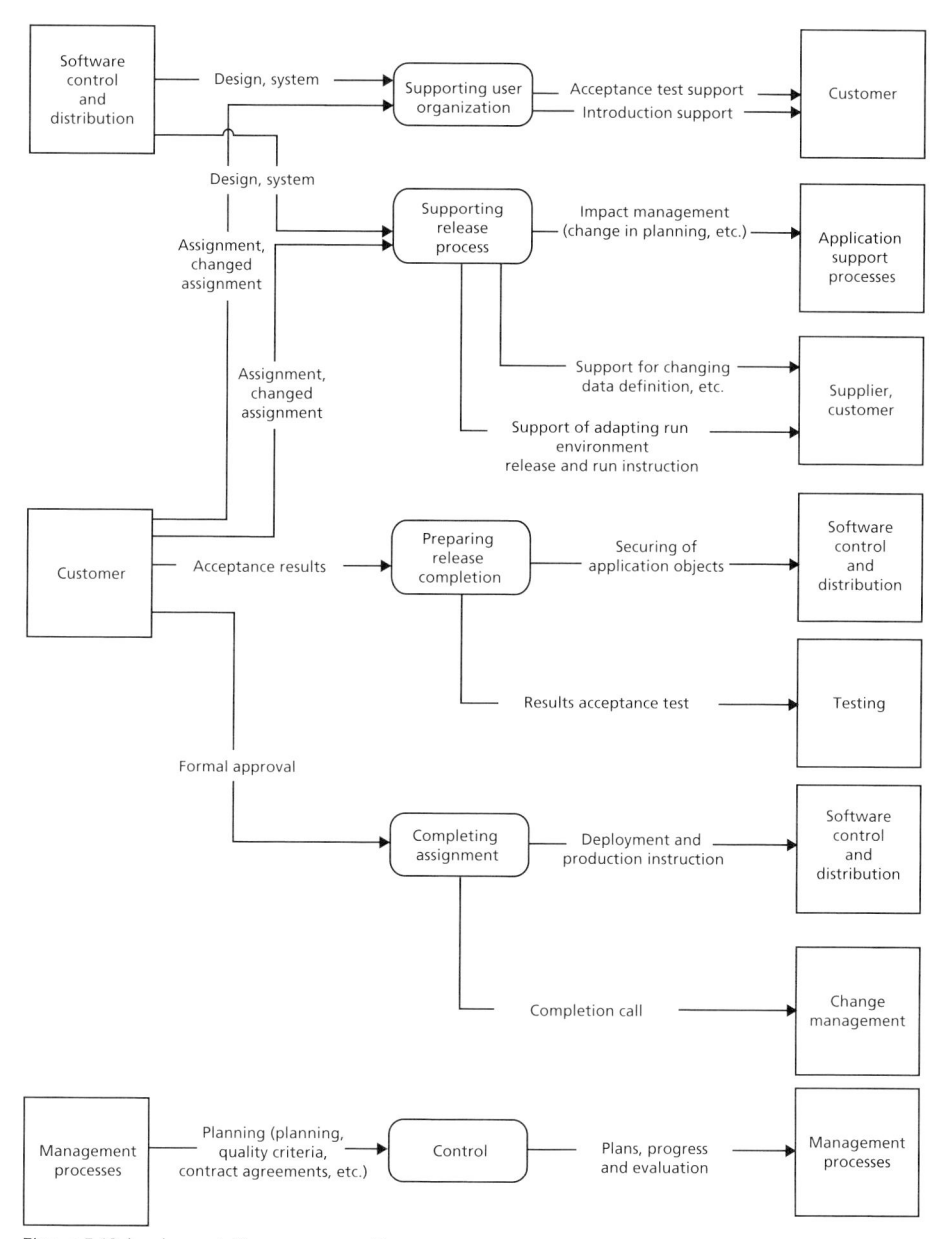

Figure 5.12 Implementation process outline

Support of user organization:
- Support during preparation of acceptance testing.
- Support during the execution of acceptance test (data, questions, processing of test results).
- Support of business information management in aid of introduction into the user organizations, such as support of changes to user manuals, support during functional conversions (functional control parameters).

Preparation for the finalization of the release:
- Archiving documents, preparation of discharge protocol, initiation of evaluations.
- Adjusting test defects resulting from acceptance test.

Completion of assignment:
- Assignment discharge.
- Issuing production assignment.
- Status call to change management.

Management:
- Estimation of necessary capacity and working method.
- Compilation of progress reports.
- Evaluation.

5.6.4 Implementation results
Supporting deployment for use:
- Supporting acceptance test.
- Possible calls from acceptance test.
- Supporting the introduction into user organization.

Supporting taking the system into production and roll-out:
- Ensuring that the requirements of application support, maintenance and renewal, and production are fulfilled.
- Additional production information.
- Possible changes in production scheduling.
- Supporting the changing of data definitions and conversions.

5.6.5 Implementation relationships
Customer (often business information management):
- Support for acceptance test (output): support for the execution of the acceptance test.
- Discharge protocol (input): the assignment discharge for the release, change, assignment for renewal.
- Support of introduction (output): support for the introduction into the user organization (support in user manuals, changes in functional control parameters, arranging of conversion scripts, etc.)

Supplier, customer (mainly in aid of infrastructure management):
- Supporting changing data definitions (output): by means of, for instance, support of data definition changes, handing over information about files, processing jobs/steps, order of jobs, support in developing installation procedures, etc.
- Assignment for installing of processing, production assignment (output): supporting and maybe controlling the process of taking the system into production.
- Supporting installing the processing, production assignment (output): results of supporting of the introduction.

Application support processes:
- Impact operation (output): Experience gained from the production test and acceptance test containing, for instance, the necessary computer capacity, availability and continuity. As a result of the release, new planning or possible adjustments to the production scheduling may be necessary.

Software control and distribution:
- Design, system (input): changed products (change package) can be placed in the user test environment and the production environment(s) at the stipulated time.

Change management:
- Reporting completion (output): changes in the status of the developments or the release (approved and subsequently in production).

Tests:
- Findings from acceptance test (output): the results of the acceptance test that give cause for testing and/or improvements.

Management processes:
- Planning (planning, contract agreements, quality criteria, etc.) (input):
  - Planning and control: expected effort and turnaround time required (or re-planning (if necessary, in case the planning has overrun)).
  - Contract management: agreements.
  - Quality management: quality criteria, working method, indicators.
  - Supplier management: agreements with suppliers and parties involved (such as application management).
- Progress, evaluations, problems (output):
  - Planning and control: planning and estimates, realization.
  - Quality management: problems, evaluations, possible audit results, peer testing, incidental checks.
  - Contract management: realization of agreements with the customer, perception.
  - Supplier management: realization of suppliers' agreements.
- Plans (output):
  - Planning and control: estimated capacity necessary for implementation.
  - Quality management: possible deviations in quality system, working method, quality criteria, etc.
  - Contract management: suggested relationships and communication with customers.
  - Supplier management: possible deviations in the interaction with suppliers.

6 Connecting processes

> **ASL statements**
>
> - The connecting processes synchronize the application support processes and the maintenance and renewal processes. They address the logistics within application management.
>
> - The complexity of these processes has increased due to the growth in complexity of services and the increased use of standard solutions, so the necessity to effectively implement these processes has also increased.

6.1 Introduction

The connecting processes are found between the application support cluster and the application maintenance and renewal cluster. These connecting processes take care of the synchronization and alignment between application support (the use of applications in a stable situation) and application maintenance and renewal (the adapting of applications as a result of requirements and developments).

More and more often, you will find an n-to-m relationship between application support, maintenance and renewal:
- Releases and versions are used in multiple locations, and often different versions are used. This means there are more instances and versions to manage.
- However, there is a need for the simple execution of maintenance and renewal processes, which is not always possible. Sometimes the same functionalities or improvements need to be implemented into multiple versions of the same application.

This means that it is necessary to control this synchronization. For this reason, there are two connecting processes:
- Change management: change management forms the 'inlet valve' to the Application maintenance and renewal cluster. Here it is decided by whom, which and when changes will be made to applications.
- Software control and distribution: this process acts as the 'outlet valve'. In this process logistics around application object within the Application maintenance and renewal cluster are handled, as is the distribution to production and operation. It also forms an 'inlet valve' for the application objects that are created by other application management organizations.

6.2 Change management

6.2.1 Goal of change management

The goal of change management is to ensure that a standardized working method is used for changing applications, so that harmonized and prioritized changes can be built to improve the supplied functionality of applications.

In the change management process, the various desired changes are gathered, clustered and planned into releases or projects. This constitutes, as it were, the production planning[1] of the application and the application management – how we plan the changes in the change 'production line' (after all, maintenance and renewal is nothing but a change factory).

The change management process works in close cooperation with impact analysis. Initial ideas or assumptions can be validated and adjusted within impact analysis. Impact analysis can also be used to gain insight into these assumptions or ideas; this is why there can be iterations between these processes. Change management results in the final definition of the change and in agreements about the detail, as well as release delivery data (under the auspices of contract management).

6.2.2 Change management topics

a. Release and change

Change
A change is the desired or required alteration of application objects. This includes software and files, but it also applies to documentation and other objects. The goal of a change is often to alter application functionality, but a change can also relate to a different operation, behavior, or correct functioning.

Release
A release is a set of grouped changes that are simultaneously and collectively undertaken. A release is a round of changes of an application, leading to a new version of the application.

The recognition of the release concept and its use has more than one advantage:
- Improvement of efficiency: by clustering changes, less capacity for design, building and testing is necessary than when changes are handled separately.
- Improvement of predictability and control. There is a mechanism in place for the planning of changes, which leads to greater predictability and easier control.
- The management and scheduling of capacity will run more smoothly.

---

[1] In the sense of a regular company, such as a bicycle factory, building contractor, etc.

The recognition of release has – or appears to have had – a negative effect on the time-to-market. A limited number of releases take place in a year and a customer has to wait for the deployment of the release.

Effective organization considerably limits such a disadvantage:
- The identification of sufficient annual releases.
- Not completely filling the releases in an early stage, but leaving some margin in releases, so as to be able to implement (important) last-minute changes. In short: do not plan all releases filled up completely at the beginning of a year.

On the other hand, the cost benefits are often also obvious.

Coherence between release and change
The core activity of change management is the gathering of changes and fitting them into releases. There can be a number of relationships between releases and changes:
- A release contains multiple changes.
- A change can also be covered by multiple releases (as in the case of renewal). This is, however, quite rare.

Emergency change
An application is not always error-free upon delivery. Sometimes defects are of such a nature that they must be solved quickly. This leads to a change that must be quickly executed. In such a case, the usual maintenance process regularly takes too long, so it is not unusual to define an emergency procedure as well: a change process in case of serious failures, defects or shortcomings. Part of this process is the identification of a regular flow in order to deal with such changes quickly.

Structural renewal
Besides emergency changes, major changes may also be desired with such a scale that other projects will have to be run in parallel with the regular maintenance - for instance, the renewal of a significant part of the application. In this way, a number of releases can run simultaneously. The synchronization of all the changes in these flows is important in order to prevent previously encountered defects or changes, recurring in later versions. Monitoring to enable prevention of this situation also forms part of change management.

b. Design and implementation factors

The set-up of the decision-making process to determine which changes are allowed and which are not, has a number of implementation variables, such as:
- The location in the chain and the authorization of application management to make decisions. Sometimes the decision-making authority lies outside application management, and sometimes entirely within.
- The extent to which formalization and consultation are necessary. Some organizations and customers have an extremely formalized process with many consultation steps. In other organizations, this process is very simple.

- The dynamics and the degree of iteration. Some environments are very changeable and sometimes there is a strong need for multiple iterations (for instance, because the impact of a change often leads to the readjustment of the change content and its prioritization).

c. Stages of change

Changes can go through various stages. This is also one of the aspects to be agreed upon. Usually there is a minimum of three stages, but there can be more:
- Received and not yet finalized/scheduled (desired, a change proposal).
- Taken on in maintenance (in progress).
- Executed (finalized).

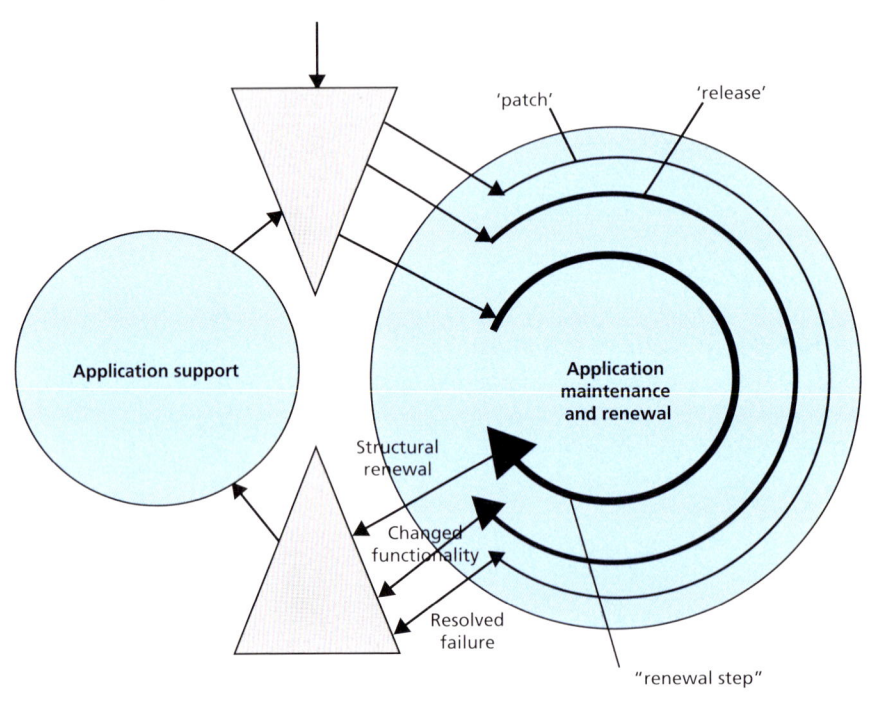

Figure 6.1 Multiple parallel releases

6.2.3 Change management activities

Registration of changes:
- Receiving and inventory of change proposals.
- Storing and registering of change proposals and corresponding initial data (regarding scope, duration, priority, origin).

Scheduling of release:
- Determining assumptions and conditions about releases.
- Incorporation and clustering of change proposals into releases.
- Determining whether these releases comply with starting points and conditions.

- Preparation of decision-making for the release.
- Initiation of execution of changes/release.

Adjustment and monitoring of release:
- Establishment and validation of assumptions about the release.
- If necessary: adjustment of releases based on more detailed data from impact analysis or from next phases in the maintenance/renewal process.
- Monitoring of interaction between releases.
- Monitoring of completion, removal of change proposals after completion of a release.

Control and reporting:
- Creation of reports about, among others, changes still to be carried out, pending, completed (etc.) changes, and the extent of 'backlogs'.
- Drawing up evaluation reports and reports about problems, time, money, etc.

Information and communication:
- Provision of information about changes.
- Provision of information about changes in releases, or about releases.
- Provision of information about proposed releases or changes in the information system at a functional level.

6.2.4 Change management results
Release:
- Series of changes.
- Scope of the release and its duration.
- Changes or components of changes carried through.
- Impact of the release.

Change:
- Requested change.
- Cause, expected impact.
- Status.

6.2.5 Change management relationships
Customer:
- Change request (output): changes that belong on the change calendar from an application perspective.
- Feedback (input): feedback on the change proposals or remarks about the possible scheduling of a release.

Supplier:
- Change request (input): change desired by the supplier.
- Feedback (output): feedback on this.

Note: The design of the process depends on the control over the application or related components. For both customers and suppliers, the arrows can possibly be fully reversed. (i.e. output instead of input).

Use support:
- Changes (output): information about the changes for the benefit of communication.

Application support processes:
- Call, change request (input): desired or required changes to the application from an information system management point of view.
- Status request (output): feedback about the status of the change request.

Change processes:
- Information (output): information about the changes.

Impact analysis:
- Adjustment of human capacity requirement (input): estimated deviation of size of the release or change based on a more detailed problem analysis within impact analysis.
- Release (output): content of a release.

Implementation:
- Completion call (input): call from the Implementation process about the completion of the release.

Planning and control:
- Plans (release and required capacity) (output): expected estimate of the human capacity necessary for the change or release.
- Planning (human capacity and timelines) (input): available human capacity, the capacity reserved for the release or development in relation to the time (calendar).
- Planning, progress and realization (input): progress of the release or development including human capacity used, with possible necessity for adjustments.
- Plans (possible adjustments to release) (output): possible adjustments to the release with their impact on capacity and turnaround.

These flows are taken on within planning and control, following customary practices.

Contract management:
- Plans (output): first proposal towards a release or estimation of the feasibility of the proposed release.
- Agreements, scope (input): the proposed or determined release along with changes to be carried out and additional conditions.
- Agreements scope (input): criteria relating to possible adjustments to the release.
- Plans (output): release adaptations or adaptation proposals.

These flows are taken on within contract management, following customary practices.

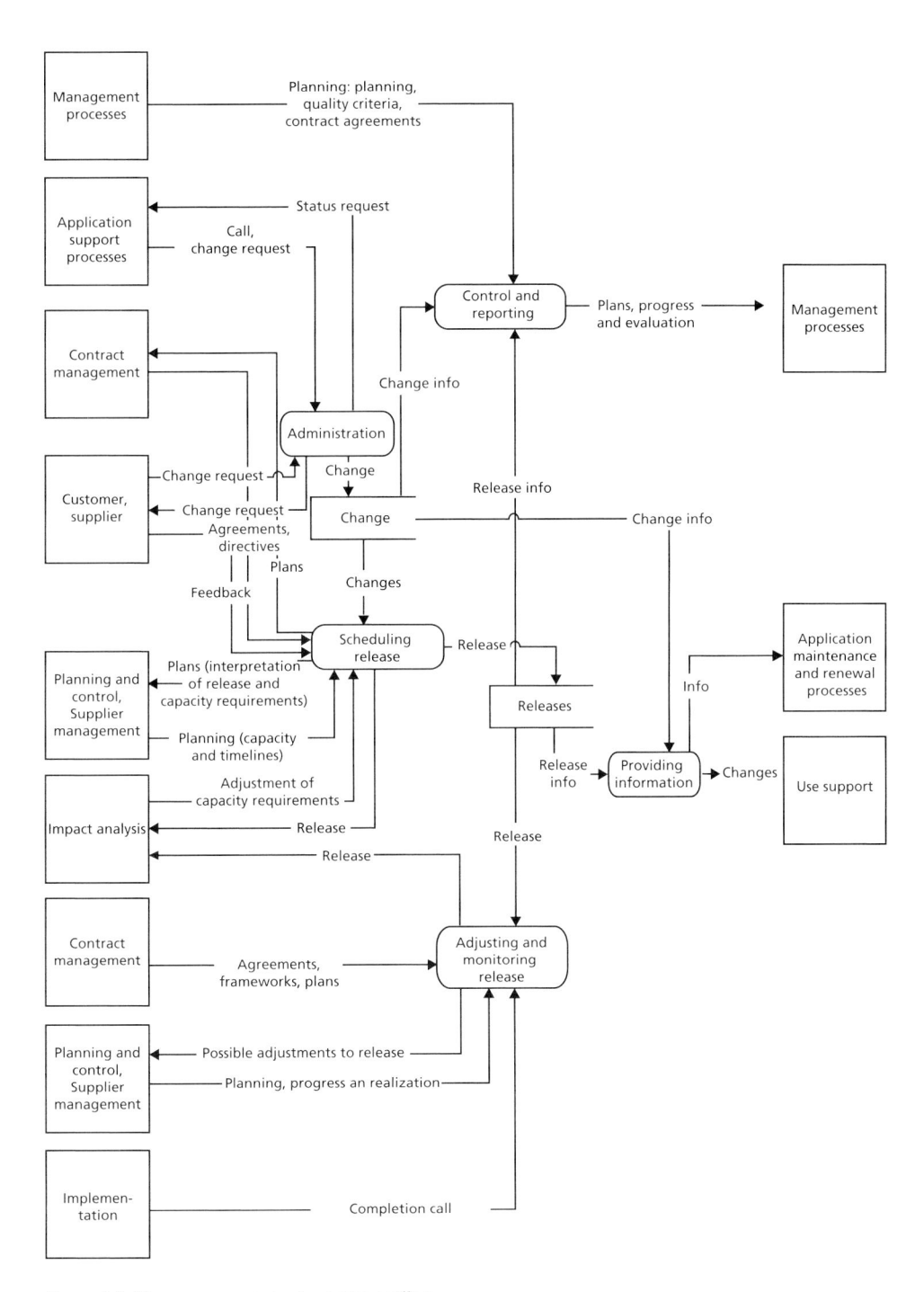

Figure 6.2 Change management process outline

Supplier management:
- Plans (output): proposal for a release including its impact on customers (in other words: the desired release for suppliers).
- Planning (input): agreements with suppliers about human capacity, delivery period, services and/or functionalities related to this release.
- Plans (possible adjustments to release) (output): release adaptations or adaptation proposals.
- Planning, progress and realization (input): progress made by suppliers.

In addition, in order to support 'control and reporting', there are information flows that also occur in the other processes, from and to the management processes.

6.3 Software control and distribution

6.3.1 Goal of software control and distribution

The second connecting process is software control and distribution, which ensures the recording, distribution and control of application objects. Application objects (in this context) are the files/components that are used to build an automated system. Objects to be considered here include applications and modules, data definitions, designs, test sets, compilation scripts, etc.

Software control and distribution takes care of the physical distribution of these objects by, for instance, transferring software to the production environment or transferring the correct objects (such as designs) to the design process.

The goal of software control and distribution is making the correct application objects (or information about them) available to the correct processes at the right time.

This process must offer a safe working method that limits the risks posed by unauthorized use, unauthorized change, and destruction. The process can be regarded as a product tollgate: adapted application components are transferred to production (infrastructure management), and the information about this is made available to the application management application support processes. Also, this process takes care of the logistics of the objects between the various steps of the maintenance process.

6.3.2 Software control and distribution topics

a. The logistic process

The need to effectively and stringently organize the logistic process within application management has intensified over the past years. Besides increased expectations for quality, the need for 'compliancy' (the compliance with legal or operational requirements about the insightfulness and reliability of information processing) is also a factor.

In addition, the implementation of the process can become complex:
- Often, a situation may occur in which multiple versions and releases of an application need to be supported simultaneously. The impact of a change (e.g. a change necessary to correct a critical error) on the other releases (such as the regular release) thus becomes an issue and must be known.
- Applications are built up from many objects (software programs, modules) and there are various types of objects (such as software, modules, purchased modules, scripts, various types of designs, test sets, etc.). The number of objects may be quite large.
- Sometimes, objects or components are used in an application from other suppliers, who have their own version control processes.
- Often, the next step in the maintenance process cannot be taken if not all the versions in the preceding step have been completed. For instance: meaningful testing can only take place if all changed (and to be changed) programs are available.
- Because of this, and also because of compliancy requirements, software release must be explicit and demonstrable, and it must be possible to prove accuracy and comprehensiveness.
- Comprehensiveness is always an issue. During a later stage of the maintenance cycle, it may become evident that more objects need to be adapted. The extension of the 'change set' must take place in a controlled manner.

The situation and the demands that are set have a major impact on the way in which software control and distribution is established.

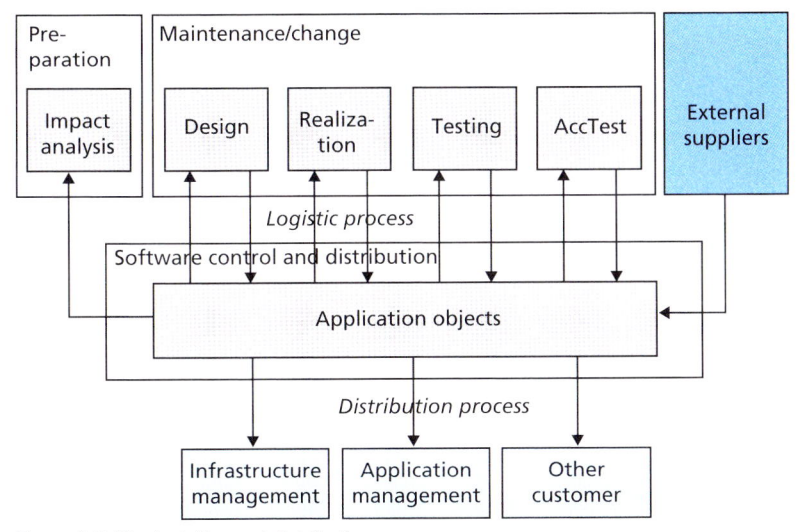

Figure 6.3 The logistics and distribution process

b. The distribution process

Besides the logistic function within the Application maintenance and renewal cluster, software control and distribution also performs a distribution function to parts of the external community, such as infrastructure management. Here as well, many variants are possible, which in turn have an impact on the establishment and scope of the process, and also on the link with configuration management (within application management as well as within infrastructure management). There are various forms of distribution:

- Transfer to multiple external environments. A software package supplier often hands over software or updates to multiple infrastructure environments. Often, deployment to the final production environment cannot and may not take place (the package cannot be automatically installed). In almost all organizations, it is 'poor practice' if this can and does take place. In virtually all organizations, this is not acceptable from a security, fraud-sensitivity and integrity point of view. This is why sources or executables are distributed, which infrastructure management must install itself.
- Transfer to multiple external environments that are responsible for application management. In some cases installation (automated or not) is possible. In order to make this possible, application management will need to have an overview of the infrastructure environment and will have to check that the correct versions, etc. are installed.
- Transfer to an infrastructure environment that is integrated into the service portfolio of the application management process. Here, the process is linked to similar infrastructure management processes. The organization of this process requires a lot of harmonization because infrastructure management will place numerous conditions on this. On the other hand, this makes linking with configuration management possible and can lead to a demonstrably reliable process.
- Transfer to a unique external environment without this integration.

Besides an output side, software control and distribution also has an input side – more and more often, base modules (components) are used in which the version management process of third parties must be incorporated into the organization's own environment.

c. Products

A number of concepts play an important role within software management. These include:
- Change set
- Change packages
- Shipments

Change set
The change set is the collection of objects, which may undergo change as the result of a release. These are the objects that are (more or less) allocated to a release or change.

Change packages
A change package is the collection of objects that have been changed and approved and will be transferred to the production environment (in a broad sense; the current system documentation environment is also included here). In case of multiple releases, there are – similarly - multiple change packages.

Shipments
A shipment is a collection of changed objects that are integrally transferred to one or more production environments, including implementation instructions.

The actual distribution to the production environment can also take place in steps. This means that multiple distributions (shipments) may be necessary or desirable.

6.3.3 Software control and distribution activities
Registration of objects in the maintenance process:
- Registering of the change set: indicating that the objects can be changed as a result of a release.
- Possible transferring of the various objects between the different environments in the maintenance process.
- Transferring to the production environments.

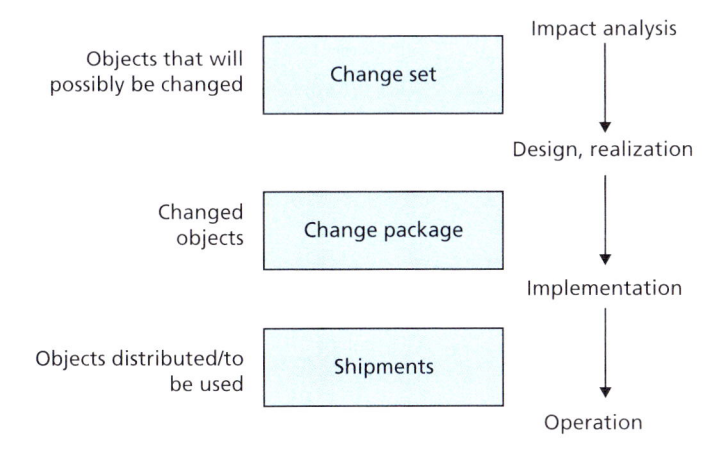

Figure 6.4 Objects within software control and distribution

Issuing of objects:
- Storing versions of objects.
- Provision of various types of documentation to design or realization.
- Provision of software items (programs etc.) to realization, testing, acceptance testing, etc.

Information and communication (to maintenance process):
- Identifying related objects (with respect to a change) and defining change sets.
- Identifying possible 'interferences' (overlaps) in the various change sets.

- Provisioning of software and documentation in a certain status of a specific release.
- Determining the change package.

Transfer to production:
- Determining the various possible shipments based on the present change packages.
- Approval of transfer to production.
- Transfer of shipments to the production environment (in a broad sense).
- Transfer of current information about the new or changed application objects to configuration management.

Control:
- Creation of reports about the software control and distribution process.
- Monitoring progress, execution, agreements, working method, identification of problems, etc.

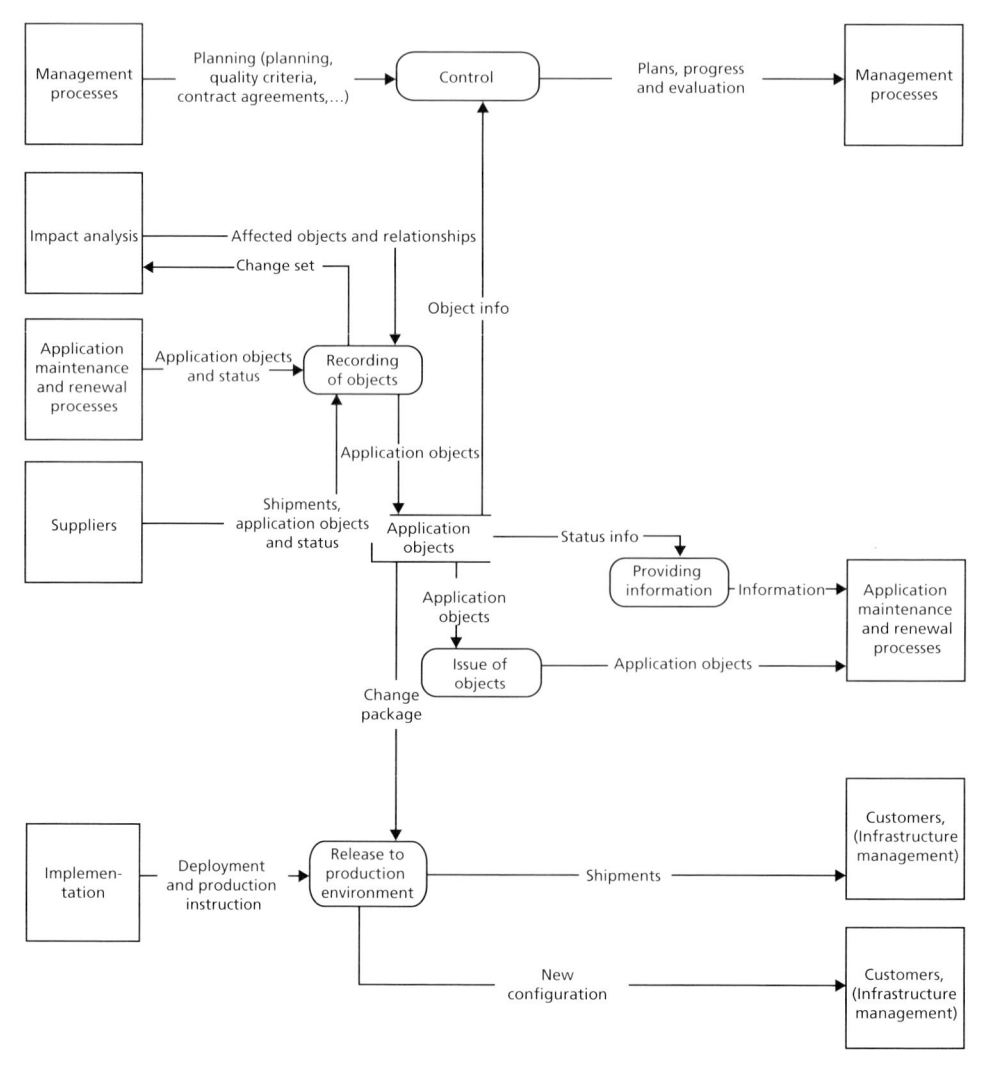

Figure 6.5 Software control and distribution process outline

6.3.4 Software control and distribution results
Application objects:
- Various types of objects necessary for operation, maintenance, renewal or the possible use of an application.
- Status and information about the object.
- Versions and history.

Application object deliveries:
- Change sets.
- Change packages.
- Shipments.

Support for transition between environments and phases:
- Transfer of software and documentation.
- Transfer to production.
- Information about the new configuration.

Information about objects and statuses:
- Support in determining impact and relations.
- Relationships between releases.
- Other information.

Control:
- Reports.
- Evaluations, problems.

6.3.5 Software control and distribution relationships
Suppliers:
- Shipments, application objects (input): application objects used or to be used that are created by other organizations.

Customers (infrastructure management):
- Shipments, application objects (output): generally to infrastructure management, but also supply to customers (or other application management organizations) is possible.

Impact analysis:
- Change set (input): collection of application objects that can be altered as a result of a change or release.
- Affected objects and relations (output): answer to an information request from impact analysis concerning application objects and the relationships between them. This information is used within impact analysis to determine the change set.

Implementation:
- Transition and production transfer (input): assignment for the distribution of a new release or system to infrastructure management or to a different organization.

Change processes:
- Application objects (input and outgoing): application objects that are adapted or used within the process, and application objects that are created or used within the process.
- Information (output): necessary or relevant information about application objects.

Configuration management:
- New configuration (output): provision of information about the new version and about the customer organization.

Management processes:
- Planning, contract agreements, quality criteria:
    - Planning and control: (annual) planning (scheduling and capacity), re-scheduling.
    - Contract management: agreements.
    - Quality management: quality criteria, working methods, indicators.
    - Supplier management: agreements with suppliers and parties involved (such as application management).

- Progress, evaluations, problems:
    - Planning and control: plans and estimates, realization of budget.
    - Quality management: problems, evaluations.
    - Contract management: realization of agreements with the customer, customer perception.
    - Supplier management: realization of suppliers' agreements.

7 Management processes

> **ASL statements**
>
> - Market dynamics impact the management processes significantly. Continual evaluation and reassessment of agreements with customers is necessary
> - Management processes also form the link between operations and policy.

7.1 Introduction and management topics

Management processes are positioned at the center of the framework and are described in this chapter. These processes probably need to be more flexible than the other processes: major changes in the dynamic IT sector have been influencing both process design/implementation and management for years.

Application management is managed from various perspectives. ASL recognizes five management processes:
- *Contract management:* the agreement and management of customer expectations regarding services and supplied products.
- *Planning and control:* the management and monitoring of time, human resources capacity and delivery dates.
- *Quality management:* monitoring of the power to supply and the quality of the organization, application and services.

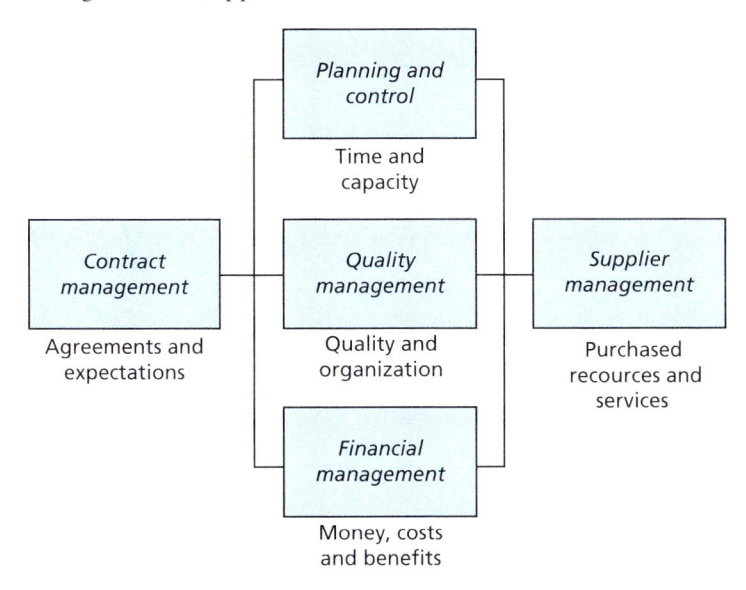

Figure 7.1 The management processes

- *Financial management:* management of the production factor relating to money (costs, benefits).
- *Supplier management:* management of services and products that are acquired.

7.1.1 Management at the center between operational and strategic processes

Management processes are positioned at the center of the framework, between the operational and strategic processes. As a result, three change portfolios converge at management level:

- The strategic change portfolio: changes from strategic processes that must be implemented at management level.
- The tactical change portfolio: this contains the short/medium term changes and goals to be achieved (scope of six months to two years). Many of these demands are business-driven and too short-term to be recognized in the strategic change portfolio.
- The operational change portfolio contains the changes and improvements from an operational perspective. Budget and scope for regular application support, maintenance and renewal are determined at management level.

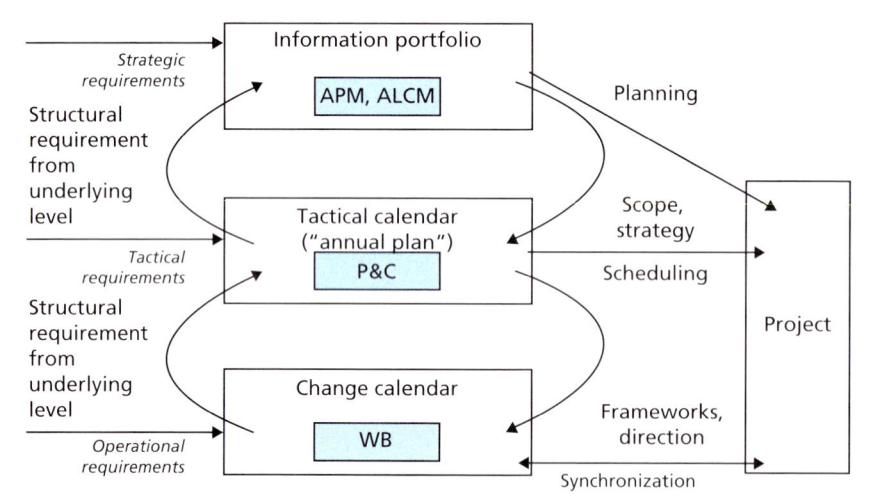

Figure 7.2 Portfolios and their correlation

The correlations between these portfolios are illustrated in Figure 7.2. In addition to the external demands placed directly on the portfolio, there are also bottom-up and top-down demand flows.

Demands with an overly structured nature are passed up to a higher level. Below are two examples.

> *Example 1*
> Over the past few years, the number of defects in the TTT-module has increased. More corrective maintenance is needed. There are also more approved changed proposals aimed at improving the low quality of the module. At the higher management process level, quality management takes the decision to structurally improve the module as part of the next release.
>
> *Example 2*
> A planning and control analysis has indicated that the relationship table frequently needs many changes and that maintenance costs are always high. Quality management has also observed much dissatisfaction with the possibilities. The application is considered not to be future-proof. The issue is dealt with in application life cycle management and application portfolio management, where the idea is developed of separating the customer functionality from the application and replacing it by customer relationship management (CRM).

There is also a top-down management flow, giving scope and direction to the processes in the lower-lying cluster.

> *Example 3*
> Within application life cycle management, it has been decided that the customer and relationship functionality must be removed from the application; a roadmap for this enhancement has been outlined. The scenario is designed in such a way that the release calendar does not need to be changed. The first step in this direction will be taken in the first release in the following year. As a result, the release budget has been doubled, ensuring that regular urgent changes can be executed as usual. Consequently, business operations are not hindered.

> *Example 4*
> The budget for application support, maintenance and renewal was based on significantly higher norms. In the previous year, system defects caused negative publicity.
>
> Management decided that reliability must be the top priority. With regard to the application maintenance and renewal processes, it has been determined that system reliability must be improved step-by-step and that maintenance must not lead to production outages. Designs must be verified more thoroughly and extensive testing must take place. The budget has also been increased to allow the solving of a number of persistent and dormant errors.

Monitoring the right balance between the change portfolios has become a significant activity.

> In the wake of these dramatic defects, an analysis has exposed a severe imbalance between the various portfolios. The management change portfolio had been overshadowing the other portfolios. This caused reduced operational quality and at the same time fewer strategic improvements because of an excess of projects aimed at fulfilling medium term demands. As a result, during budgeting at management level, explicit annual planning budgets have been allocated to strategic improvements (30 percent), tactical needs (35 percent) and operational improvements (35 percent).

7.1.2 Levels of management

The management of application management takes place at a number of levels. Examples of these levels are:
- The level of a release and/or a component of an application.
- The level of the entire services concerning an application or group of related or similar applications.
- The level of the services of the entire application management organization.

For the sake of efficiency and effectiveness, it is advisable to link and mutually adjust these levels as much as possible. The greater (higher) level can act as an escalation level or a safety net, while the underlying level can act as the pilot.

> Here are a number of examples:
> - There is too little capacity for a release. Capacity is brought in from the organization in order to realize the release.
> - The departmental quality system acts as the starting point for the quality system for an individual application. Specific modifications are made to this system.
> - The application management organization's policy of adopting a new tool is put into practice by deploying this tool for a release. Along with this, additional necessary investments (extra capacity) are also introduced by the organization.
> - Shortcomings are observed in the planning of various releases for many applications. A program is started to take the planning process for the whole organization to a higher level.
> - Version problems in various projects lead to an organization-wide introduction of a version management system.
> - A new successful approach to the use-oriented design of application A is broadly implemented within the organization.

7.1.3 The management cycle

The management processes are subdivided in a similar manner. The three sub-processes are:
- Planning and structuring;
- Monitoring and adjusting;
- Evaluating, learning and readjusting.

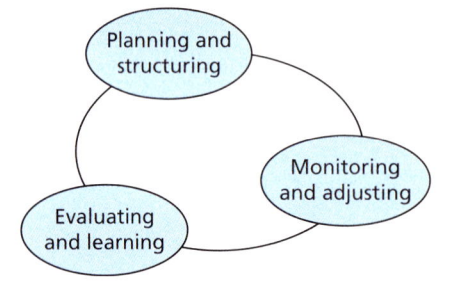

Figure 7.3 The three sub-processes

Planning and structuring
The first sub-process is planning and structuring: setting the required results and determining or budgeting and allocating the resources that are needed to achieve these results.

A result of the outlined growth in dynamics (see Chapter 2) is that management structures (systems) are subject to drastic change. Contract structures, cost charging structures, responsibility structures and numerous other structures change more and more each year, and will certainly not be stable for a number of years, so part of the first sub-process is the setting up or adapting of the structures for management and execution of activities.

> An example of greater dynamics is customer demands and expectations. For example: if the reliability of services is acceptable, the focus frequently shifts to costs.
>
> A change of contact within the customer organization can lead to desired changes in the management structure: for instance, the new person requires less insight and control with respect to the content of the services and focuses more on less costly results. Likewise, the new person can demand more influence and control over the way in which service is provided. In this case, the 'contract' is not a stable document that will remain unchanged for years.

Monitoring and adjusting
The second sub-process is monitoring and adjusting, if necessary. Adjustment can lead to extra measures in order to achieve the goals. The goals might also be adjusted (to a lower ambition level, for instance).

Evaluating, learning and readjusting
The third step is the evaluation and analysis of the results, and learning lessons from them. This will often lead to a change in the needs or the way management is fulfilled, which is then, in turn, addressed in 'planning and structuring'. This creates a learning and adaptive organization.

7.1.4 Design and implementation factors
In each chapter you can find a section concerning design and implementation parameters. Examples of these parameters include the constellation (the role in the chain and integration with the environment), the customer, whether or not integration-responsibility forms part of the services, authority over the application, invoicing structure, etc.

The management level in particular is characterized by strong flexibility and dynamics. Flexibility and dynamics are explicitly included in the planning within the management processes, as indicated in the previous section.

7.2 Contract management

7.2.1 Goal of contract management

The goal of the contract management process is the realization of services according to agreements (or deviating from these agreements by mutual consent), in order to fulfill or exceed the expectations of the customer.

The contract management process forms the front end of services at management level within ASL.

7.2.2 Contract management topics

Chapter 2 outlines the fact that services are provided in service constellations, following a black-box approach. This renders agreements broader, more functional and less technical, more outcome-oriented and less focused on the (internal) production process.

The content of contract management is strongly dependent on the type of customer, the customer's requirements, the structure and form of the agreed services, and the expectations. The critical success factors for contract management are a sufficiently broad coverage in agreements and an adequate focus on the individual (personal) customer. This is why the following topics are addressed:
- The role of the customer;
- Intentions and structure of services;
- Agreements;
- Documenting agreements.

a. The customer
The application management customer is not always a user organization (i.e. business information management). Application management services can also be used by other organizations, such as:
- A different application management organization that supplies a complete package, part of which is formed by the application management organization's application.
- Infrastructure management. In organizations in which only standard applications and standard solutions are used, infrastructure management often acts as the first point of contact for IT services.
- An organization that fulfills a system integration role for a user organization.
- Multiple user organizations (business information management organizations): a standard total solution is supplied to various organizations.

It is evident that the type of customer has a major impact on the content and further specification of the contract with the customer.

b. Intentions and structure
Intentions and emotions of services
Customer satisfaction is, to a large degree, determined by how the customer perceives the services. This means that the external character of the services is an issue. It is

strongly influenced by the way in which the customer is approached, for instance, an open approach (or the opposite), the acceptance of responsibility, a large degree of commitment, etc. Personal characteristics (such as being energetic or calm) also play a role.

Such behavioral characteristics are neither good nor bad: the customer's perception strongly depends on their character and what they expect and appreciate. Sometimes a customer might not want an open approach or want the supplier to accept responsibility.

> Bob Black of ETON is a quiet, thoughtful man who values care and diligence. After being GTR's customer for four years, Bob is succeeded by Theo Wilde. Theo is cost-driven by nature. He aims to get everything for a low price and has made it his goal to make GTR cost-conscious once again.
>
> This change of customer staffing has an enormous impact on what ETON expects from the relationship, communication and GTR's behavior.

Customers tend to want everything and they often think that this is possible. But quality criteria are generally at odds with each other, so it is important to determine the relative importance of the criteria. This is why it is important to know what the 'real expectation' is: the thing that is most essential to the customer with respect to the services or the supplied solution. Examples might include low price, certainty and reliability, or the prevention of undesirable situations.

Almost always, this actual expectation also depends on the person or persons who commission the order. And often, different people have different intentions. The supplier must clarify these expectations by discussing them explicitly.

Structure of management
To a large extent, a contract also defines the responsibility structure. How the services are managed is defined in the contract. This structure is determined by answering questions such as:
- Who is responsible for the delivery process?
- Who takes the final decision about which functionality is added to an application?
- Who decides on the appearance of the functionality?
- Who is responsible for managing and controlling risks?
- What does the supplier constellation look like and what is the application management organization's role and place in it?

These outcomes cannot be disconnected from the financial component of the contract.

c. Agreements
Agreements between customers and suppliers address the following topics:
- Agreements are made about the solution (the product, the supplied application or information system) and services (the service and activities performed by the supplier).

- With regard to applications as well as services, there are agreements about integration with the environment, actual content and demands and/or preconditions.

This leads to a structure as illustrated in Figure 7.4. A contract will generally apply to all six blocks. These topics are described in detail in the rest of this section.

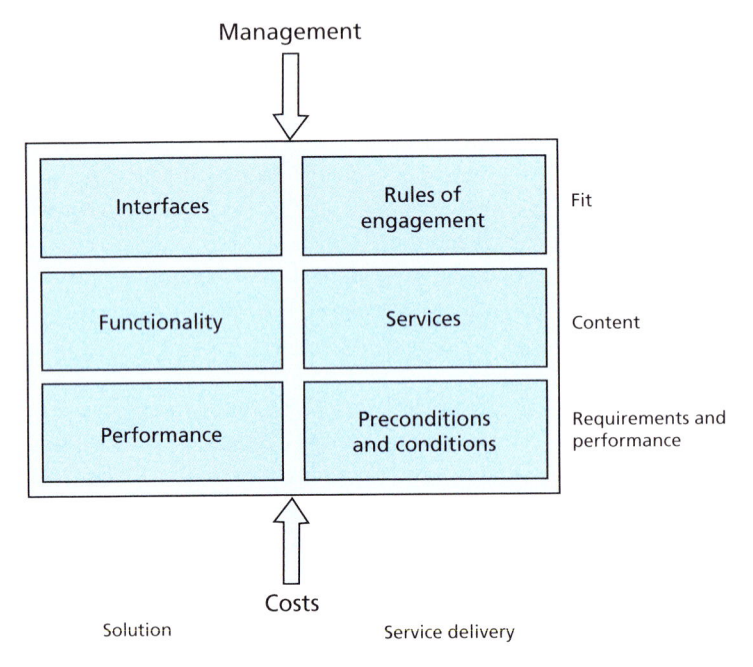

Figure 7.4 The agreements

Interfaces
Interfaces outline the method by which the managed or developed application communicates with the environment, and how it interacts with other components of functioning information provisioning or the environment (messages, data, events, event handling). In a process such as design, these interfaces are further established (or reference is made to other documents).

Functionality
Functionality refers to what an application/information system provides, the reason why customers acquire it, its functions, which services it provides, which information it contains. Functionality is defined in more detail in designs or specifications.

Performance and preconditions
Agreements can also be made about the performance of applications (e.g. with regard to response times and reliability). Applications always have limits and, beyond these limits, applications do not operate according to the agreed quality demands. Applications usually also place demands on the environment in which they operate. The agreements about these topics are gathered under the heading 'performance and

preconditions', although an application's durability and validity form a part of this. Examples of relevant questions are:
- What does an application demand of its environment, e.g. in terms of infrastructure, versions, other applications or other resources?
- Under which conditions can an application be expected to operate effectively, up to what amount of data is its performance and reliability guaranteed, and what are the behavioral characteristics in terms of performance in that case?
- In which situations is it evident that the supplier will not be able to comply with an agreement (exception)?

Requirements can also be placed on an application and the method used to build it – whether it complies with (given) criteria for operation, maintenance and design, for example. The rollout topic is addressed in the quality management chapter.

An SLA often contains the concrete details of part of these agreements.

Rules of engagement
The fourth type of agreement is summarized under the rules of engagement heading. This refers to agreements about how the organizations (customer, supplier or suppliers) cooperate, communicate, report and exchange information. These agreements document much of the interfaces and design/implementation variables mentioned in this book. Here, the following questions are answered:
- How are the customer-facing aspects of services integrated into the environment? Who communicates with whom, who supplies to whom, when and in which sequence?
- What kind of information is divulged by the services processes, what interfaces are defined, what do they look like, what forms of consultation are there and how often does this take place?
- How are possible needs defined for firm quality requirements regarding internal processes?
- Who takes action in which situation?

Services/services
The content of service provisioning is the fifth type of agreement. Here, the services of the supplier (application management) are determined:
- What kind of services are supplied and what is not? For example: maintenance and implementation support, but no operation services.
- On which services and support can the customer count?
- Who has the various (management) responsibilities?

Preconditions and conditions
Even services are subject to durability and validity. So agreements are also made regarding this issue. These can be boundaries or agreements such as:
- A disruption will be addressed within four hours.
- Services are ZZZ-compliant.
- Apart from disruptions, changes will only be handled in releases.

- There is a three-month guarantee period or, after approval following the acceptance test, application management is no longer held liable for defects.
- Under which conditions are services supplied? When is application management liable and when is it not liable?

d. Contracts and underlying documents

A contract outlines the services and other aspects. There are underlying documents which describe the services, solution and approach in more detail. These products will not always be created in the contract management process (e.g. acceptance criteria, specifications or design), but they will generally form part of the complete set of agreements that make up a contract.

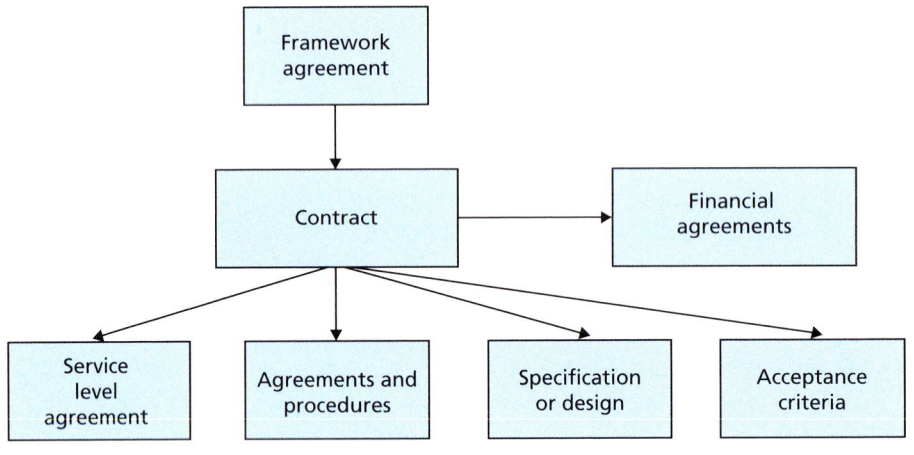

Figure 7.5 Contract and underlying documents

Framework agreements are contracts that usually overarch a services contract. Within ASL, framework contracts are addressed by contract management. A framework agreement is generally a contract in which there are no concrete service obligations.

7.2.3 Contract management activities

The contract management process has three underlying processes:
- Determining and negotiating contracts.
- Monitoring and adjusting of contracts.
- Evaluation of contracts.

Determining and negotiating contracts
- Designing or adapting the supply constellation.
- Designing or adapting the areas of responsibility and management latitude.
- Designing the desired parameters for management and invoicing / cost charging.
- Determining the services and criteria.
- Determining the costs.
- Re-adjustment of all of the above.
- Documenting and approving.

Monitoring and adjusting of contracts
- Monitoring progress and degree of realization.
- Monitoring the desirability of the agreements.
- Where necessary, taking measures to eliminate undesirability or shortcomings.
- Monitoring the results of these measures.

Evaluation of contracts
- Evaluating the results of the services and the application in relation to the agreements made and the agreements actually expected.
- Evaluating the management and remuneration model employed.
- Analyzing the desired form and determining possible changes to this form.
- Documenting and agreeing future activities.

7.2.4 Contract management results

Contract and underlying agreements
See description of topics.

Realization reports
Reports about performance delivered in relation to agreements.

Evaluation of contracts
See activity with the same heading.

7.2.5 Contract management relationships
Customer:
- Requests and demands (input): requests and demands concerning services and applications.
- Draft contract (output): provisional version of a contract.
- Approved contract (input): approved version and with it the delivery assignment.
- Contract realization (output): information about realization.
- Measures (input and output): measures or communication about measures, in case of services issues.

All processes (except management):
- Plans (input): proposed agreement with the customer and its impact.
- Agreements, frameworks (output): contract agreements and intentions. These can also be adaptations of the existing agreements (adapted agreements). In various processes, this is part of the planning input flow.
- Reports (input): realization of agreements and the degree to which they come up to expectations.

Change management
- Plans (input): proposal for a release or assessment of the feasibility of the proposed release. See *plans*.

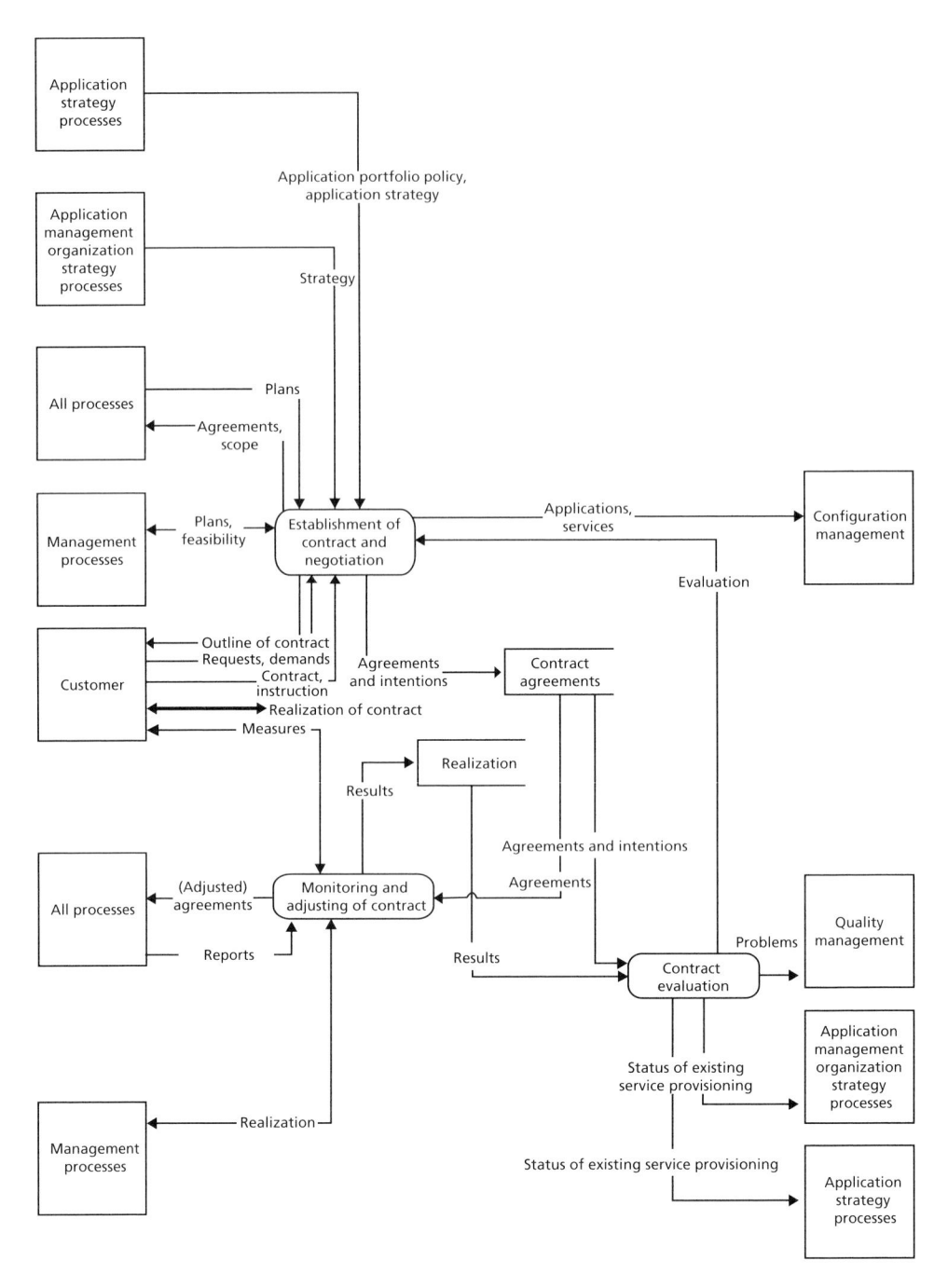

122 ASL® 2 – A framework for Application Management

Figure 7.6 Contract management process outline

- Agreements, frameworks, approval (output): the proposed or established release with the changes to be implemented with additional frameworks. See *planning*. This can also be re-planning.
- Consultation, priorities (output): criteria with respect to possible re-adjustment of the release.
- Adjustments (input): changes to the release, or proposed changes. See *reports*.

The information flows from change management can be similarly integrated into the information flows of other processes. This is why they do not appear in the process outline.

Management processes:
- Plans, feasibility (input): demands set by other processes addressing services for, and agreements with, customers and the feasibility of conditions for agreements, stemming from (draft) contracts for the organization. Examples:
  - Demands (or expectations) set by financial management: required margin or requirements for the remuneration structure.
  - Demands (or expectations) set by planning and control: expected delivery date or capacity necessary for the next year for the application support processes. Feasibility of the delivery date required by the customer, and its impact.
  - Demands set by quality management: degree of services quality (content-based input for SLAs). Impact of guarantees required by the customer regarding price/capacity.
- Plans, feasibility (output): demands or expectations placed on other processes stemming from (draft) contracts for services, and the feasibility of demands placed by other processes on contract management or contracts.
- Realization (output): degree of realization of the approved agreements and the required agreements (in the contract).
- Realization (input): realization of agreements and demands placed by other management processes with respect to the contract or services (e.g. expected delivery date or capacity for the rest of the year, costs of services versus budgeted costs, quality and results of audits of delivered products).

Application management organization strategy processes:
- Strategy (input): detailed as follows:
  - Service delivery definition: policy outline.
  - Account and market definition: the account strategy.
  - Capabilities definition: (impact of the) capabilities strategy (for customer and demands and expectations with respect to the relationship).
  - Technology definition: (impact of the) technology strategy (for customer and market).
  - Supplier definition: the supplier strategy.
- Status of existing services (output): for all Application management organization strategy processes.

Application strategy processes:
- Application life cycle management (output): status of existing services.
- Application portfolio management (output): status of existing services.
- Customer organizations strategy (output): status of existing services and needs.

7.3 Planning and control

7.3.1 Goal of planning and control

The goal of planning and control is to ensure that the agreed upon services are realized, using the agreed human resources capacity and in accordance with the agreed delivery date, by the correct deployment of human resources capacity at the right time.

The complexity of planning and control has greatly increased due to the ongoing componentizing of services, because the application management organization has to deal with subcontractors or suppliers whose internal capacity is not always externally manageable.

7.3.2 Planning and control topics

a. Capacity

The most important challenge within planning and control is to balance three topics as best as possible:
- The amount of human resources capacity required: the amount of application management capacity necessary to, for instance, carry out the desired changes on an application.
- The current (available) capacity: The capacity available for the execution of these activities.
- The desired and possible timelines (delivery dates): the points in time at which changes to applications, for instance, must/can be realized.

Most of application management human resources capacity is used for two groups of activities:
- The execution of application support and (regular) maintenance and renewal.
- The implementation of major changes to applications, managed from the strategic and tactical change portfolios. These changes can be executed in regular maintenance, but they are often carried out in separate projects.
- The delivery date for the realization of a release can be fairly easily determined based on the available capacity, provided the human resources capacity is known. Realizing the *desired* delivery date and the realizing the *desired* human resources capacity complicate planning and control.

To realize this, it is evident that there must be transfer of human resources capacity between operation, regular change and tactical/strategic change, although the possibilities are limited. Other possibilities for realizing the desired delivery dates include:

- The deployment of extra human resources capacity.
  By employing extra capacity, the feasible delivery date can sometimes be brought forward. However, these possibilities have their limitations too. Maintenance and enhancement require a high degree of knowledge of the business processes and the application and, in some cases, it can take many months or up to a year for capacity to be efficiently deployed.
- The transfer of activities and parts of the solution to subcontractors. Here the same arguments apply as in the previous point.
- Reduction of demand, adjustment of the delivery date, adjustment of the requirements, or execution in a simplified form.

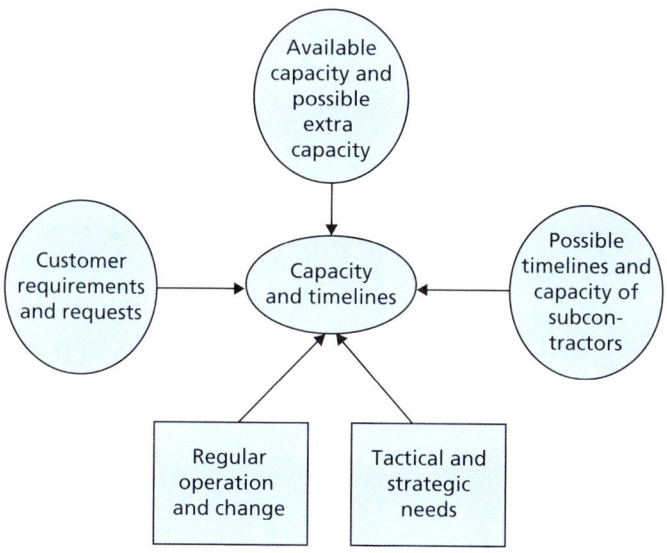

Figure 7.7 Planning and control

Planning and control is complex because of the dependency on plans, possibilities and limitations of customers and suppliers. Customers and suppliers have similar issues with respect to available capacity and feasible delivery dates.

Often, timelines and the availability of functionalities are fixed. Here is an example: the supplier support for version 9.04 expires on January 1st. Because support is required, it is necessary to migrate to version 9.1. For the conversion to take place, settings must be changed and the system must be tested again.

Sometimes, suppliers force customers into performing upgrades by certain dates, and these upgrades lead to additional effort. Suppliers of frequently used solutions do not allow the timelines of their versions to depend on the individual requirements of customers.

The planning and control process, the setting up of capacity and timelines, the monitoring of results and adjustment can become very complex and create a puzzle that is difficult to solve.

Topic: Project versus line

Application management - and the other forms of IT management - are essentially regular line activities. Business processes are, in principle, 'perpetual' and, as a result, information systems continually support the business processes (this is welcomed by user organizations). Operation, maintenance and the renewal of information provisioning are line activities, and so the same also applies to the operation, maintenance and renewal of applications.

There is a strong tendency to regard the execution of changes (releases as well as large-scale renewals) as projects: activities that are performed in a project-based manner. This perspective can easily be justified.
- The development of new applications was, and still is, executed as a project – a collection of activities that must be completed by a certain point in time.
- There is much support for the effective execution of projects, including best practice approaches such as PRINCE2.

A project-based approach also has risks. Projects have a strong focus on the completion of work by a specific point in time, after which the work is regarded as finished. The system can then be handed over to maintenance or to operation. This often results in lack of understanding that the actual work starts after project completion.

Often, in order to meet the required deadlines or to prevent costs from exceeding budgets, major compromises are made about the quality of applications, their maintainability or their manageability. These shortcomings will only arise after the completion of a project. They will not, however, be the project manager's problem.

The costs of shortcomings will often be many times higher than the amount that has been 'saved':
- During the lifespan of an application, its maintenance costs are much higher than its development costs. Difficult-to-maintain software leads to significantly higher maintenance costs.
- Difficult-to-manage systems generally have shortcomings in use, leading to higher costs for the user organization and increased costs for operation.

The use of projects and the implementation of project management techniques and approaches can significantly improve the manageability of maintenance and renewal. But, in all cases, one needs to realize that:
- The end of a project is the start of the next project. After the development of an application or a new release, another release will come. Then all the shortcomings will need to be faced once again.
- Knowledge of the (development) project or a previous release, etc. is also necessary for the next release. Application support, maintenance or project resources overlap one another.

Application management is line (not project) work, so the following points require attention:
- Do not only manage the capacity and quality for the development (building) phase of a release, but also for development, support, maintenance and renewal as a whole.
- Do not only manage the capacity for a single release, but for all upcoming releases.

> *Example*
> An organization has decided that all changes that require more than 40 hours are considered to be a project. These projects are executed separately from maintenance. Anything smaller can be executed by the maintenance department.
>
> If projects are too large, application developers assigned to maintenance are planned into projects without discussing it with the manager who is responsible for maintenance. Often, there are also arguments about the quality of releases. Maintenance blames the projects for developing systems that are not manageable. Defects that have previously been solved often re-occur in new versions.

b. Planning and estimates

An important planning and control activity is the estimation of maintenance. The core of the estimate is usually created in other processes. A release is often estimated in the impact analysis; suitable methods for this are (Maintenance) Function Points, Product Breakdown Structure, and Work Breakdown Structure.

These outcomes must be modified to take the environment into consideration. There are many reasons for further modification of these outcomes. Risks must be taken into account with respect to the current quality of an application, the service levels to be achieved, experience or expertise available within application management, the necessity of a faultless introduction, experience gained from previous projects, possible holidays, etc. This adjustment takes place in planning and control.

Further sources of information and tooling are necessary for this adjustment, such as the presence of norms like productivity factors, availability percentages (sickness), risk analyses, etc. Information about these factors is often provided by other processes.

7.3.3 Planning and control activities

Planning:
- Listing of the expected capacity required for both application support and maintenance and renewal processes.
- Detailing these capacity requirements to a level of activities/releases and subcontractors.
- Determining of requested specified timelines provided by customers and suppliers.
- Determining available capacity, required capacity and, where applicable, extra capacity that could be made available.
- Identifying risks and appropriate mitigation measures.
- High-level allocation of capacity to activities.
- Updating and monitoring of norms for operation, maintenance, releases (such as function points, maintenance function points, availability and productivity indicators, etc.).

Control:
- Monitoring of available hours (sickness, holidays, training, etc.).
- Monitoring of the number of hours spent on work packages.
- Monitoring of progress.
- Readjusting based on current insights.
- Taking of further measures (in combination with other processes such as contract management), such as rearranging tasks, reallocation of capacity, rescheduling milestones, reducing the scope of work packages.

Review:
- Evaluation of the results.
- Identifying and documenting the lessons learned.
- Identifying problems and initiating improvement proposals.

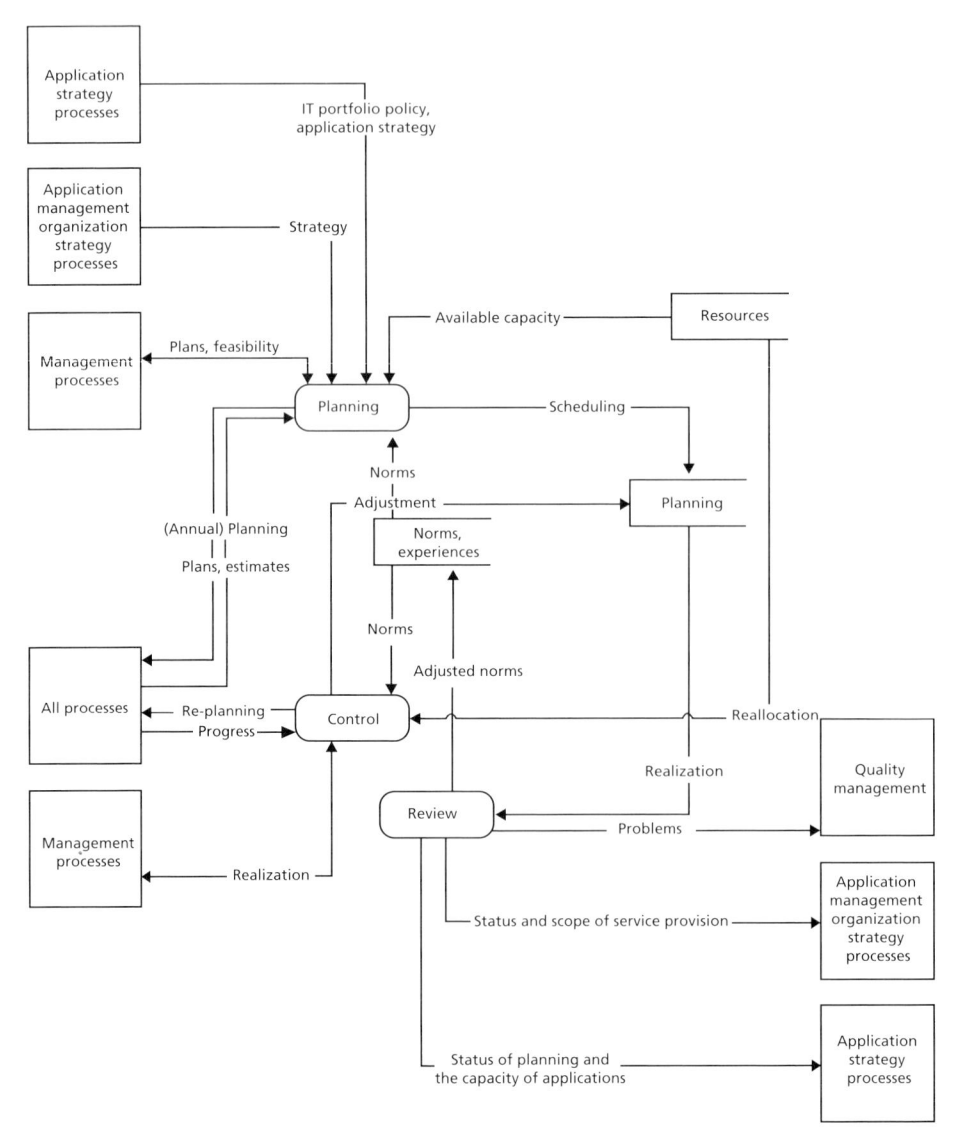

Figure 7.8 Planning and control process outline

7.3.4 Planning and control results
Plans: annual plan and/or rolling quarterly plan, including:
- Estimated work and/or changes.
- Required capacity, timelines.
- Reservation/scheduling of capacity (operation, maintenance/renewal, management processes, etc.) and extra capacity for quality improvement, etc.
- Changes compared to previous plans (in the case of rolling planning).

Resources (human resources capacity):
- Available capacity.
- Already allocated and reserved capacity.
- Free capacity.

Planning:
- Desired/required capacity.
- Allocated capacity.
- Timelines.

Norms:
- Productivity figures etc.
- Approximate norms, empirical figures.

7.3.5 Planning and control relationships
Change management:
- Release and capacity requirements (input): capacity required for a release. See *plans and estimates*.
- Capacity (output): capacity for a release or for development. See *planning*.
- If necessary, readjusted capacity requirements (input): changes to the release that have an impact on capacity. See *progress and realization*.
- Planning, progress and realization (output): realization of application maintenance and renewal processes, impact on delivery. See *adjusted planning*.

Information flows for change management are integrated in the normal planning and control process. However, small changes in the process do occur. In the process outline, these flows are included as part of 'all processes'.

All processes (except management):
- Planning and estimates (input): expected capacity and planning needed for the execution of processes.
- (Annual) planning (output): planning and capacity available for operation, maintenance and development (releases) and the other processes.
- Adjusted planning (output): re-planning (if necessary). The processes that handle this output often refer to it as 'planning'.
- Progress and realization of planning (input): capacity used and the realization of progress with respect to the planning.

Management processes:
- Plans, feasibility (input): demands set by other processes with respect to capacity and planning and control (in a broad sense), and the feasibility of demands (placed on other management processes by planning and control).

Examples: availability of the new version of a component from a supplier via supplier management, customer deadlines via contract management, etc.
- Plans, feasibility (output): demands placed on other processes and the feasibility of demands placed on planning and control by other processes.

Example: the human resources capacity required to improve the quality of services (for quality management).
- Realization (output): degree of realization of the agreed and required planning, time spent by, and budgets for, human resources (e.g. the hours spent on quality management, hours spent on application support, maintenance and renewal, etc.), identified problems (for quality management).
- Realization (input): realization of planning and capacity and demands of other management processes with respect to planning and control. Examples: the delivery date is adjusted by the customer (via contract management). The hours spent are forwarded to financial management for cost charging.
- Problems (output): for quality management.

Application strategy processes:
- Application life cycle management:
  - Application strategy (input): strategy containing the renewals to be scheduled.
  - Status planning and capacity of applications (output): developments and available capacity.
- Application portfolio management:
  - Application portfolio policy (input): strategy concerning the renewals to be scheduled, or renewals of adjacent applications.
  - Status planning and capacity of applications (output): developments and capacity available.

Application management organization strategy processes:
- Strategy (input):
  - Service delivery definition: policy outlines.
  - Capabilities definition: (capacity issues of the) capabilities strategy.
  - Technology definition: (capacity issues of the) technology strategy.
  - Account and market definition: (capacity issues of the) account strategy.
  - Supplier definition: (capacity issues of the) supplier strategy.
- Scope of capacity and its developments (output), for example: growth or limitation of application support or application maintenance and renewal and the nature of human resources capacity over the past years.

7.4 Quality management

7.4.1 Goal of quality management

The goal of quality management is to ensure the (internal and acquired) quality of the acquisition process, product, resources and organization by defining and monitoring these, and also ensuring that the relevant regulations are implemented and followed. A second, derived goal of quality management is to determine possible and desired improvements and to ensure that these improvements are realized.

The separation of external and internal quality (see section 2.4.2.) has made it essential to explicitly monitor and manage the capabilities of the organization and the application. This also applies to the integration issue. This refers to both the degree of alignment between the (agreed) services and the customer, and to the coherence, accuracy and comprehensiveness of the agreed services by subcontractors, combined with the internally supplied services. Quality is related to the acquired quality (the quality of acquired services and products) as well as internal quality.

In this definition, services include the delivered solution (application or integration of applications).

7.4.2 Quality management topics

Quality management focuses on four topics:
- Quality of the supplied *product* (application, documentation and possibly the underlying infrastructure). Aspects concerned are the quality of software and data structure (structured, relevant – based on insightfulness, understandable, correct, maintainable), quality of documentation (correct, comprehensive and up-to-date).
- Quality of the *(production) process*, including the quality of the process design, the roles, responsibilities and procedures. Examples: the clarity (no risk of ambiguity) and employees' knowledge of the approach for testing or design, the implementation of concrete processes; clear and agreed transfer times, concrete agreements regarding the way realization has been set up (e.g. we use tool Y).
- Quality of the *organization*. Topics include the quality of human resources, skills, place within the organization, competences, culture etc. Examples of the quality of the organization are: having enough experience in the area of realization using tool X, adequate training facilities and knowledge management abilities; clear agreements with other parts of the organization.
- Quality of the *quality system*[1]. Quality system refers to infrastructure for application development and application management in a broad sense, such as tooling, aids, methods and techniques. Examples of quality are: the presence of an adequate development environment, support of standard information by means of spreadsheets, detailed methodology for testing, including tooling.

---

1 In this book, the term 'quality system' is used in two different ways. First, the concept can be used in the narrower sense: this is the definition that is explained here in this topic. Beside this definition, the name 'quality system' is sometimes also used in a broader sense, describing the whole - that is, also including the other three topics. 'Quality system is commonly used in both senses. When the term is used in this book to indicate the broader scope, this will be indicated.

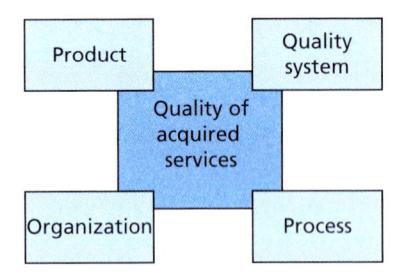

Figure 7.9 Quality management topics

Quality management is also responsible for the degree to which suppliers' services and products are aligned with the organization's own services and products. This responsibility includes ensuring that the services and products as a whole (from suppliers and IT's own organization) cover the customer's requirements and agreements made with them.

This is why quality management will place demands on the products, services, quality system and process of both the supplier and the customer. Quality management therefore provides input for supplier management and for contract management. The actual formulation of agreements with customers and suppliers is part of these processes.

> **Topic: Rollout**
> Rollout' is currently a hot topic on both the supply side (as part of the contract) and the acquisition side (supplier management). This theme is relevant to new applications as well as new releases, especially if the party that manages or maintains the application has not developed the application.
>
> In order to perform application management well, applications must comply with further demands or requirements. Operation requirements are called operation criteria, while change requirements are called change criteria. Quality management is responsible for determining the application support, maintenance and renewal criteria. Often, applications or releases are created under severe time pressure. Complying with support, maintenance and renewal requirements is then often given a low priority. This, in turn, promptly results in long-term extra costs for support, maintenance and renewal.
>
> In order to prevent this, several measures have to be taken.
>
> It is important that the criteria are known during specification and the initiation of the assignment. Subsequently, fulfillment of these criteria must be reviewed during the assignment.
>
> The responsibility for this lies with the customer as well as the service provider. The provider must ensure that, at the end of (or shortly after) the assignment, it does not become evident that the application will be difficult to support, maintain and renew. A solution that is not functioning optimally should never be 'pushed' into application support, maintenance and renewal (even by brute force of the customer). Quality management plays a managing role in ensuring this.

However, the customer must also ensure that this transfer to operation and/or change takes place smoothly. Any bottlenecks in operation and/or change will, eventually, affect the customer organization. Giving the (future) application management party (if another party then the developer) an explicit role in the development process is a step in the right direction.

Referring to the use of suppliers and the supplier management process, the application management organization fulfills the role of the customer, so this theme is also relevant for acquisition.

Topic: Problems
Many other process models include a problem management process. This is not the case with ASL. You can read about the basis for this in the use support and FAQ sections. For the sake of comprehensiveness, we will also deal with this issue here.

Problems are shortcomings in the quality system in a broad sense: they are the result of evaluations and can be generated by every process within the ASL framework. Problems form one of the most significant means by which quality management gains insight into quality. Consequently, problems are collected in quality management and are processed– decisions are made about whether or not they will be solved and whether they will lead to changes in the quality system or product. Problems can be extremely varied; here are a number of examples:
- The designs in the ATS subsystem are incomplete and not up-to-date, leading to software errors.
- Testers are of poor quality: the testers have insufficient training and experience.
- Releases are always delivered too late. A structured planning methodology is required.

7.4.3 Quality management activities

Quality planning:
- Estimating the ability of the organization and the subcontractors to deliver the current and required services.
- Estimating the required quality level and the current quality level.
- Creating a quality plan containing quantifiable and feasible improvement measures, required ambition levels and the necessary investment.
- Initiating of improvements in the quality system: setting up guidelines for tooling, standards, approaches, processes, and organization.

Quality monitoring:
- Detecting and dealing with problems and providing proposals for improvement.
- Periodic examination of the process, product, infrastructure and the organization, for instance by performing reviews, and product and process tests.
- Readjustment/improvement of the organization, processes, and infrastructure.
- Monitoring the progress of the quality improvement activities.

Quality review:
- Evaluating how releases have been developed, based on the executed assessments, reviews and tests.

- Evaluating the total quality of product and process.
- Evaluating the problems that have been solved.

7.4.4 Quality management results

Quality plan:
Plan for maintaining, improving or innovating the quality system with the aim of improving the quality of the organization and the services. The quality plan addresses the strategy, existing shortcomings and necessary changes to the quality system, and the concrete way of working in the organization in relation to the environment.

Quality system:
See the relevant description under Topics. The way of working, production process, aids, methods, tools, techniques, demands placed on process and product, manuals.

Problems and evaluations:
Identified problems (shortcomings in the quality system), their status, proposed solution direction, planning and resolution.

Plans, feasibility:
Requirements (agreements) are communicated by the other management processes, for instance in the field of customer agreements, quality demands, cost demands. These requirements can have an impact on the way of working, the implementation of processes, the organization of the quality system.

Feedback is provided about the feasibility of these requirements.

In its turn, quality management places demands on the other management processes, including the maximum feasible demands with respect to services (e.g. for contract management), necessary demands placed on subcontractors (supplier management), the costs of changes to the quality system, etc. Feedback is also provided about the feasibility of this.

7.4.5 Quality management relationships

All processes (except management):
- Demands (output): demands set by quality management in relation to the way of working, the quality of the supplied product, etc.
- Plans and feasibility (input): quality agreement proposals and the feasibility of possible demands.
- Resolution of problems (output): status of the resolution of problems.
- Evaluations, problems, realization of quality (input): reports about the realized quality, supplemented with evaluations of the execution of processes and/or possible problems.

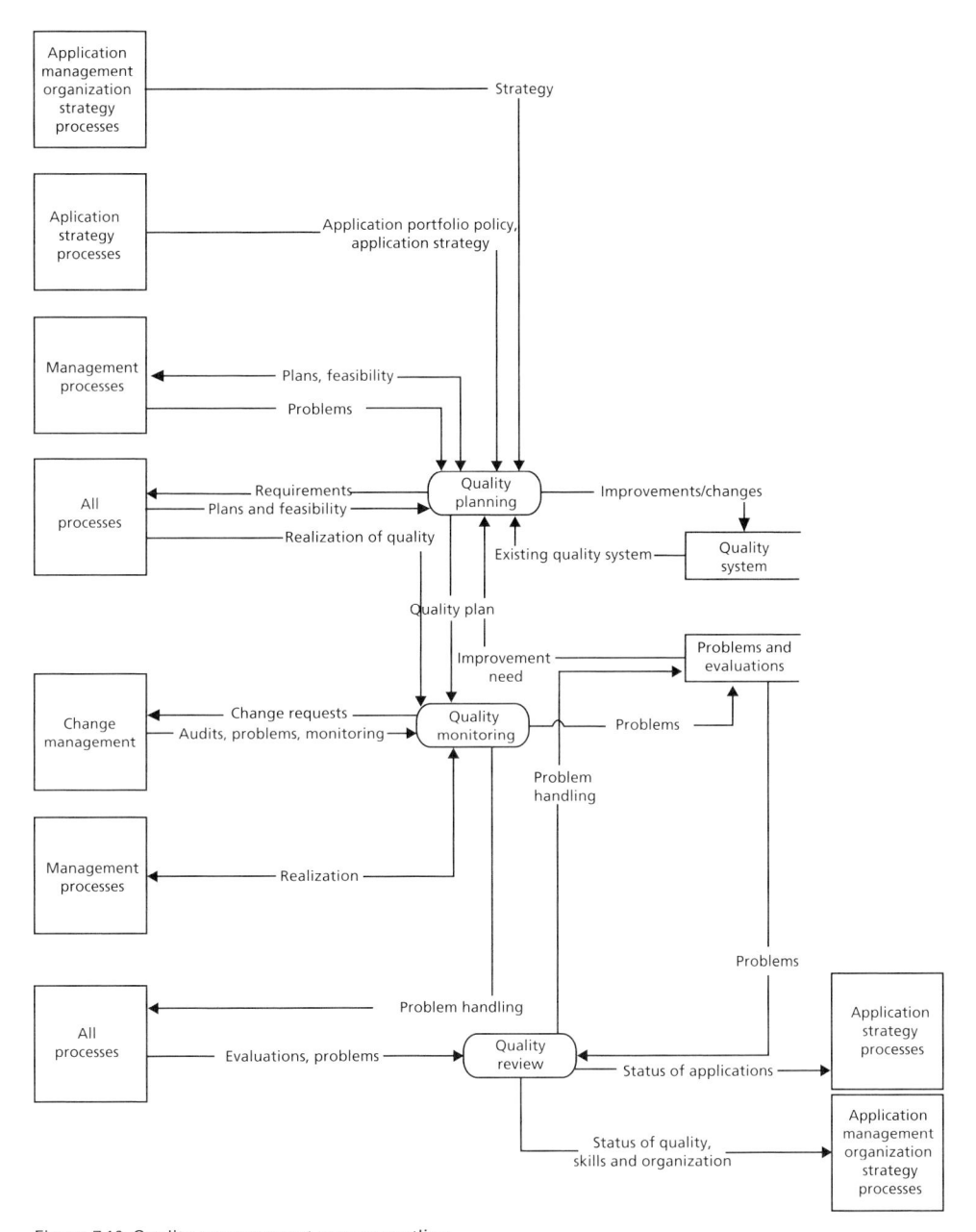

Figure 7.10 Quality management process outline

Management processes:
- Plans, feasibility (input): demands placed on the quality system (in a broad sense) by other processes and the feasibility of demands (placed on other management processes by quality management).
- Plans, feasibility (output): demands placed on other processes and the feasibility of demands placed by other processes on quality management.

- Realization (output): degree to which the agreed and required quality agreements are realized, improvements to the quality system or the finalization of problems.
- Realization (input): realization of agreements and demands from other management processes with respect to the quality system, way of working, etc.

Application management organization strategy processes:
- Strategy (input):
  - Capabilities definition: (quality and skills issues of the) capabilities strategy.
  - Technology definition: (quality issues of the) technology strategy.
  - Account and market definition: (quality issues of the) account strategy.
  - Supplier definition: (quality and alignment issues of the) supplier strategy.
- Status of quality, skills and organization (output):
  - Capabilities definition: status of quality system and skills.
  - Technology definition: status of quality system and technology.
  - Account and market definition: current services and skills.
  - Supplier definition: quality of the supplier with respect to delivery and integration into services.

Application strategy processes:
- Application portfolio management:
  - Status of the current application landscape (output): quality and structure of the existing applications/application landscape.
  - Application portfolio policy (input): strategy, demands and structure of the application landscape.
- Application life cycle management:
  - Status of current application (output): quality and structure of the application.
  - Application strategy (input).

7.5 Financial management

7.5.1 Goal of financial management

The goal of financial management is to ensure that the costs incurred for supplying/maintaining an application and/or services are planned and managed and are in balance with the benefits generated by application management. A further precondition is that whatever is supplied is competitively priced.

It is preferable that the structure for control and charging of costs for the agreed services is as much as possible in keeping with the customer's perspective.

7.5.2 Financial management topics

a. The business case concept

In application management, there are two different business cases:
- The customer business case: a customer consumes services and will incur costs.

- The supplier business case: the method by which an IT organization charges for the costs of products and services that are consumed.

The customer business case
The customer business case is the business case of the customer (not of the application management organization). The customer organization decides whether investments in applications or changes to applications are sufficiently beneficial in terms of business benefits. The benefits are the responsibility of the customer and can be best estimated by the customer. The costs involved do not only include IT costs, but also costs of transition into use, etc.

IT organizations do have an interest in this business case (if the IT costs are too high, investments will not be made), but do not have responsibility for this business case. It is especially important for application management that the costs of applications and services are competitive.

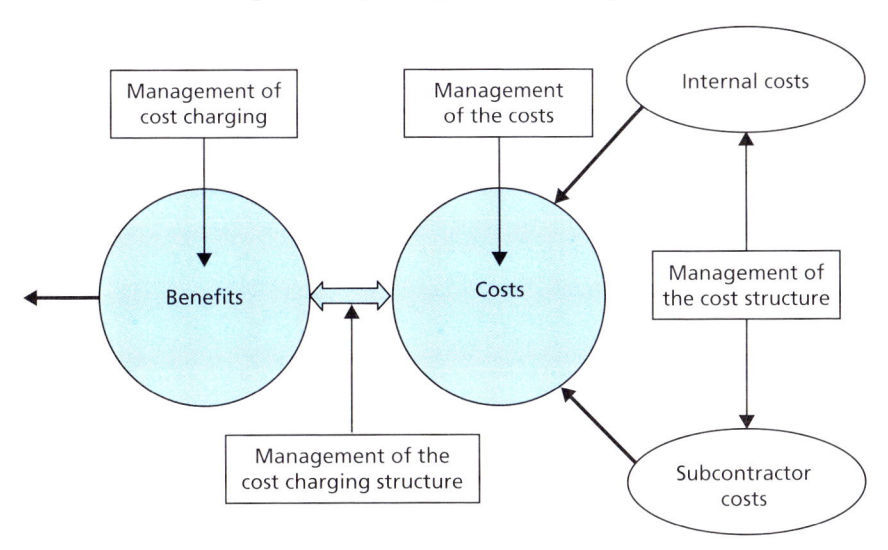

The application management business case (supplier)
However, application management has its own business case. Increasingly, this involves shared solutions (such as packages) and application management also charges according to result-based pricing, where the price is not directly related to the internally incurred costs.

An application management organization acquires solutions, creates solutions and integrates them where necessary. There are costs involved in doing this. Application management supplies the whole package according to fixed financial agreements with customers. These prices constitute the application management's benefits. This business case is a responsibility of application management.

Figure 7.11 The application management business cases

b. Management topics
Costs need to be translated into benefits. As a result, there are four topics to be managed.

Management of the internal cost structure
The first topic is the establishment (or adjustment) of the internal cost structure and cost allocation structure. Relevant questions are:
- How are the costs determined and according to which standards are they measured?
- In what form and how are they allocated to applications (or components), or supplied services?
- How are they budgeted and what is their predictability?

The cost structure describes the structure according to which the internally incurred costs are charged. This also includes the costs related to contracted suppliers and their products, such as the use of the development environment, acquired basic components, maintenance of basic components, etc.

The cost allocation structure describes the method by which these costs are assigned to the products and services supplied to the customers.

Management of the costs
The second management topic is the management of costs. This entails budgeting of costs and an assessment of the degree of predictability, monitoring the utilization of budgets, and evaluation of how accurately budgets have been predicted.

Management of the cost charging structure
Because the 'real' costs often cannot be directly assigned to customers' individual orders, a cost charging structure is necessary. A cost charging structure charges costs to customers according to predetermined units (such as prices per function point, user licenses per user, etc.) Often, invoicing also takes place according to this structure. The determining, monitoring and evaluating of this is the third topic. The cost charging structure has a close relationship with contract management (in which this is agreed upon with the customer). Questions asked here include:
- Which rates are identified?
- How are these determined and calculated?
- What is the ratio between these and the 'actual' costs, and what is the relationship between the behavior of the cost charging structure and the behavior of the actual costs?

Management of the cost charging
A final topic is ensuring that the correct details are used in invoicing, monitoring of benefits, and also the evaluation of the predictions of expected benefits.

Financial administration, accounting, and monitoring accounts payable lies outside the scope of application management.

7.5.3 Financial management activities
Financial planning:
- Setting up or adjusting the cost structure and cost charging structure (in consultation with contract management).
- Predicting the costs of the required development, maintenance and management activities.
- Predicting the costs incurred due to suppliers or subcontractors.
- Predicting the expected benefits and an estimation of its market conformity.
- Readjusting and adapting the financial plan and the possible readjustment of the costs and cost charging structure.

Financial monitoring:
- Monitoring the costs.
- Monitoring the benefits and the cost charging.
- Identifying and initiating measures in case of deviation.

Financial evaluation:
- Evaluating the costs incurred and the benefits realized.
- Evaluating the functioning of the cost structures and the cost charging structures.

7.5.4 Financial management results
Financial structures:
- Cost allocation structure (this will often be generic within the organization).
- Cost charging structure (this depends on the market and can be generic or specific for a kind of services).

Financial plan:
- Costs.
- Benefits.
- Developments and long-term perspective.

Financial review:
- Results.
- Evaluation, change proposals and problems.

7.5.5 Financial management relationships
Financial administration:
- Invoicing (input) (to be monitored).
- Invoice information (output).

All processes (except management):
- Financial estimates (input): plans, estimation by process of the expected costs or consumption of units, plus a unit-price.
- Financial planning (output): financial planning and budget.
- Financial realization (input): realization of the costs and financial units.
- Evaluations (input): evaluation of the applicable financial structure and the estimates.

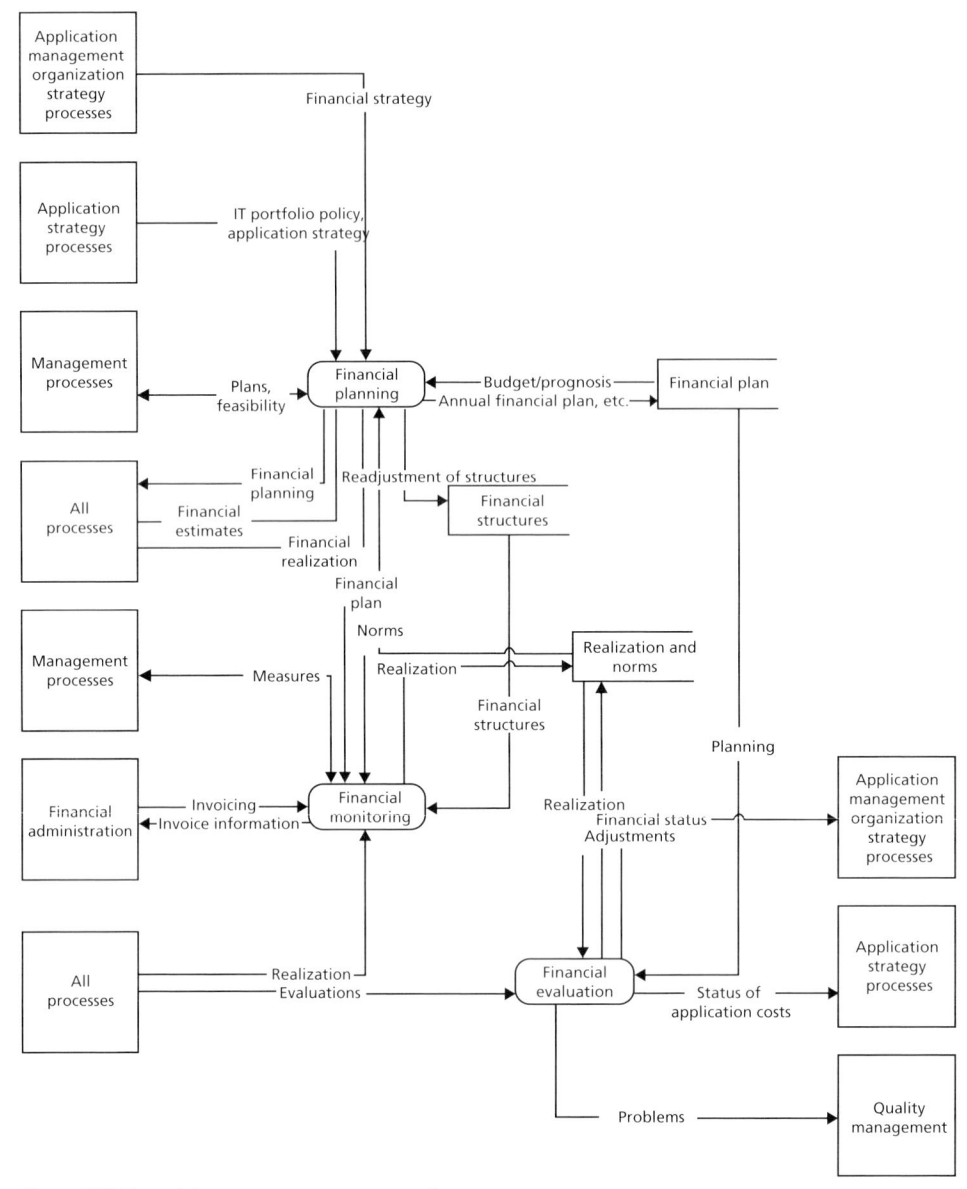

Figure 7.12 Financial management process outline

Management processes:
- Plans, feasibility (input): plans and agreements of other management processes (such as planning and control, quality management, supplier management) and feasibility of plans or demands set by financial management.
- Plans, feasibility (output): financial plan (costs, benefits, cost structure, cost charging structure) and financial feasibility of other process plans.
- Realization (output): degree of realization of agreed and required agreements (regarding the financial aspects).

- Realization (input): realization of agreements and demands of other management processes with respect to the contract or services (for example, extra supplier costs related to unforeseen functionality).
- Problems (output): for quality management.

Application management organization strategy processes:
- Strategy:
  - Service delivery definition: policy outlines.
  - Capabilities definition: (financial aspects of the) capabilities strategy.
  - Technology definition: (financial aspects of the) technology strategy.
  - Account and market definition: (financial and cost charging aspects of the) account strategy.
  - Supplier definition: (financial aspects and cost structures of the) supplier strategy.
- Financial status (output): for all Application management organization strategy processes.

Application strategy processes:
- Application portfolio management (output): financial status.
- Application life cycle management (output): financial status.

7.6 Supplier management

7.6.1 Goal of supplier management

The use of suppliers and subcontractors (these are also suppliers) has become self-evident. In the past, suppliers provided the development environment or infrastructure, for instance. Nowadays, the use of a broader variety of subcontractors and suppliers is commonplace, for example:
- A hosting party, for example for an Application Service Provider (ASP) solution.
- Supplier of a configurable platform.
- Supplier of a component.
- Supplier of a custom built system or component, for which the application management organization will, for example, perform the support, maintenance and renewal functions.
- Supplier that provides a defined functionality as a separate solution.

Supplier management is responsible for agreements regarding services and/or solutions provided by third parties (suppliers), and for evaluating, monitoring and improving them.

7.6.2 Supplier management topics

The topics in this process are, to a large degree, similar to the topics that play a part in contract management. Of course, this makes perfect sense. The supplier's contract management communicates with supplier management. There is, however, a fundamental difference. Here, application management is the consuming party.

a. The demand
This difference results in a different interpretation of the process. To a large degree, emphasis is placed on clarifying the demand and on the conditions under which the solution should be provided (therefore, there is much less emphasis on whether and how it should be provided).

Why use a supplier?
The first issue concerns the demand and the conditions – in what way does the supplier contribute to services?
- Why use a supplier and what do they contribute?
- What contribution needs to be provided? Contributions can include competences (expertise), resources or products, infrastructure, capacity (activities).
- What are the essential aspects of the services and the solution that is sourced? What kind of behavior is expected from the supplier?
- Which topics should the suppliers manage? Which topics does the organization not want to manage or know about, which topics does the organization not necessarily need to manage/need to know?
- Which form of management should be retained and what information about the sourced services or solution (application or infrastructure) is necessary?
- What are the expectations regarding costs and which kind of cost charging is preferred?

Many of these questions are answered in conjunction with the other management processes (quality management, financial management, planning and control and contract management).

What does the supplier want to do and what are they capable of?
Rarely will the supplier provide exactly what is desired, nor will this happen according to the desired conditions. This leads to a negotiation process. So it is advisable to research the supplier's attitude and position in advance – what can they do, what would be feasible to them, what makes it – or why is it – attractive to the supplier, etc.

Identifying many forms of engagement in advance can lead to a stronger negotiation position and proceedings can converge towards an outcome more quickly. Information Services Procurement Library (ISPL) is a framework that can contribute to selection and contracting.

b. The agreements
The agreements are illustrated in Figure 7.13. Section 7.2.2 mentions the topics about which agreements must be made.

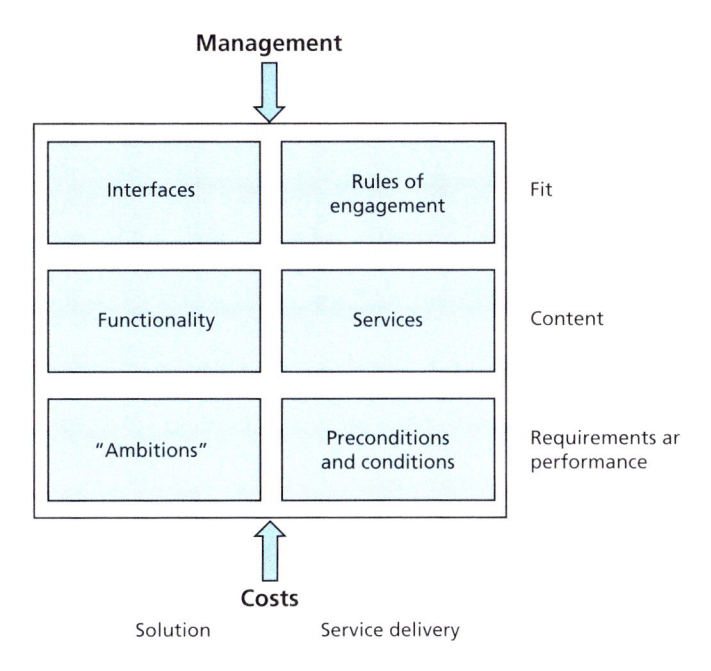

```
                Management
                    ⇓
┌─────────────────────────────────┐
│  ┌──────────┐  ┌──────────┐     │    Fit
│  │Interfaces│  │ Rules of │     │
│  │          │  │engagement│     │
│  └──────────┘  └──────────┘     │
│                                 │
│  ┌──────────┐  ┌──────────┐     │    Content
│  │Function- │  │ Services │     │
│  │ality     │  │          │     │
│  └──────────┘  └──────────┘     │
│                                 │
│  ┌──────────┐  ┌──────────┐     │    Requirements ar
│  │"Ambitions"│ │Preconditions│  │    performance
│  │          │  │and conditions│ │
│  └──────────┘  └──────────┘     │
└─────────────────────────────────┘
                    ⇑
                  Costs
        Solution        Service delivery
```

Figure 7.13 Financial management process outline

Topic: Rollout

The operation or change rollout topics are important with respect to suppliers. There are situations in which organizations have products or components developed or modified by external parties, but subsequently would like to operate or change these themselves.

It is also important to set demands regarding the quality of the product, including demands regarding documentation structure, the speed and comprehensiveness of data access, programming standards, etc.

Criteria will be needed for operation, and acceptance.

It is important that these demands and standards are not only registered as requirements (primarily by quality management), but that compliance with them is monitored.

Experience has shown that 'serious concessions' occur due to deadline pressure and project focus (this is a euphemism for the fact that often nothing is done in this regard, since the project has to go into production). Often this is a precursor to problematic application support, maintenance and renewal.

7.6.3 Supplier management activities
Supplier planning (establishment of contract and negotiation)[2]:
- Determining of actual need, demand and scope.
- Selection of supplier(s).
- Matching supply and demand.
- Drafting an engagement model and a contract model.
- Designing the desired parameters for management and invoicing.
- Determining services and criteria.
- Aligning and determining of costs.
- Evaluating, adjusting and mutual adjustment of previous topics.
- Documenting and approval.

Supplier monitoring:
- Evaluating the progress and the degree of realization.
- Acceptance of the interim results and the results.
- Possibly, taking measures for correction of undesirable aspects or shortcomings.
- Monitoring the results of these measures.

Supplier review:
- Evaluation of the results.
- Evaluation of the management and invoicing model employed.
- Analysis of the desired form or readjustment.
- Documentation and agreeing next steps.

7.6.4 Supplier management results
Contract (from supplier) and drafted contract:
See the description above.

Realization:
Realization of supplier services and the degree to which agreements and expectations are fulfilled. This also includes the non-rational aspects (including experience) that are described, among others, in sections 2.4.2 and 7.3.2.

Status of suppliers:
Information about suppliers' capabilities and services, and (possibly) the technology they use, capacity and developments in the supplier market.

7.6.5 Supplier management relationships
Supplier:
- Requests and demands (output): requests and/or demands with respect to suppliers' services or solutions.
- Draft contract (input): draft contract for suppliers of services or solutions.
- Contract (assignment) (output): signed contract/assignment.
- Realization of contract (input): information about the realization of supplier services.

---

[2] See also ISPL

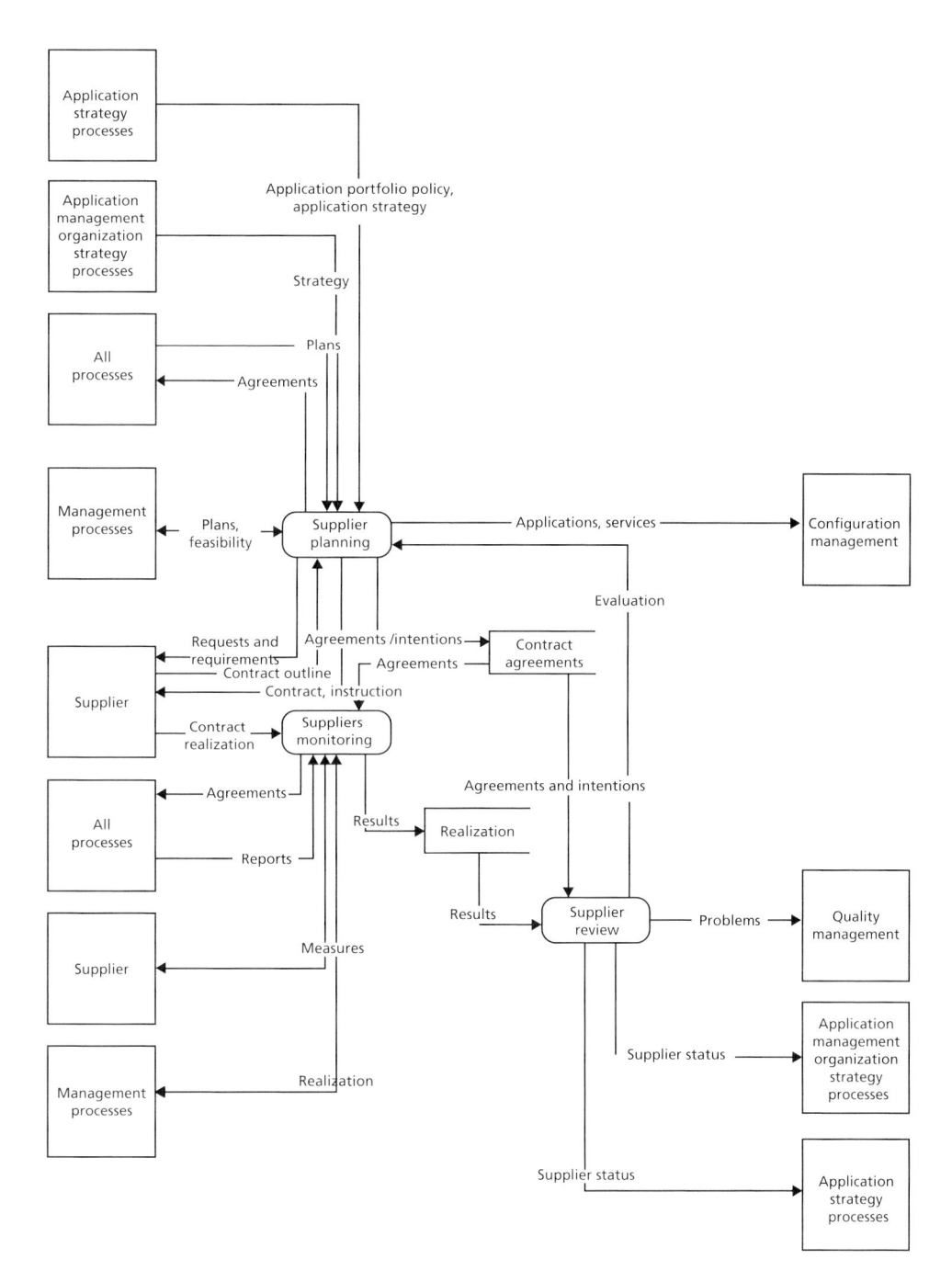

Figure 7.14 Supplier management process outline

- Measures (input and output): measures, or communication regarding measures, in the case of services issues.

All processes (except management):
- Plans (input): proposed agreements with suppliers and/or demands placed.
- Reports (input): information about the realization of suppliers' services and possible necessary measures.
- Agreements (output): agreements with respect to suppliers' services or products. This can include adapted agreements with suppliers (re-planning).

Configuration management:
- Application, services (output): new services or versions of suppliers' applications.

Change management:
- Plans (input): draft proposal for a release (or new services/solution) including capacity estimate and impact.
- Agreements, frameworks, approval (output): feedback about this release and possible agreements.
- Adjustments (input): adjustments to the release or adjustment proposals.

The flows are included in 'all processes'.

Management processes:
- Plans, feasibility (input): demands set by other processes with respect to (projected) contracts with suppliers and the feasibility of conditions for the organization as a result of these (projected) contracts. Examples:
    - Demands (or expectations) of financial management with respect to costs or the invoicing structure. Feasibility of the supplier's costs – as indicated in the projected (sub)contract – in relation to the costs of the complete services.
    - Demands (or expectations) of planning and control with respect to the delivery of services. Feasibility of timelines – as indicated by suppliers – in relation to final delivery to the customer.
    - Demands of quality management with respect to the quality system used by the supplier, integration issues, etc. Degree of acceptance of products and services set up by the supplier in relation to the application management organization's services.
- Plans, feasibility (output): demands of, or impact on, other processes as a result of (projected) contracts and the feasibility of demands, placed on supplier management or contracts, by other processes.
- Realization (output): of the supplier's agreements (financial, timelines, quality, etc.).
- Realization (input): of agreements of other management processes regarding the contract with the supplier (e.g. delivery period of the organization's own products, etc.).
- Problems (output): for quality management.

Application management organization strategy processes:
- Strategy (input): more detailed:
  - Service delivery definition: policy outlines.
  - Supplier definition: the supplier strategy.
  - Capabilities definition: (impact of the) capabilities strategy (on suppliers or services).
  - Technology definition: (impact or urgency for suppliers due to the) technology strategy.
  - Account and market definition: (financial and cost charging aspects of the) account strategy.
- Status of suppliers (output): for all Application management organization strategy processes.

Application strategy processes:
- Application portfolio management:
  - Status of suppliers and developments (output): developments with respect to suppliers' technology/solutions and organizations.
  - Application portfolio policy (input): strategy, demands and structure of the application landscape.
- Application life cycle management:
  - Status of current application (output): developments with regard to suppliers' technology/solutions and organizations.
  - Application strategy (input).

8 Application strategy

> **ASL statements**
>
> - Renewal and innovation of the business process will increasingly have to come from the existing applications; starting from scratch is becoming less of an option.
>
> - Managing the applications as a whole (the portfolio) is becoming an important issue within application management.
>
> - Understanding of the developments in respect to the user organization, the user organization's environment and technological developments plays a decisive role in the alignment with the customer's business process.

8.1 Introduction

8.1.1 Goal of application strategy

Application strategy focuses on the future and the life cycle of the objects (applications) within information provisioning.

There are several reasons why this cluster is so important.
- We live in a world of replacement. The majority of future applications already exist and we live increasingly in a world of replacement: the majority of new applications replace existing applications. The quality of the information provisioning will be improved by executing application support, maintenance and renewal within a good strategy for the future.
- Referring to the world of replacement, improvement, renewal and innovation of the existing information provisioning are becoming the preferred scenario for the improvement of the information provisioning. Large parts of the information provisioning work well, but there are several bottlenecks. The goal is to avoid rebuilding from scratch, by preventing the reasons for rebuilding. This is achieved by solving the issues and shortcomings preemptively.
- User organizations never like the idea of radical disruptions such as initial development. Application management organizations also often do not benefit from it: for them an initial development could potentially mean discontinuity in the services, which is an opportunity for a customer to choose another solution or another supplier.

This is why the alignments between applications and the business process requirements and continuous improvement have become important goals. The scope of these activities is two to five years, which results in strategies and improvement initiatives for a similar or slightly longer period.

8.1.2 Application strategy processes

The cluster has two kinds of processes:
- Three processes that provide insight. They collect information about the developments and determine their generic impact on the applications.
- Two processes that determine the strategy and take decisions. Within these processes, and based on the insight into the current state of affairs and future trends, blueprints and future strategies (scenarios) are created and a scenario is chosen.

The 'insight' processes are:
- IT developments strategy. The focal point of this process is technological developments (including standard solutions) and the impact these have on the applications.
- Customer organizations strategy. Here the core subject is developments in the user organization and the impact these have on the applications.
- Customer environment strategy. This process reacts to developments in the information provisioning in other organizations with which the customer interacts (the information chain).

Decision-making takes place at two levels: at the application level (application life cycle management) and at the level of the applications as a whole, the application landscape (application portfolio management). The status of the applications and/or application landscape is determined within these two processes. Scenarios are also developed, and where possible a decision is made about which scenario is to be followed.

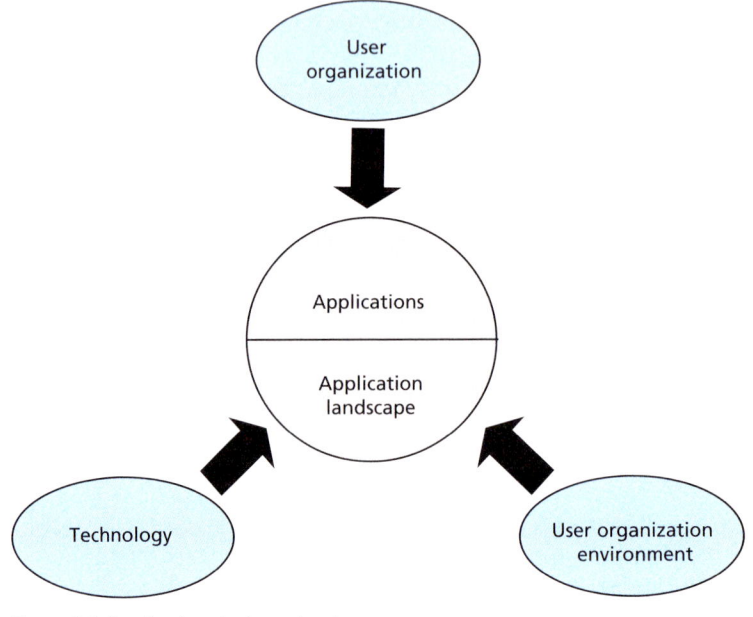

Figure 8.1 Application strategy structure

8.1.3 Design and implementation factors

The design, implementation and organizational execution of the application strategy processes can be complex. Several factors play a role.

Subject and scope

The first subject is the scope. In Chapter 2 it was already explained that application management operates in many different situations.

The scope of the application strategy -processes can vary a great deal for each application and for each application management organization; this particularly applies to application portfolio management. When an application management organization provides a service to a large coherent area (for example, the information provisioning for an insurance company), the logical step would be to define the application portfolio management accordingly.

However, some organizations focus on a market segment while others works in multiple segments. The second kind of organization deals with applications that operate in several varying and disconnected information landscapes.

It is therefore vital to determine the scope and the impact that it will have on the process.

Cooperation with other organizations
As a rule, these processes are always executed in close collaboration with other parties.

Application life cycle management and application portfolio management can rarely occur by themselves and independently. In most cases, other organizations have influence, authority or final responsibility regarding parts of the broader applications landscape:
- Other organizations that provide other services for the same domain. An example is infrastructure management that supplies the infrastructure on which the applications run. Often they are responsible for the result or have ownership of part of the information provisioning and therefore have the autonomous right to make decisions for that particular part.
- The customer (often business information management within the user organization) usually makes the final decision.

These other organizations perform similar processes. In order to achieve an integrated and accepted solution it is essential to organize a co-production, whereby roles are determined (for example 'has final decision' or 'following/supportive').

Dynamics
The dynamics also play an important role. For stable and large-scale legacy systems it would be logical to perform a fundamental re-evaluation once a year or once every

other year. Other applications require a higher frequency. The market can be so dramatic that this will be a continuous process. This too will need to be predetermined.

Quality of design and implementation
In the long run, application strategy usually has a major impact. This means that the life cycle management has to be performed well. The right people, the right expertise and the right skills are usually more important than how the process is designed and implemented.

A combination of a very detailed process and people with inadequate experience, or not able to think laterally, rarely has good results (although a detailed design would suggest otherwise).

8.2 IT developments strategy

8.2.1 Goal of IT developments strategy
The goal of IT developments strategy is to determine the impact of technological developments on the application portfolio.

IT development strategy examines which technological developments in the IT sector may be interesting for the organization's information provisioning. Most of the attention is focused on the technology for application development (development and management tooling), although new infrastructures (such as networking, image/sound, etc.) can also create opportunities for applications for the user organization.

8.2.2 IT developments strategy topics

a. Tooling

Technology comes in a variety of guises and has varying consequences for the business process of application management and the applications. Examples of technology are:
- Design and development tools: these are the tools, or resources, with which programs and systems are designed and built, such as compilers and interpreters (Java, C #, Cobol), and related development and design environments.
- Functionality: these are the basic functionalities which are part of the application that are built or maintained - for example, software packages, ASP solutions, etc.
- IT management tooling: these are resources which provide control for the application management organization - such as version control software, helpdesk and monitoring systems.
- Infrastructure (target environment): these are the platforms, managed by infrastructure management, for which the application is developed and which the application uses to be able to run. An infrastructure is also necessary for the development of software; however, this could be a different platform.

b. Position within the life cycle

Technology and tools, like applications, also have a life cycle. These could be:
- End of life: this technology is still used but its future is uncertain. This can be corporate, functional and technical by nature.
- Stable: there is no ageing. However, even in the stable phase in the life cycle there are continuous developments that should be taken into account (such as releases and upgrades).
- New: new technologies and solutions appear on the market that have not yet been implemented, but could be attractive.

The generic life cycle (the market life cycle of the tool) can vary from the life cycle to the specific situation in which it is being used. Therefore, it is conceivable that a component could be in a stable phase in the generic market, while its use within a specific solution is no longer appropriate.

c. Impact

Determining the precise (factual) impact of technology on an application takes place within application life cycle management. The generic impact is determined within IT developments strategy, such as the broad impact on an application or the rules for determining the impact and costs, generic replacement scenarios, alternative scenarios, implications for other developments, etc.

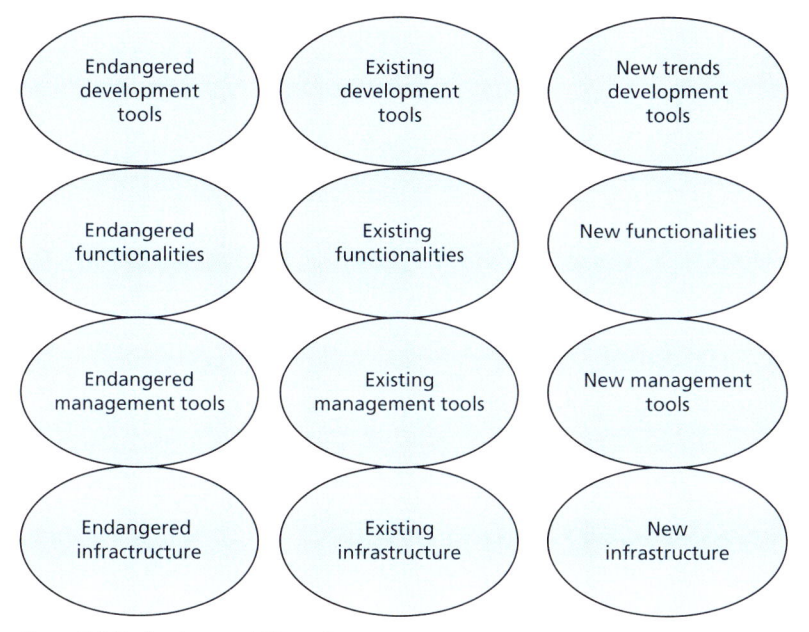

Endangered development tools	Existing development tools	New trends development tools
Endangered functionalities	Existing functionalities	New functionalities
Endangered management tools	Existing management tools	New management tools
Endangered infrastructure	Existing infrastructure	New infrastructure

Figure 8.2 Technology and life cycle

8.2.3 IT developments strategy activities

Technology development inventory:
- Identifying the technology tools/solutions used, and determining their status (life cycle).
- Identifying the need for upgrading or phasing out.
- Determining the affected applications or areas within the application landscape.
- Making an inventory of possible scenarios for this.
- Identifying new technology tools or solutions.
- Determining the possible needs and threats that these tools or solutions could address.
- Selecting any potentially interesting technology, and gaining more insight into their applicability such as costs, ability to integrate, risks, investment, and growth path.

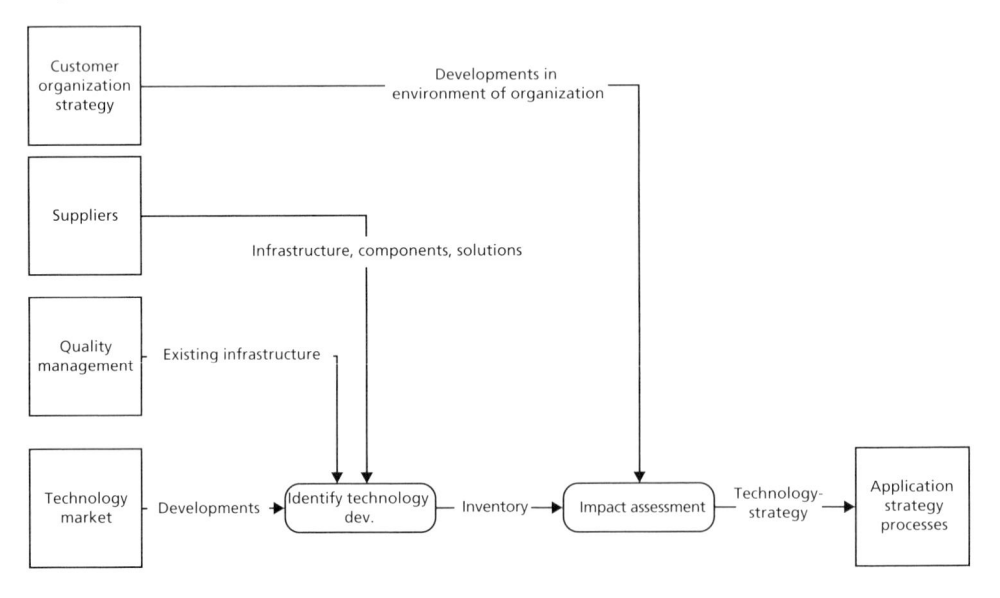

Figure 8.3 Process diagram for IT developments strategy

Determining impact:
- Identifying an overall policy or desired approach for the technology or solutions used.
- Identifying the impact on the existing application (portfolio).

8.2.4 IT developments strategy results

Technology strategy:
- Current technology and its developments.
- New technologies and opportunities.
- Impact of all developments and opportunities.
- Potential implementation scenarios and phase-out scenarios with key figures.

8.2.5 IT developments strategy relationships

Suppliers:
Developments regarding infrastructure, components, solutions (input).

Technology market:
Developments (input).

Customer organizations strategy:
- Developments in the organization (input): needs and developments of the organization as far as they relate to the technology, the impact they have on the technology or as far as they create the need for technology.

Application strategy processes:
- Application life cycle management (output): technology strategy/analysis.
- Application portfolio management (output): technology strategy/analysis.

Management processes (mainly quality management):
- Status of current infrastructure (input).

8.3 Customer organizations strategy

8.3.1 Goal of customer organizations strategy
The second process within application strategy is customer organizations strategy.

This process identifies the developments in the customer organization(s). The objective of this process is to determine the impact of developments in the user organization or the user organizations on the application portfolio. For most organizations the time horizon/scope for this will be two to five years.

Customer organizations strategy proactively determines the impact for applications, so it is clear which constraints these applications will have for these developments, and the best way to respond to these constraints.

As indicated in paragraph 8.1.3, the scope depends on the kind of services provided. Depending on the place and role of the application management organization, the ´customer organization´ under consideration could be a single customer organization (for example in case of bespoke software), but it could also be more than one organization, or a collective organization that represents a number of organizations.

8.3.2 Customer organizations strategy topics
The need for change can originate from the 'controlling' side or the 'logistics' side of an organization.

When we talk about the 'controlling side', we mean changes in the structure or design/implementation of the customer organization(s), such as mergers, a reorganization (towards market oriented units or product oriented units), a change in the financial management structure, etc. Changes in the infrastructure (housing/location, machines or possibly IT) are also part of this perspective.

The 'logistics chain' refers to the changes in the customer's primary production process: the chain of suppliers (for the customer's business process) from raw materials to products, and finally the customer of the customer's business process.

Structural (fundamental) changes in this logistic chain have a remarkably strong impact on the structure of the information process and therefore on the structure of the application and application landscape. Applications are always based on a certain structure and a certain scale of the underlying business process and its communication streams, so any alterations to these will result in the need for large-scale change.

> *Example*
> An organization is accustomed to selling directly to end-users. Because of market consolidation, end-user customer cooperatives have been created. This, in turn, results in framework contracts, which involve several end-user customers. However, not every end-user customer is bound by a master contract.
>
> The sales system was based on a situation with a number of uniform customers who had a standard contract. Now there are unique framework contracts, bulk users as well as the old uniform contracts. It is difficult to incorporate these changes into the sales system.

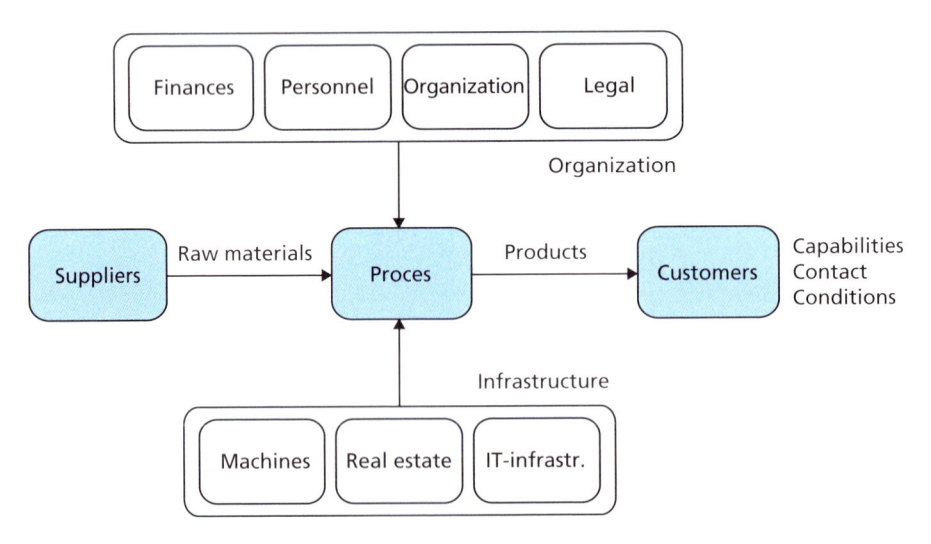

Figure 8.4 Topics of customer organizations strategy

Recognizing the changes in the logistics chain and the control chain will provide a good starting point for change requirements (from the perspective of the user organization) for the applications and application landscape.

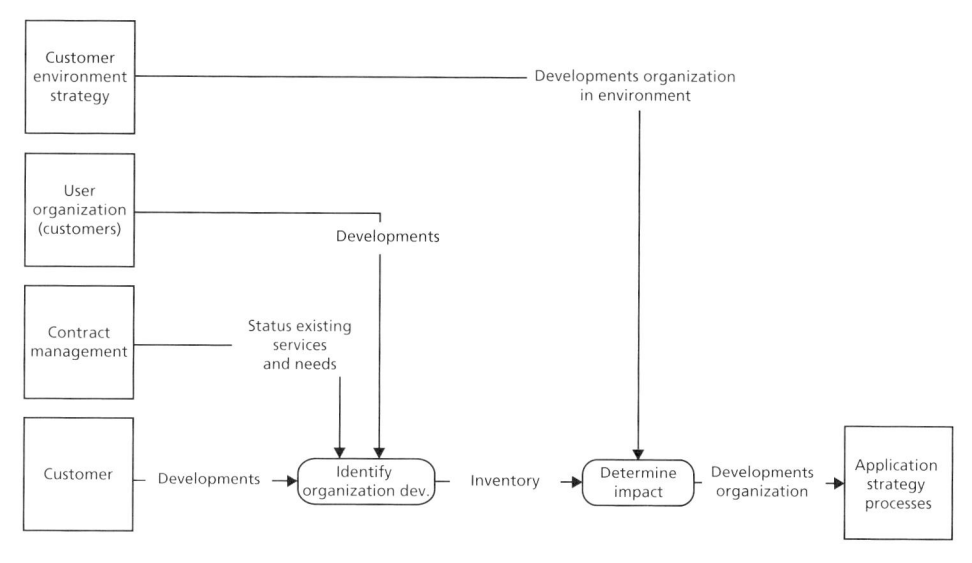

Figure 8.5 Process outline for customer organizations strategy

8.3.3 Customer organizations strategy activities
Inventory of organizational developments:
- Identifying the changes in policy.
- Identifying the changes in the business process (including customers and suppliers).
- Identifying the infrastructure.
- Identifying the organizational changes (changes in organization structure, responsibilities, financial standards, staffing aspects).
- Identifying changes regarding the IT-control.

Determining impact:
- Identifying existing applications that have been affected by the developments.
- Identifying shortcomings (blank spots) in the business support by existing information systems.
- Identifying the basic impact for existing and potential new information systems.

8.3.4 Customer organizations strategy results
Developments organization:
- Changes in the user organization(s).
- Estimated impact on the information provisioning.

8.3.5 Customer organizations strategy relationships
User organization (customer):
- Developments (input): (customer and user organizations can be the same).

Customer environment strategy:
- Organizational developments in environment (input): developments in the environment and the impact on the user organization/customer organization.

Contract management:
- Status of existing services and needs (input): existing shortcomings, needs and developments of the existing applications.

Application strategy *processes:*
- Application life cycle management (output): organizational developments.
- Application portfolio management (output): organizational developments.
- Customer environment strategy (output): organization developments.

8.4 Customer environment strategy

8.4.1 Goal of customer environment strategy

Customer environment strategy analyses developments in the exchange of information and data between various organizations (information chains), and uses this to gain insight into the requirements and opportunities regarding the applications.

The objective of customer environment strategy is to determine the impact that developments in the environment of the customer organization or user organization have on the application portfolio.

An ever-increasing number of organizations are operating as units in a production chain that consists of multiple organizations. This structure creates strong dependencies in the field of information provisioning between organizations and the applications of other organizations.

In addition, there is a rapidly growing trend towards the use of centralized records databases, for example in the public sector. These developments lead to the emergence of 'information chains'. The word 'chain' will be used in this section to indicate an information chain.

A consequence of this that the capabilities of the information provisioning for a particular organization now depend on developments of other organization's information provisioning, and the decisions made in this respect.

The opportunities to determine the changes or to prevent changes from happening become highly dependent on the place and position (of the customer's organization) within this chain.

8.4.2 Customer environment strategy topics

a. The chain

The chain does not exist
First of all (the same applies to service chains) the chain does not exist. The chain depends on the position of the application (organization), on what the application

(organization) does, and with whom information is exchanged. Because many information chains are linked, everyone will view their own specific chain.

> *An example*
>
> The customer makes use of the TWK-application. In the past a customized link has been created to the XXX -administration. Blue Pink is responsible for the maintenance. In addition, the application is connected to the financial administration. This is managed by ITM.
>
> The application management organization manages TWK and also acts as the overall system integrator for TWK. They are not involved with other applications and business information management is responsible for the internal functional integration issues. System integration for TWK does not imply that they do all the work themselves. TWK also runs on Getrad's infrastructure. The system integrator takes full responsibility for this, and as a result business information management is hardly aware of the infrastructure. However, sometimes this creates a few (internal) control problems, due to the fact that Getrad has another 25 customers using the mainframe.
>
> In order to verify data, system integration uses a clearinghouse. The payments and collections go through Interpay. TWK is based on a package with a fair amount of customization. The supplier of the standard application has 212 applications, primarily in a different market segment.

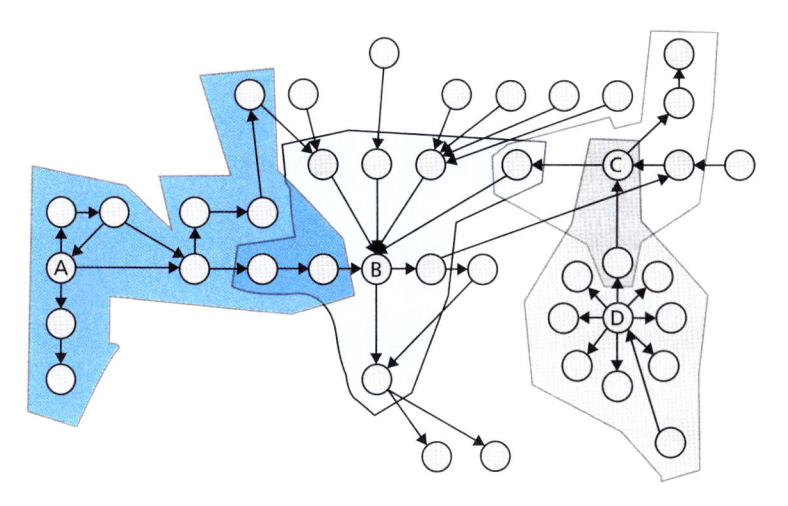

Figure 8.6 Examples of chains

Party A (or application component A) in Figure 8.6 sees a completely different chain from B, C, D or E. No one oversees the whole picture.

Chains are not controllable
A consequence of this is that chains are hard to directly control:
- The organizations in the chain are often independent and often lack an overarching enforcing authority. The parties within the chain have their own responsibility,

their own and other chains, their own resources, their own control and their own interests.
- Each party sees a different chain, and this means that they have to deal with other interests of other parties in other chains. Moreover, these other parties have to deal with other possibilities and yet more parties. As a result the whole setting becomes entirely unpredictable.

> A modern trend is the use of centralized records databases. A centralized records database is difficult to change, because all customers rarely agree on what exactly should be changed and why. One reason why a 'change request' for centralized records database functionality is so difficult is because many customers do not see the need for that change (it does not bring any benefits but it does result in costs).
>
> When a centralized records database changes, then this change is hard to stop because the owner of the registration will be aiming for one single model. As an environment can rarely switch in its entirety in one go, this results in maintaining both the new and the old models and interfaces over a long period of time.

All this complicates the control within the chain and the control of a chain. A negotiation model is often the way to achieve change.

This does not imply that chains cannot be corrected or that chains cannot work. It simply indicates that direct or directive control is seldom possible. Therefore, it usually ends as a matter of negotiation, and this requires an intelligent and often complex form of management and organization. Usually it is necessary to support both older and newer forms of information exchange and this creates longer delivery dates, as not every customer is willing or able to switch - which means that the process will be time consuming.

b. Push and pull

There are several ways in which chains are created, and can be improved or modified.

Push
Chains can be created as a consequence of the policies or strategies of multiple organizations.

> *Example: government architecture*
> The Dutch government has embraced a type of architecture that allows its citizens to provide information once and once only. This centralized records database structure is enforced top-down.

Pull
Often, the infrastructure already happens to be in place. This means there is already an existing structure, and adding or creating requirements will be a simple matter. This time, the growth will originate more from the bottom up.

> *Example: the automation of government information exchange*
> Many Dutch government departments already exchange information because this obviously results in improvements in efficiency and reliability. Exchanging information is relatively easy because the information exchange infrastructure was already in place. Employees were already familiar with the interfaces they needed to use to write or read data with - the knowledge was there. This made it a simple matter to exchange information between government departments. Creating links made it possible to economize and increase reliability. Therefore, this approach was less top-down and more bottom-up.

In order to link information streams, the different organizations have to be linked at four levels:
- The (technical) infrastructure must allow information exchange to take place and allow mutual linking (e.g. middleware).
- The information or functions between the various data domains have to be interchangeable. Differences in syntax and semantics must be reconciled.
- The content and the status of the information need to correspond. The different demands that each chain partner makes regarding reliability, completeness, topicality and the amount of detail also have to be reconciled.
- Information exchange with third parties should be aligned with the business process, the steps of the process and the policy of the organization (for example privacy, delivery dates).

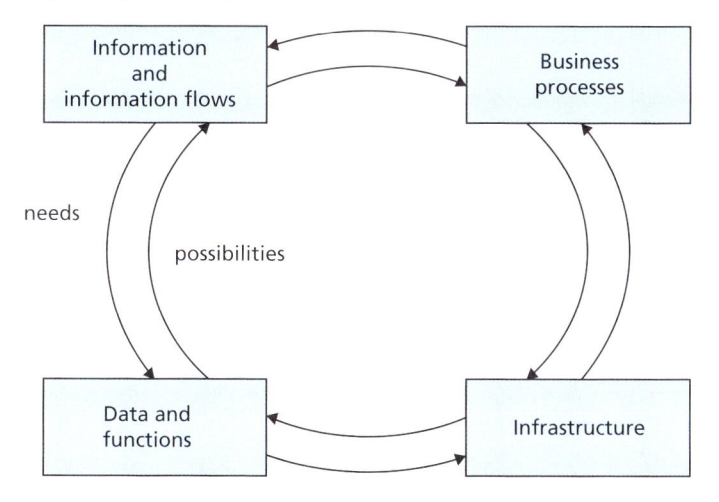

Figure 8.7 Objects and links

Many organizations already have many facilities in place for chains. In many cases, the bottom-up approach leads to the creation of small and more profitable chains. The process customer environment strategy identifies the opportunities for components in the application landscape in a structured way.

8.4.3 Customer environment strategy activities

Creating a list of the developments in the organization:
- Identifying the relevant developments in business processes that overarch several organizations, including any related standards.
- Identifying the developments in respect of generic requirements in the field of information exchange or centralized records databases.
- Identifying organizational requirements when working with the relevant organizations, including the user organization's customers.
- Identifying any modifications that are needed regarding existing information exchange.
- Identifying the opportunities and possibilities for any further alignment or information exchange.
- Identifying and selecting any necessary or possible 'communication infrastructure', such as middleware, networking, etc.

Determining the impact:
- Indicating the global policy or desired direction for the chain processes and their implementation.
- Indicating potentially interesting opportunities for implementation chain processes, starting from existing infrastructure and applications.

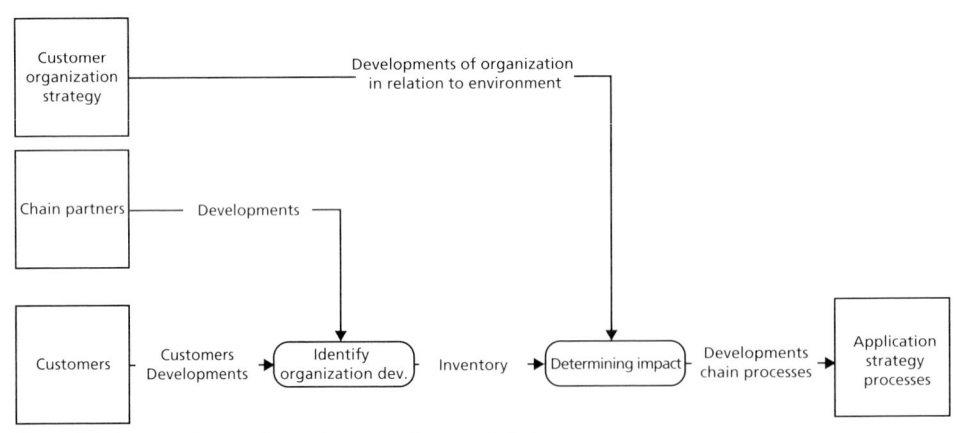

Figure 8.8 Process diagram for customer environment strategy

8.4.4 Customer environment strategy results

Developments in chain processes:
- Developments in respect of communication, technology, and exchange standards.
- 'Reciprocal' or requirements and opportunities that apply to a specific market segment.
- Limitations and bottlenecks.
- Impact on applications and application landscape.
- Any requirements in respect of standards for messaging, including those in the fields of applications and infrastructure.

8.4.5 Customer environment strategy relationships

Customers:
- Developments (input): information about developments in respect of the customer or customers (this will usually be the user organization or user organizations), regarding information exchange with third parties.

Chain partners:
- Developments (input): information about developments in the chain or affecting the chain. These could be general guidelines or Application strategy type plans made by the chain partners.

Customer organizations strategy:
- Developments in the organization in the relationship with environment (input): development or strategy of the customer's organization regarding its environment.

Application strategy processes:
- Application life cycle management (output): developments in the chain processes.
- Application portfolio management (output): developments in the chain processes.

8.5 Application life cycle management

8.5.1 Goal of application life cycle management

The goal of application life cycle management is to determine the future strategy of an application, translated into actions, so that the application can provide support for the company processes in the future.

We have already explained in this chapter, and in Chapter 2, that applications are often active for a longer period than planned or expected. Increasingly, the question is more about replacement than about a new information system. In practice, parts of the applications are now more often renovated, resulting in a system comprising old and new parts. It is now less easy to distinguish between development, maintenance and enhancement.

According to ASL's vision, application management encompasses the support of the company processes for their entire lifespan using the information systems. Application management is therefore not the management and maintenance of an application during its lifespan. It represents a shift from the application to the company process.

This means that an application's long-term perspective is vital. Choosing the existing situation as the starting point towards the future is a logical consequence.

8.5.2 Application life cycle management topics

a. The roles played by customers and suppliers

Any decisions to be made about the future of an application cannot be made without interaction with its environment. Infrastructure, business information management (the customer of application management), users, external users, decisions made by customers outside the application management organization: all these elements have to be taken into account. The interactions can differ, depending on the application.

> For suppliers of custom systems, it is almost always a matter of a paying customer who will determine the strategies and the specifications. The customer's business information management almost always takes the lead and has the final say.
>
> Often the infrastructure is split because the platform is used by multiple customers. Infrastructure management will often offer the infrastructure as a facility, in which the control of the platform and the strategy it uses will be determined by the infrastructure management organization.

The role and authority of application management regarding the strategy to be followed can be different for each application: sometimes the final responsibility will reside with the application management, at other times application management can only advise the customer. The nature of other parties with whom information is exchanged will also vary. The set up and execution of application life cycle management must be carried out for each separate application, and the position of this process in the environment has to be determined for each individual application.

There is not a pre-determined sequence and coherence between application life cycle management and application portfolio management. In a highly centralized structure with strong top-down control, it will be logical to see the results of application portfolio management as the source of inputs for application life cycle management. Unfortunately, many organizations simply do not have this strong kind of top-down management with regard to information provisioning. In these situations, the inputs of application life cycle management will mostly serve as the control for application portfolio management. The set-up and execution will have to be determined separately for each process: what the sequences will be and what form the decision-making will take. There is no pre-set standard formula.

b. Approach

As we explained in paragraph 2.4.4, there is an increasing demand for replacement or adaptation. In these situations (and this is almost always the case) it is more efficient and effective not to define what an application should look like in an ideal state, but rather to determine the modification requirements for the existing information provisioning. There are several reasons for this:

- It is difficult to determine (in advance) what something should look like in its ideal state. It is easier to answer the question 'what can be changed', than to answer the question 'what would the ideal application look like'[1].
- Concrete change requirements make it easier to come up with concrete solutions.
- Any proposed ideal situation will not still be ideal in three years time: by then the outlook will have changed (and therefore the proposed architecture), the organization's set up will be different, etc. The ideal situation is also often out of reach (too expensive, takes too long, etc.).

Usually (but not always) the easiest way to identify the desired situation is to collate the various ways in which change is required. There are two types of requirements for change:
- Shortcomings in the current situations. These can be subdivided into:
  - Technical quality: the quality of the application from the maintenance point of view (maintainability).
  - Functional quality: the quality from the user's point of view (such as suitability, ergonomics, information quality).
  - Operation quality: continuity, manageability.
- Changes that result from policy or strategy or that result from a change in the environment. With regard to these developments, the work will already have been carried out in the customer environment strategy and the customer's organizations strategy processes.

In order to present an idea of the way in which solutions can implemented, it will be necessary to have an idea of the opportunities presented by technology, or of the solutions. The IT developments strategy process will provide the necessary input.

The result of application life cycle management is a description of solution strategy; this will consist of both a blueprint/architecture (what will it actually look like) and a scenario/strategy (how do we make it happen).

It would be advisable not to produce just a single scenario (solution approach) but several scenarios. The selection of a scenario cannot actually be made without looking at its impact in terms of costs, risks, timescale, and consequences. Managers cannot afford to separate aims and policies from their consequences and costs. People often do not realize what the impact of their demands will be.

Having a choice means that you have to think in advance about what people really want (or what needs to be sorted out and whether or not they have considered the costs and effort required). This often leads to a scaling down of their ambitions. This explicit choice leads to a major increase in the basic needs and acceptance by the management board and/or customer. In the follow-up phase of the process this commitment will be required.

---

1 However, the answer to this last question is often translated into a need to change the existing system ('this and this should be more flexible').

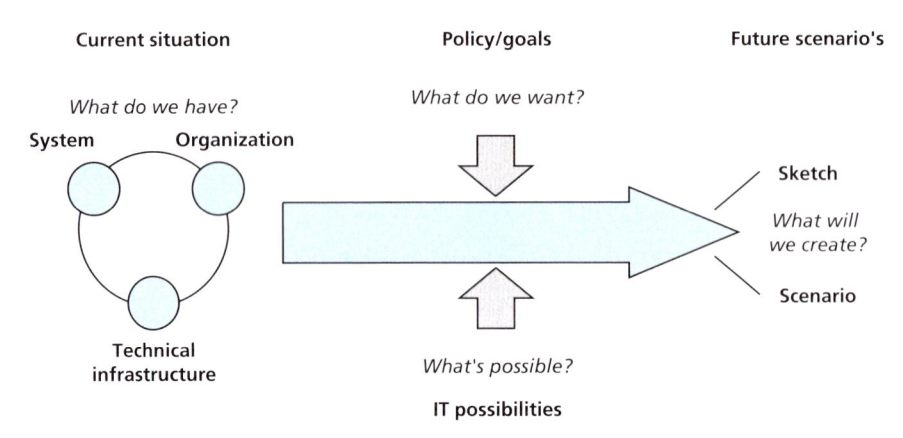

Figure 8.9 Renewal

8.5.3 Application life cycle management activities

Determining the status of the current situation:
- Determining the technical quality (future stability, maintainability, flexibility) of the application.
- Determining the functional quality (the connection with users and the business process).
- Determining the operational quality (continuity, manageability, efficiency, reliability).

Determining the impact of the policy:
- Determining the impact of developments and changes in the business process, policy and the environment of the application.
- Determining the impact of the changes in the organization, users, information provisioning and other applications.
- Determining the commitment and willingness to invest, and other preconditions.

Determining technical possibilities:
- Determining potentially interesting or necessary technology.
- Determining the developments of existing technology.
- Determining the availability and the value that it will provide for the application.

Determining strategy and scenarios:
- Creating possible scenarios and blueprints.
- Determining the investments, benefits, advantages, disadvantages and the extent to which the requirements are met.
- Advice/choice of scenario.

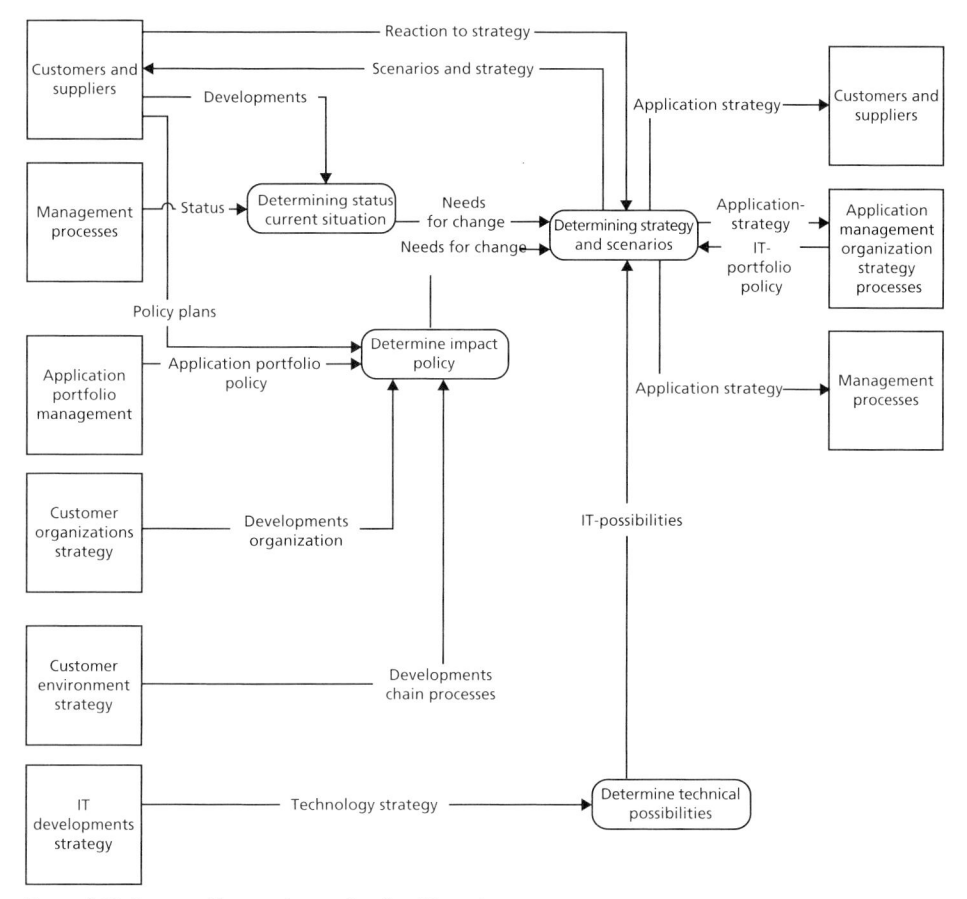

Figure 8.10 Process diagram for application life cycle management

Iterative process
What the process scheme implicitly makes clear (and the relations more explicitly) is that application life cycle management can (and often will) be an iterative process. The customer's policy plans can serve as information, but can also be a starting point. These policy plans depend on the design of a similar Application strategy process within business information management. The plans can be adjusted by the results of application life cycle management.

8.5.4 Application life cycle management results
Application strategy:
- Existing structure and quality of the application.
- Most important developments.
- Possible future scenarios including impact assessment and sketches, and a general blueprint of the structure/architecture.
- A choice of scenarios, possibly more developed, towards a concrete plan that can be implemented at the controlling level.

8.5.5 Application life cycle management relationships
Customers and suppliers:
- Developments (input): developments/needs/status of quality regarding the application, the resources or how they are used.
- Scenarios and strategies (output): the devised or established strategy of the supplier or customer and potential scenarios for the future of the application (and its impact).
- Reaction to strategy (input): reactions or decisions of the customer and/or suppliers.
- Application strategy (output): the established sketch/scenarios/architecture.
- Policy plans (input): policy plans or proposed policies of the customer with respect to its information provisioning.

Management processes:
- Status (input): the quality of the application, described from several approaches, for example:
  - Quality management: the quality of the application and application parts.
  - Contract management: experiences and needs of customers and the extent to which the agreements are fulfilled.
  - Financial management: costs, gains, market conformity, trends.
  - Supplier management: supplier developments, supplier performance.
- Application strategy (output): impact on contract management, quality management, planning and control, supplier management.

Application strategy processes.
- Customer environment strategy (input): chain process developments.
- Customer organizations strategy (input): organizational developments.
- IT developments strategy (input): technology developments.
- Application portfolio management (output): application strategy, frameworks for the application portfolio strategy or changes to the application strategy following the application portfolio strategy.
- Application portfolio strategy (input): application portfolio policy.

8.6 Application portfolio management

8.6.1 Goal of application portfolio management
Application portfolio management aims to align and coordinate the various components in an application landscape (or the entire information provisioning as a whole) and to mutually adjust and optimize the larger or radical investments and changes.

The process identifies the significance and the performance of the various applications for the user organizations with respect to a particular application landscape. It translates the company policy to various objects in the information provisioning and, based on this, it then works out a strategy for the future of these objects in the portfolio. At the same time it makes provisions for the collective nature of the different objects.

Application portfolio management looks at:
- Whether application maintenance and renewal processes in applications also fit into the broad perspective of the information provisioning.
- Whether all the changes and projects are feasible for the customer organization(s) and/or for the application management organization.
- Whether investments could offer a greater return or added value in a different area.

8.6.2 Application portfolio management topics

a. Which information provisioning?

Determining the scope of the application portfolio management demands extra accuracy. Application portfolio management looks at the complete set of applications, meaning the information provisioning as a whole. The difference between an application and an application landscape is somewhat arbitrary: some organizations view certain groups of applications in an application landscape as a single application.

An additional complication is that applications can have different environments in different situations. Not only that, but the definition of what the application landscape actually is can also differ for each situation, because there are several definitions to consider (see also section 8.1.3):
- The information provisioning/application landscape of the customer.
- The application portfolio, which is maintained by their own application management organization.
- The application portfolio in the chain or the branch in which the applications operate.

It is evident that this scope is inseparable from the place, role, and market position of the application management organization. And sometimes there are multiple portfolios.

Examples

For a supplier of packages for local government the focus of application portfolio management will mainly be on supplying a complete solution for this market segment. In this case the scope is a market segment.

A custom application organization (for example an internal IT department) for a single customer will have a strong focus on the information provisioning of the customer.

A supplier of a clearinghouse will concentrate on the applications and solutions that provide and collect the data from the clearinghouse. Here the scope is an information chain landscape in which the clearinghouse operates.

Also, the design of the process is highly dependent on the scope and the information provisioning. The decision-making process in the second example will largely take place outside the application management organization; in the first example this can take place within the organization.

b. Methods and techniques

For the realization of application portfolio management there are many methods and methodologies that incidentally also may exhibit large principal differences. The subjects and images in this book (such as Figure 8.11) are taken from NIP, the new information provisioning.

ASL has no specified method, which means multiple methods and techniques can be used (TOGAF, 9-level model, NIP).

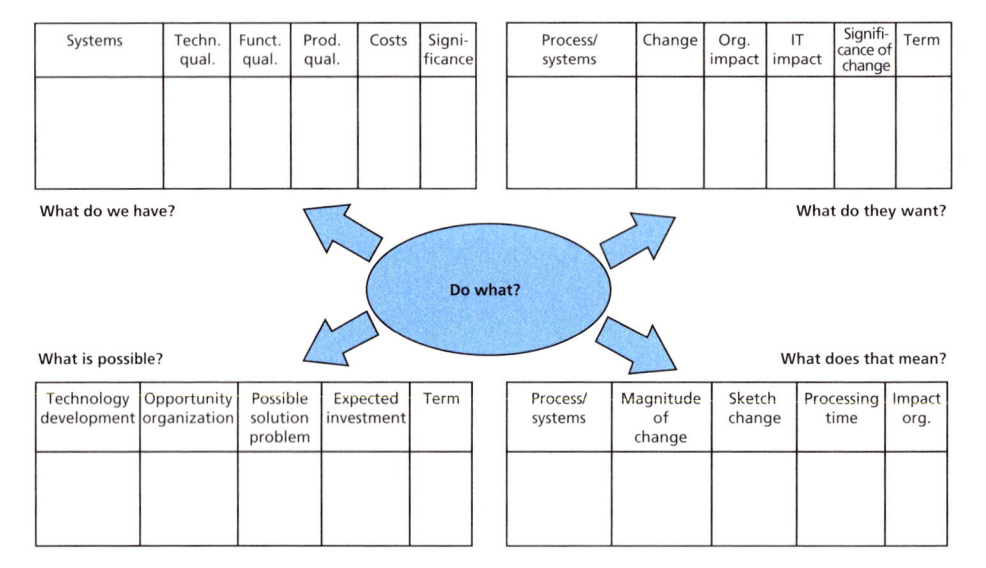

Systems	Techn. qual.	Funct. qual.	Prod. qual.	Costs	Signi-ficance		Process/ systems	Change	Org. impact	IT impact	Signifi-cance of change	Term

What do we have?   What do they want?

Do what?

What is possible?   What does that mean?

Technology development	Opportunity organization	Possible solution problem	Expected investment	Term		Process/ systems	Magnitude of change	Sketch change	Processing time	Impact org.

Figure 8.11 Topics of application portfolio management

c. Application portfolio and application portfolio policy

The next topic is the subject that application portfolio policy addresses.

Application portfolio management aims to optimize the application policy for the entire domain of the information provisioning.

This can often be more complicated than it would seem at first glance, because there are usually different and independent decision makers for the various parts in the applications landscape (see section 2.2.2). They would rarely be directed from a single point; in addition to this, such an approach would often be counterproductive.

Increasingly, the negotiating approach or the coordinated approaches ('being on the same page') appear to be dominant approaches for application portfolio management.

The coherence and common ground of information provisioning are monitored by application portfolio management. This coherence and common ground are reflected in three areas:
- The individual applications in the application landscape and their interdependence.
- The shared components and standards.
- The change portfolio of the applications.

Coherence/application landscape
The first topic in application portfolio management is the application landscape and how it is subdivided. The application landscape describes which applications are present, what the characteristics are, and what the relationship between them is or should be. This means that it describes the whole structure (architecture) as well as the limits of the components (applications).

Regarding these components, there are also several characteristics that will be defined, such as size, replacement cost, the quality as observed from different angles, continuity and major developments (the application portfolio).

Shared resources and standards.
The second topic covers shared resources. Another widely used expression for this is 'setting the standards'. The use of shared resources (such as the system that is used for workflow or document management, the basic payment application, etc.) can lead to increased flexibility and lower costs for the organization. The objective is to find out which technologies and features are or should be included in the standard/shared landscape. Achieving this standardization in an existing application portfolio can be costly and can require a great deal of effort. The feasibility and desirability of such shared functions and standards need to be an explicit topic of conversation during the identification of requirements: standardization can never be a goal in itself.

A theme that is very topical and closely related is the rationalization of the application portfolio: reducing the number of applications by phasing out applications with similar functionality. This underlying need is not new - the theme has existed for years - but because of the growing dynamic within organizations it is becoming a higher priority on the agenda. ASL also raises this question. However, one must realize that application rationalization is a functional question first and foremost, and much less of a technical question.

Change portfolio
The change portfolio indicates if and which large-scale changes have been considered for applications in the portfolio. Application portfolio management assesses whether it is still feasible as a whole. A situation in which everything is updated simultaneously is rarely feasible. The relations between different application maintenance and renewal processes also need to be identified. Based on this information it may be decided that the planned changes are too demanding for the organization and that it would be more advisable to stop. These considerations and the results of this decision should be seen as the change portfolio at the strategic level (the strategic calendar).

8.6.3 Application portfolio management activities

The structure of the activities of portfolio management application is similar to that of the application life cycle management process. However, the content, depth, scope, and process differ.

Determining status of current situation:
- Identifying or updating the current portfolio (existing and used applications, size, used resources, relations between them, replacement or investment value).
- Determining the current quality of the IT portfolio in a broad sense (strengths/weaknesses), functional quality, technical quality and operational quality.
- Determining bottlenecks or generic bottlenecks in the current situation.

Determining the *impact of policy:*
- Creating an overview of the developments at the generic level (from the environment and the user organization) and of all the appropriate changes at the level of the various applications.
- Determining the impact of these developments, the mutual impact and overall impact.
- Assessing the total capacity for change of the organization, the users and the IT.

Inventory (of the suitability of new) IT-possibilities:
- Determining the scope, appropriate or forced changes and developments in the field of technology.
- Determining connections between the various technological developments at the application level.

Creating strategy:
- Determining the total impact.
- Creating several basic scenarios and overall architectures (or modifications).
- Decision-making, attuning or coordination.
- Designing the form in which development takes place (outside the scope, within the scope, comprehensive maintenance, project).

8.6.4 Application portfolio management results

Application portfolio:
- The various applications with their descriptions.
- Consistency of the applications and the relations between applications.
- Indications of size and quality.
- Relevant developments for the applications etc.

Application portfolio policy:
- Proposed connection between applications or changes for all applications.
- Use of (future) standards and technology.
- Strategic change portfolio.
- See Section 8.6.2.

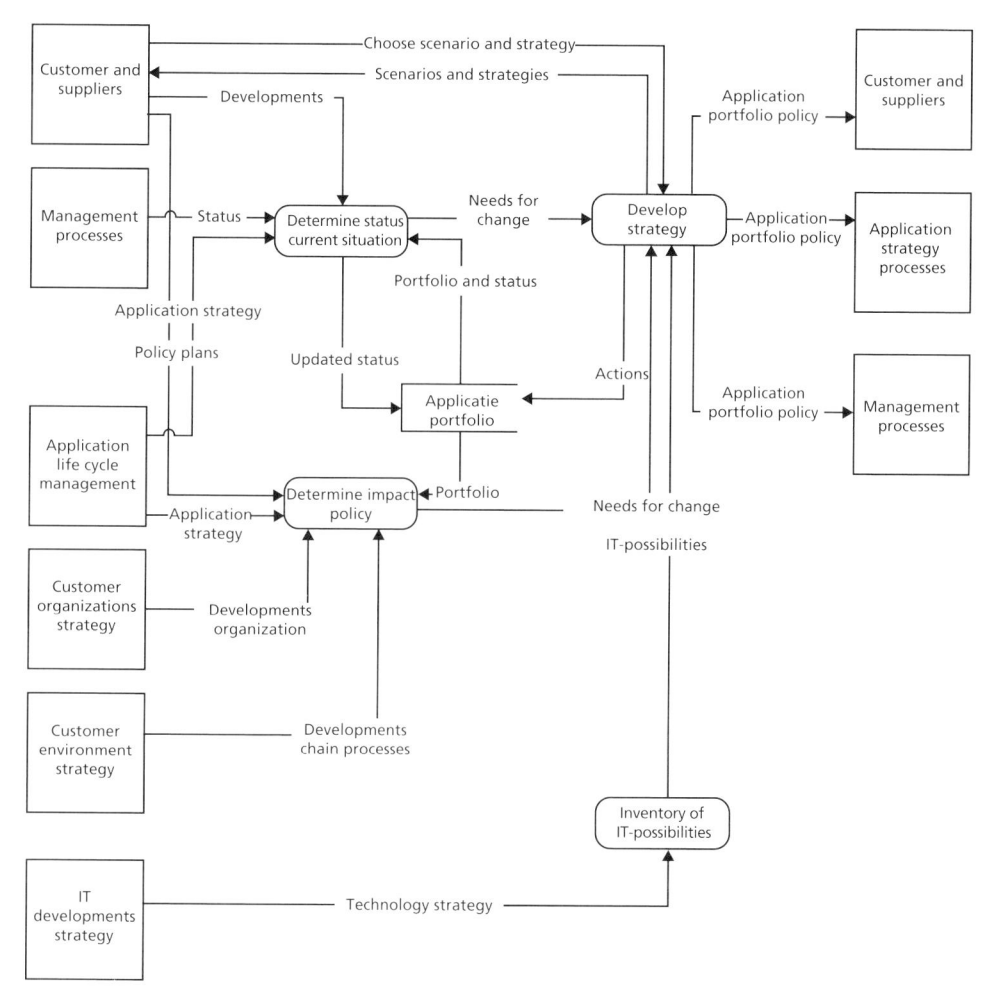

Figure 8.12 Process diagram for application portfolio management

8.6.5 Application portfolio management relationships

Customers and suppliers:
- Developments (input): developments from customers and suppliers.
- Policy plans (input): proposed or adopted policies of customers.
- Choosing scenarios and strategy (input): possible choice regarding a potential strategy to be followed.
- Scenarios and strategies (output): one or more strategies for application portfolio policy.
- Application portfolio policy (output): the established application portfolio.

Application life cycle management:
- Application portfolio policy (output).
- Application strategy (input): life cycle application strategy of an application.

Additional Application strategy processes:
- Customer organizations strategy (input): developments in the user organization.
- Customer environments strategy (input): developments in chain processes.
- IT Development Strategy (input): technology strategy.

Management processes:
- Status of the management processes (input).
- Application portfolio policy (output).

9 Application management organization strategy

> **ASL statements**
> - The commercialization of services has resulted in Application management organization strategy becoming vital for the future of the application management organization.
>
> - There is a large degree of freedom within services. However, the opportunities for an organization to supply multiple kinds of services are rather limited.
>
> - Therefore, there is great need to choose a strategy and form alliances with other organizations. This requires a conscious strategy.

9.1 Introduction

9.1.1 Goal of application management organization strategy

The objective of the application management organization strategy cluster, is to make choices about future services, to justify these choices, and to translate this into strategy and implementation.

Determining the organization's future services is vital for the application management organization. Application management manifests itself in many forms and decisions within these degrees of freedom have to be taken with respect to the future services (please also see paragraph 2.2.5):
- There are a great many forms of service provision, technologies and markets where people can excel. One single organization cannot supply all the various combinations.
- The needs of the customers and buyers are many and varied, both in the type of services, the type of management, as well as for example the most important acquisition driver (such as costs and innovation). Even one customer can present so much variety that the field would be too broad for just one supplier.
- Increasing componentization will further increase the complexity of IT. There are lots of technologies and/or technology tendencies to be considered, as well as the complex question of integration.

> *Examples*
> Within the internal IT departments of the larger organizations, employees have to ask themselves what their role is going to be. Some internal IT departments have been outsourced, others are forced by the customer to transfer services to third parties, and sometimes the customer will demand a level of services that is difficult for the IT department to manage and provide (alongside all the other existing and required types of services).

> Various internal IT organizations are moving towards a system integration function for the user organization. This means that they take on the integration of the subcontractors as well as their own standardized forms of services.

This is further complicated by the fact that customers expect the services organizations to supply and be familiar with the services. The policy of 'learning on the job' at the customer's expense is no longer self-evident.

The investment costs involved here (and therefore the costs of the learning curve) will be borne by the supplier. This means that there is less scope for investing in a number of different markets and services, and different types of services.

9.1.2 Application management organization strategy topics

Application management organization strategy distinguishes between four topics, with 'future services' as its central theme. Each of these topics corresponds to a process within Application management organization strategy.

Customer and market
The account and market definition process focuses on the first specialization axis (see paragraph 2.2.5), which is the customer. To a large extent, application management's theme is 'customer organization intimacy' or 'market segment process intimacy'.

Used and required technology and solutions
Technology (which also includes solutions) is the second specialization axis and is highly dynamic. Investments in new technology are enormous, partly due to the need for supplying high quality services using people and tools. The technology definition process determines the strategy with regard to the technology used within application management.

Core competences and skills
The core competences (skills) of the organization and the skills of its employees are at the center when defining capabilities definitions. It is a question of 'What is the organization really good at and where do we have to do well later on?'.

People (and organizations) cannot perform magic. The capacities for learning and change are limited and the learning curve for an organization to change its working methods could take up to three years. Therefore, making feasible and correct choices is vital.

Subcontractors and partners
One of the conclusions from Chapter 2 was that working together with other suppliers has become inevitable within IT services. Working out who the partners should be, their roles, position and contribution all form part of the supplier definition process. This includes such questions as: "What kind of collaborative partners are out there?" And, even more important: "Which ones could we work with and do we want to work with in order to realize whichever type of services we want to offer?".

Future services
The point where all these areas converge is the service delivery definition process. Investments in the four different areas have to be mutually agreed upon.

The service delivery definition process defines the future types of services and provides the structure required to realize them integrally.

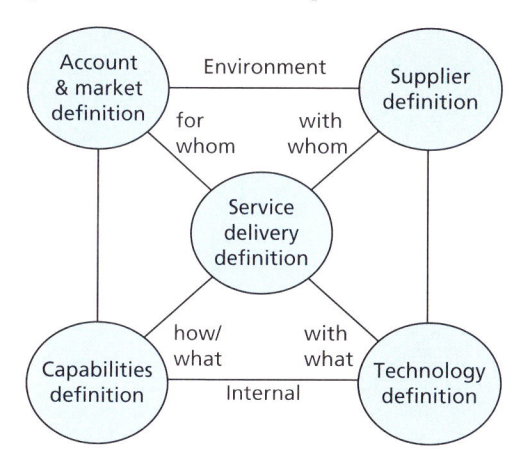

Figure 9.1 Structure of application management organization strategy processes

9.1.3 Coherence and approach
The different processes are highly interdependent.

> *Example*
> Within account and market definition it is acknowledged that in TZS, there is a pressing need to move to standard applications in the insurance field. The organization does not have the facts at its disposal about which kinds of applications are available on the market. Within the capabilities definition process they have assessed that gaining the knowledge and experience will not fit in with the current service and will be difficult to realize. It could be possible to build up this kind of expertise within the organization, but an alternative option is to use another company that already has the knowledge required in this particular field. A preferred supplier could carry out the implementation, after which the internal application management organization can carry out the support, maintenance and renewal.

The process approach (excepting service delivery definition) comprises four steps, the first two having a bottom-up character and the last two a top-down character:
- Making an inventory of the existing shortcomings and strengths and identifying developments and expectations.
- Based on this, determining the possible trends (or positions).
- Finalizing the agreed definitive strategic objectives.
- Translating the agreed objectives into a working strategy and implementation plan.

The results of all the application management organization strategy processes will be fine-tuned between the second and third steps. After the second step, the intermediate results will be collated within service delivery definition. This is where the trends and feasibilities from the various areas will be mutually fine-tuned, and translated into a clear and coherent strategy. For the different units, this strategy will be crystallized once again in the surrounding processes in the two steps we have just mentioned.

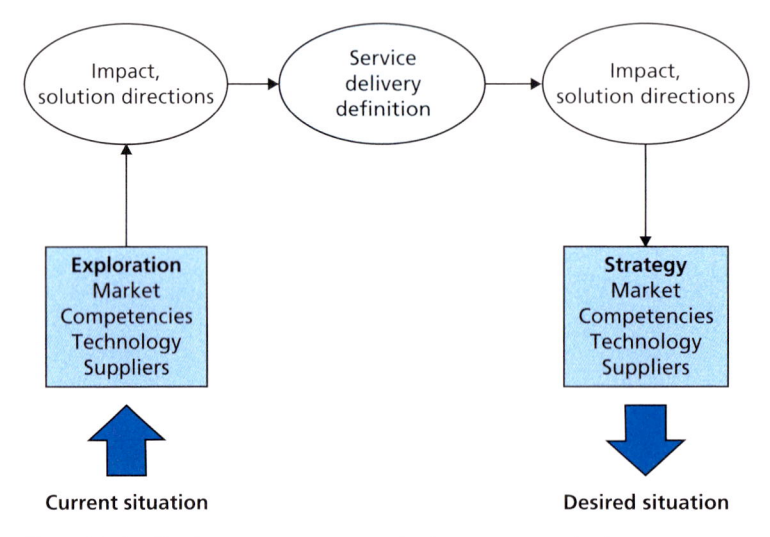

Figure 9.2 Application management organization strategy method

The approach starts as bottom-up and then changes to top-down. The advantages of this are:
- Decisions are based on concrete, complete and factual information.
- Subsequently, a strategy is drawn up and this will be completed top-down. This means that we can really talk about a cohesive and integral strategy.

9.1.4 Application management organization strategy relationship with the management processes

The processes within application management organization strategy prefer specific processes within the management processes: in this way, capability definition has a strong relationship with quality control. There are other processes within application management organization strategy that can provide frameworks for quality control. This also applies to the other management processes. The application management organization strategy processes therefore communicate with all the other management processes.

9.1.5 Application management organization strategy design and implementation factors

The application management organization strategy processes are often executed on a yearly basis; that is, when the application management organization policy is being determined. However, the environment can often be more dynamic, so that application management organization strategy has more of a continuous character.

The layout of the application management organization strategy processes is dependent on the internal structure, but it can be loosely coupled with the environment. Only when very high maturity levels exist (see Chapter 10.5), will there be a formal link to the outside world.

That last remark reflects our practical experience. Practical experience shows that (operational) employees are often a goldmine of up-to-date and reliable information about what is going on with the customers, how effective the service is, and where the organization's weak points are, etc.

Involving the employees in application management organization strategy contributes enormously to the quality of the decision-making process, as well as to the commitment when carrying out the policy.

9.2 Account and market definition

9.2.1 Goal of account and market definition

The place and role of an application management organization on the market is no longer self-evident. Its position is liable to change:
- Application management organizations have to consider which markets and which types of services are still large enough and still cost-effective enough to offer continuity.
- User organizations and customers are continually assessing what the roles of existing (internal and external) application management organizations should be. The position of the internal IT organization is no longer self-evident and depends heavily on perception.

> What is certain is that the large internal automation centers belonging to the big organizations have seen some huge changes in the last decades, due to globalization (within multinationals), among other things, and a pressing need for cost-cutting (resulting in offshoring). It is also becoming evident that the centers can no longer support all the required technical needs.
>
> This is why the obvious role and position known as "we do the automation for XXX" is disappearing. This is resulting in companies trying to find various ways in which to fill the gap. Some organizations have outsourced completely, others are moving towards a regional role, while some are taking on the role of (internal) integrator.

Defining the position, place and role with the customer and in the market is a precondition for the continuity of application management. Identifying the point of departure of the application management organization with the customer and in the market, and also compared to other IT organizations, is therefore vital.

The aim of the account and market definition process is to recognize the demands of future services for future customers and to make sure that the relationship and communication with the customers are good enough to realize this.

9.2.2 Account and market definition topics

Account and market definition covers the relationships between three entities:
- The *customers* (in other words, the market): what exactly is the relationship between the customer and the application-management organization, and in which direction are the needs of customers going.
- The place and role of the *application management organization* and how it is perceived.
- The position and place of *other organizations* (competitors/co-colleagues) in the IT service field in the market.

Central to the account and market definition process is not only the services itself but also the tools with which we can control the (perception of the) services. These topics are summarized in the illustration below.

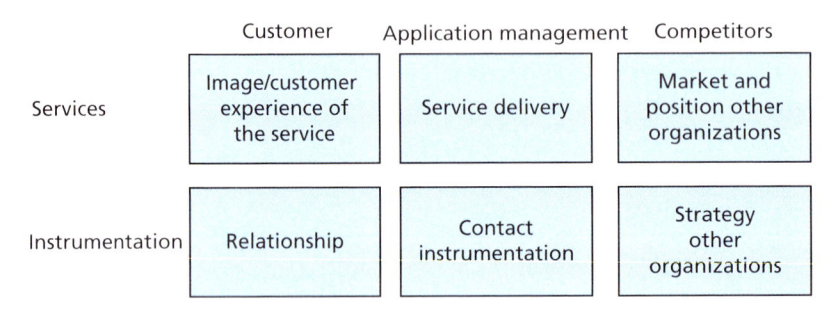

	Customer	Application management	Competitors
Services	Image/customer experience of the service	Service delivery	Market and position other organizations
Instrumentation	Relationship	Contact instrumentation	Strategy other organizations

Figure 9.3 Topics in account and market definition

Services

The central topic is the application management organization's service, now and in the future. Among other things, we will examine:
- Which service is supplied to which customer (PMC: product-market combination) and just how good is that service? How does the organization perceive its service? How far does that perception match reality?
- What kind of requirements in the fields of application maintenance and renewal and development can be expected in respect of this services or new services, stemming from the developments over recent years? Is there a call for structural improvement or modification?
- Which new combinations in products/services can be considered for which customers (PMC)?
- Could there be any new customers for the existing types of services?

Contact tools

Another important aspect of services is whether or not there are tools available to modify the perception, and whether the new service can be minimized. External organizations soon start to ask questions about the commercial side of application management. These can include:

- Who exactly is in contact with the customers and to what extent do they control the perception and services? On what level are they expected to operate?
- Is there a function within the application management organization that communicates (sufficiently) with the customers and at the right level, which corresponds to the desired and delivered services?
- Does the organization have the correct competences to communicate at that level? For example: a highly motivated technical employee is not always the right person to understand or anticipate the developments within the business. However, it can be very important to have someone who thoroughly understands communication: this could reassure the customer that there is a satisfactory level of knowledge about solutions or technology.

The image/perception of the service
It is good to have your own image of the service and application management organization, but this is not necessarily the same perception that the customer has. Relevant questions in this respect are:
- How do the customers (and those with final responsibility there) actually perceive the service and the application management organization?
- What do the customers actually want, in what direction are they going, and do they change over time? To what extent do they match current agreements?
- To what extent does the customer's image tally with reality?
- What types of services are people looking for?

Relationship
Often, the operational contacts and those making the final decisions do not necessarily have the same perception of the service.

Usually, the application management organization has no contact with the persons or department within the customer's organization that makes the decisions about information provisioning. Insight into the following would be useful:
- Who makes the decisions within the customer's organization and with whom should the application management organization discuss matters? Are they talking to the decision-makers or with the operation (or does the operation make the decisions)?
- How does the perception occur within the customer's organization?
- Are the current discussion points the same as those for future services? For example: the discussion points for outsourcing often differ from those for staff augmentation.

Market position and potential of other parties
Other parties are increasingly going to offer services within the market (customers). Making agreements or integrating with these other parties can have its advantages. The other parties could be interested in offering the services themselves. These parties could also offer replacement or competitive services. The relevant issues here include:
- Who are the other parties in the market and how do they behave?
- What kind of services do they supply and how?
- Which alternative solutions, replacements and problems could there be for the service?

Strategy regarding other organizations
The other parties also have their own image, position and capabilities. Other solutions or other parties could pose a threat to the continuity of the service. The last point will cover the question of how this can be monitored and controlled:
- How to tackle threats by substitute solutions or competing services?
- Why should other organizations be interested in cooperating? How should the contact be handled?
- What added value can organizations or solutions from other organizations bring to the services for existing or new customers? How would the customers react?

9.2.3 Account and market definition activities
Inventory of the current position (customers and needs):
- Making an inventory of current services, image of the services, image of the organization's own services and channels used for enhancing its image.
- Making an inventory of stakeholders and the customers' decision-makers.
- Making an inventory of services or possible services from other organizations.
- Making an inventory of new or expected needs for services and options to deliver this according to a customer's perspective.
- Determine need for change and options.

Definition of account opportunities:
- Making an inventory of the need to change image, services, demands in respect of contact and management tools (relationship/account management).
- Determining the scenarios, impact on the organization and any necessary investments and modifications.

Definition of account:
- Definition of the required product-market combinations.
- Decisions on the improvements required.
- Decisions on suitable measures, suppliers, quality control system, delivery, etc.

Create an account strategy:
- Elaborate to a detailed strategy and prepare the measures in respect of contact tools, image.
- Initiate these measures and actions.

9.2.4 Account and market definition results
PMC:
- Existing product-market combinations.
- Desired product-market combinations.

Account inventory results:
- Existing services to customers.
- Developments in respect of the customers.
- Opportunities and dangers.
- Possible strategy, aims, solution approaches for the market.
- Possible impact in respect of skills, technology, services, etc.

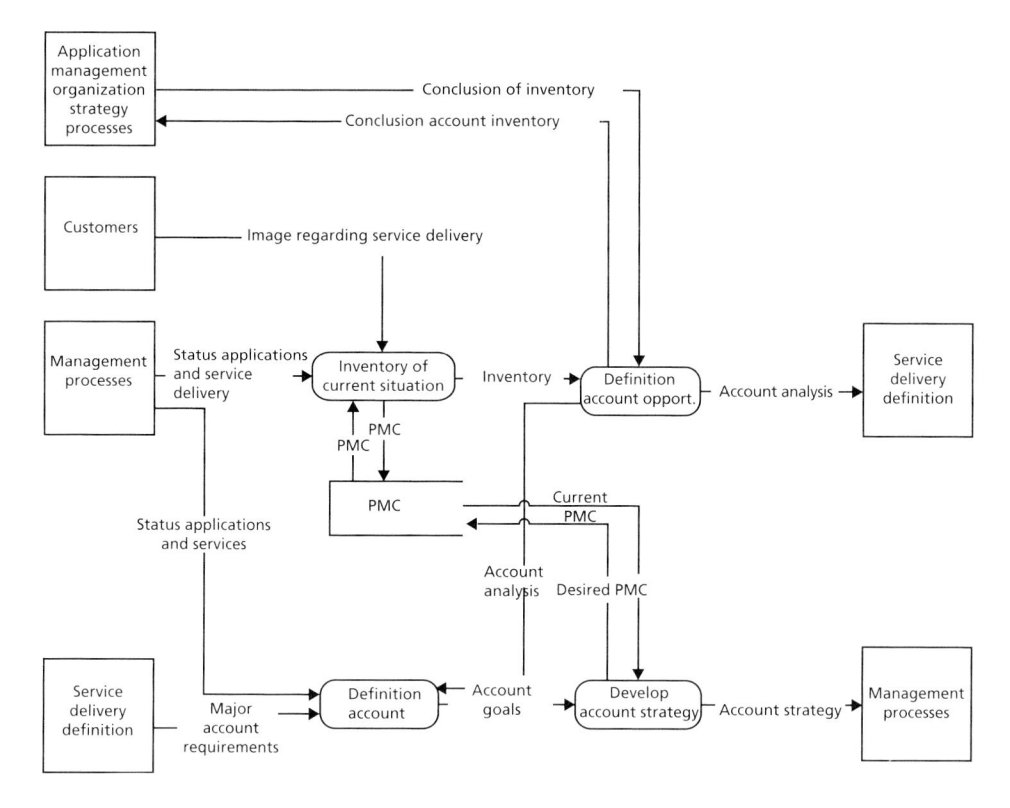

Figure 9.4 Process diagram for account and market definition

Account strategy:
- Desired position, place and role in the market.
- Strategy to achieve these, translated into actions.

9.2.5 Account and market definition relationships

Customers:
- Image of the service: information from customers about the service, the image of the organization and its services.

Application management organization strategy processes (input):
- Service delivery definition: main points of policy.
- Capabilities definition: results of the capabilities inventory.
- Supplier definition: results of the suppliers' inventory.
- Technology definition: results of the technology inventory.

Application management organization strategy processes (output):
- Capabilities definition: results of the market and accounts inventory.
- Supplier definition: results of the market and accounts inventory.
- Technology definition: results of the market and accounts inventory.
- Service delivery definition: analysis of market and accounts.

Management processes (input):
- Contract management: status of volume and development of contracts.
- Planning and control: status of the volume of capacity.
- Quality management: status of the quality management system.
- Supplier management: status of suppliers according to customers.

Management processes (output):
- All processes: account strategy.

9.3 Capabilities definition

9.3.1 Goal of capabilities definition

In order to fulfill the future needs of the market, a strategy is needed for the development and realization of the expertise and skills of the application management organization.

Capabilities definition is the process that will provide an overview of the demands with respect to skills and expertise of the organization's employees in the future. The subjects include not only the depth and scope of the expertise but also the tools (broadly speaking) that allow the expertise to be recorded and distributed.

The following experiences illustrate some of the things that can complicate this strategy even more:
- It is not unusual for a structural change in the working methods embedded in the organization's culture to take three years. It is hard to change people and organizations just like that.
- Implementing new capabilities that do not fit in with the organization's existing qualities, presents even more problems. See the example below.
- The simplest way to innovate and improve is to start from the capabilities that already exist. It is not always self-evident that an organization possesses these capabilities. In our experience, people tend to focus on what is not being done well, and sometimes forget or do not appreciate what is done well.

> Many instances of information provisioning, such as those used by banks and insurance companies, require a very high standard of precision, reliability and thoroughness. This calls for application managers who work as carefully as humans can possibly work.
>
> Using these people on projects with an experimental character goes against the grain for application managers. The same applies to applications which are not reliable and which may contain a great many errors, because they have to be really low-cost.
>
> Many application managers simply are not suited to these situations.

9.3.2 Capabilities definition topics

Central to capabilities management are the abilities of both the employees and the organization to realize the future services. These abilities (which we also refer to as expertise or capabilities) involve being able to work with specific technology, and knowledge of the market and the customer(s), and the type of services (and its core qualities such as low cost or reliability).

Capabilities definition encompasses the translation of the required services to a policy that can be followed by the employees and the application management organization's quality management. This is why there has to be a close relationship between the quality management process and the planning and control process.

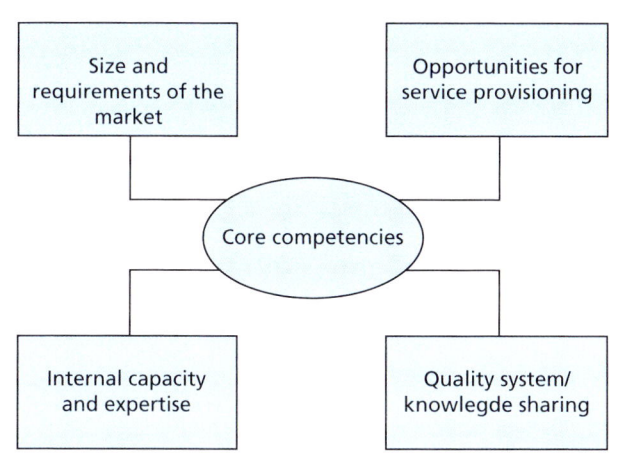

Figure 9.5 Topics of capabilities definition

Scope and requirements of the market
Our first subject is the required and expected scope of the organization's expertise and its development. Questions to be asked are:
- What are the current requirements for this kind of expertise and what are the expectations for the future?
- What kind of growth opportunities are there, both simple and not-so-simple?

Internal capacity and expertise
The growth potential of application management is limited. It is not easy to increase the capacity of application management. The question of what is actually feasible and achievable is therefore vital; it covers the scope as well as the strength and depth. It is not always easy to attract new employees and employ them effectively. Expanding the existing expertise is often the cheapest solution in order to take the employees and the organization to a higher level.

Quality management system/sharing knowledge
Experience and skills (expertise) can be shared and expanded if you have the tools to support this (the quality management system). The quality of the existing tools in the future also falls within the scope of capabilities definition. Possible tools that can be used are: knowledge sharing and coaching/training, the use of methods such as processes, templates, and guidelines.

Opportunities for services
Expertise can also be created quite by chance: by this we mean to say that it will not be a conscious development but rather just someone asking a question, having an idea, an unusual assignment, etc. Many innovations start from small beginnings.

The different types of expertise also present opportunities for the renewal or expansion of the services. The fourth subject is the recognition and assessment of broader opportunities for the current services (we could call it a 'push-approach').

9.3.3 Capabilities definition activities
Making an inventory of current capabilities:
- Make an inventory of current capabilities and expertise.
- Make an inventory of the current status of the quality management system.
- Determine the need for modifications and options.
- Determine the potential for expansion of the current services.

Definition of potential capabilities:
- Determine what kinds of expertise, skills and core qualities are needed and work out the requirements for change.
- Determine what kind of improvements are needed and assess the mutual and total impact.
- Define alternative scenarios regarding the capabilities and their impact.

Definition capabilities:
- Define further effects of the required modifications on skills, capabilities and quality control system.
- Define supplementary measures, such as trends of the suppliers, market and technology.

Setting up a capabilities strategy:
- Define and assess effect of these steps on the realization of this strategy.
- Reserve the budget and capacity.

9.3.4 Capabilities definition results
Findings of the capabilities inventory:
- Existing skills and services.
- Any identified need for internal changes.
- Options and limitations in respect of developments and expanding skills.

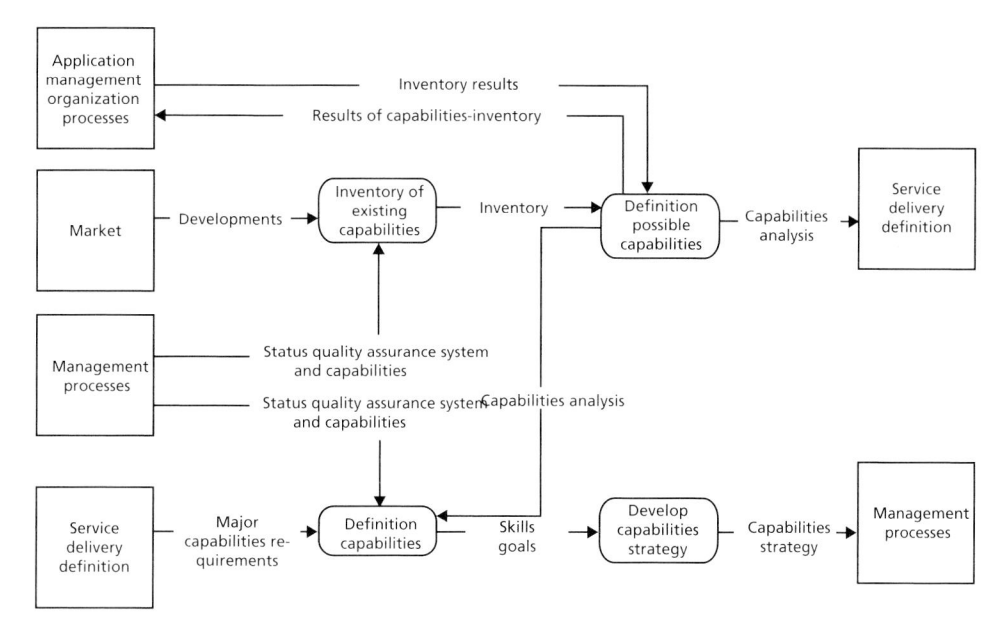

Figure 9.6 Capabilities definition diagram

- Possible strategies in respect of the organization's core competences.
- Potential impact in respect of market and customer, technology, service, etc.

Capabilities strategy:
- Required expertise from the organization, both in terms of their scope and depth.
- Strategy for achieving this expertise, translated to measures to be taken and investments.

9.3.5 Capabilities definition relationships
Market (input):
- Developments market/customers.

Application management organization strategy processes (input):
- Service delivery definition: outlines of policy.
- Account and market definition: findings from account and market inventory.
- Supplier definition: findings from suppliers' inventory.
- Technology definition: findings from technology inventory.

Application management organization strategy processes (output):
- Account and market definition: findings from capabilities inventory.
- Technology definition: findings from capabilities inventory.
- Supplier definition: findings from capabilities inventory.
- Service delivery definition: capabilities analysis.

Management processes (input):
- Quality management: status of current quality management system and skills.
- Planning and control: status of current capacity volume and developments.
- Contract management: status of contract developments.

Management processes (output):
- Capabilities strategy.

9.4 Technology definition

9.4.1 Goal of technology definition

Technology plays a dominant role in the application management organization's services. Technologies become outdated or redundant and sometimes have to be phased out and replaced. Technology that is not outdated also often requires large investments, for example when the tools it uses issue new releases. Also, new technology options are being created all the time, as well as new tools and new solutions.

Technology definition is the process that selects the tools that are used by the organization to realize the future services.

9.4.2 Technology definition topics

a. Relationship with IT developments strategy

The application strategy cluster recognizes the IT developments strategy process (see paragraph 8.2). Just as with the technology definition process, the contribution of technology is the focal point. IT developments strategy handles the contribution of technology and solutions in the information provisioning, the application or the application landscape.

The technology definition process covers the contribution of technology within the application management service.

The authority and responsibility are different for both topics, which means that the way decisions are made, as well as the outcome, will be different.

> Less relevant from the point of view of an application or application landscape is the question about which development language should be used. The market is shifting more and more towards SOA-type architectures, which means that for the customer the development environment becomes less relevant.
>
> The development environment is almost always critical for the application management organization: the employees have had the relevant training and the quality control system is set up for it.

> From a services point of view, an application management organization can also choose to migrate. The application management organization has, for example, insufficient in-house knowledge about the development environment, so that they decide to stop using it. This can also occur because the organization's market is too limited, or because the organization does not have the resources to fund further investments. The organization can decide this for itself.
>
> From an Application strategy point of view, this is a good reason to migrate: after all, other organizations might have the knowledge and the capacity. This is a choice that is often determined by the owner of the application or information provisioning (which is not necessarily the application management organization).

So, both the scope and the decisions vary. This is why they are separate processes.

> An application management organization could also choose to go for a new technology. This does not mean that this technology will be included in the existing application landscape by definition. Naturally, an organization can spot opportunities outside the existing market. Application management services can also supply to several different and mutually distinct application landscapes: it is possible to have more than one customer.

Obviously there are certain similarities and often there certainly is a link. This definitely makes it useful to use the experiences and results of the other process.

b. Tools

There are many types of technology to choose from, and their roles within the business process of the application management vary accordingly. In paragraph 8.2.2, we mentioned four types of technology. The tools mentioned were:
- Design and development tools.
- Functionalities.
- Management tools.
- Infrastructure (target environment).

c. Place in the life cycle

Technology's place in the services also has a life cycle. The analogy with paragraph 8.2.2 is as follows:
- End of life: the technology is in use but the future of the service itself is in doubt. This could be the broader market trend, or the organization's view of its own specific market.
- Stable: there is no question of ageing. However even in the stable phase of the life cycle, there are continuous developments and investments that have to be taken into account (which arise from experience with new releases and the impact on the quality control system).
- New: technologies and solutions which appear on the market that have not been used so far but could nevertheless be attractive for the services.

The examples given at the start of this paragraph have shown that there can be a difference in the life cycle in the broad IT market and that of the individual services. This means that technology can become out of date within a service, but not within the broader market.

Its place in the life cycle and also the nature of the technology has various consequences for the application management organization's policy. Here are some examples.

End of life
The 'end of life' status still has an impact. If a technology looks like it might be approaching the end of its life, the relevant information will include:
- What is its scope in the current portfolio and service?
- How pressing and vital is the need: in other words, when does 'end of life' really mean 'end of life'?
- What other alternatives can be considered and what are the scenarios for replacing the technology?
- Are there tools available for a migration, is the expertise available, can it be done independently or must others be called in to deal with the migration, the services, or a replacement where necessary?

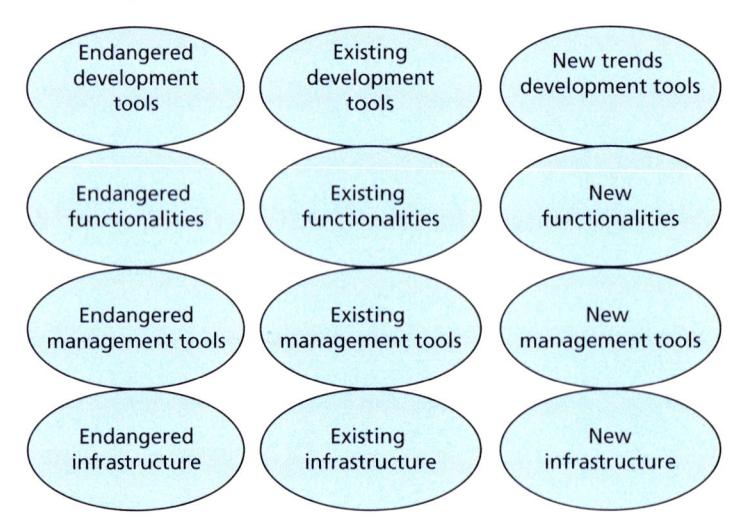

Endangered development tools	Existing development tools	New trends development tools
Endangered functionalities	Existing functionalities	New functionalities
Endangered management tools	Existing management tools	New management tools
Endangered infrastructure	Existing infrastructure	New infrastructure

Figure 9.7 Technology matrix

Stable
Even technologies or tools in the stable phase of the life cycle (not necessarily in specific situations) may experience developments such as upgrades to new versions or changes in the use of software standards, etc. In this kind of situation it would be advisable to have enough information and a policy in place, such as:
- Why is the upgrade necessary, what is its impact, how desirable and how rigid is it?
- What is the scope of the existing portfolio of services that would be affected and what would be the impact on required capacity and costs?

- What would be the impact of a potentially necessary upgrade on the regular contracts and services agreements?
- What other possible scenarios are there?
- Do everything yourselves or not?

New technology
There will also be many other technologies and tools on the market, which can support or provide opportunities for services.
- What kind of tools are there and which of them would be of interest?
- What opportunities would these solutions offer?
- What would be the chances on the market and to what extent would they overlap the current services?
- What would be the impact on the existing organization and expertise?
- How can we gain the experience?
- What kind of investment would we have to expect to make?

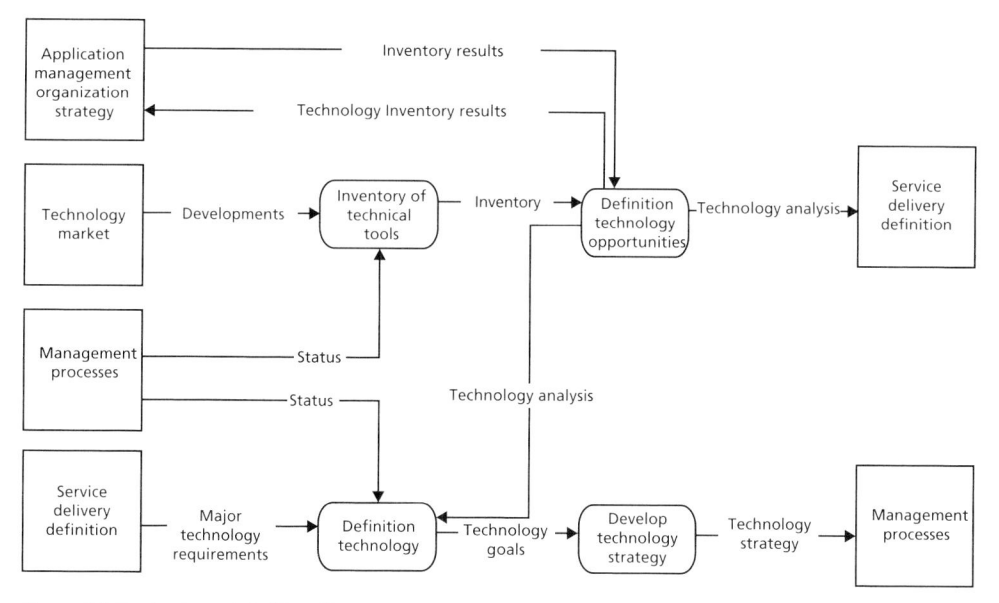

Figure 9.8 Technology definition diagram

9.4.3 Technology definition activities
Making an inventory of (existing and new) technology tools:
- Identifying the developments and threats in respect of existing technology for the services.
- Identifying the state-of-the-art in respect of technical developments in the market.
- Identifying the continuity of the existing tools and potential future trends in tools.

Definition of technology opportunities:
- Defining potential scenarios for acquiring, refreshing, or phasing out of the technology used with its impact on the services, market and skills.
- Defining the total and mutual dependency and its impact on the services.
- Identifying the alternatives and their impact.

Definition of technology:
- Defining the desired goals in respect of technology and determining internal technology policy.
- Assessing the impact on the quality control systems and the skills.

Creating a technology strategy:
- Deciding on which steps to take to acquire this technology or functionality (acquiring knowledge of), or for phasing out or innovating the technology.
- Deciding on any further steps (e.g. regarding the suppliers of skills).
- Initiating the steps.

9.4.4 Technology definition results
Findings of the technology inventory:
- Existing technology and contribution to the services.
- Developments and their impact (life cycle).
- New and interesting technologies.
- Possible strategies for the used and potential technologies.
- Impact in respect of the market, skills and competences, suppliers, etc.

Technology strategy:
- Technology used in the future.
- Strategy in respect of phasing out, the maintenance and acquisition of new technology, translated to measures and investment.

9.4.5 Technology definition relationships
Technology market:
- Developments (input): information about developments in the technology and tools markets.

Application management organization strategy processes (input):
- Service delivery definition: outlines of policy (technology).
- Account and market definition: findings from market and accounts inventory (impact on technology and customers' standards).
- Capabilities definition: findings from capabilities inventory.
- Supplier definition: findings from suppliers inventory.

Application management organization strategy processes (output):
- Service delivery definition: findings from technology analysis.
- Account & market definition: findings from technology inventory.
- Capabilities definition: findings from technology inventory.

Management processes (input):
- Quality management (to a large extent): status of current technology.
- Supplier's management: status of suppliers.
- Planning and control: status of existing volume (for each technology) and developments.
- Contract management: status/developments and services.

Management processes (output):
- Quality management (to a large extent): technology policy/strategy.
- Supplier's management: technology policy/strategy.
- Contract management: technology policy/strategy.

9.5 Supplier definition

9.5.1 Goal of supplier definition
The goal of supplier definition is to pro-actively optimize the future service by determining the role of and the involvement of external suppliers, and translating this policy to a practical, functioning organization and structure.

One important aspect of supplier definition is to determine why and how suppliers should be used in view of the application management organization's strategy.

The directional level is directed at strategy and general interpretation, across the services. Supplier management is specifically oriented towards execution within a single service.

9.5.2 Supplier definition topics
Within supplier definition, we can follow a decision chain by answering the following questions: why, what, when and how?

a. Why?
The first question is: "What is the purpose of the relationship with the supplier?" What needs must the supplier fulfill and what preconditions/requirements are involved? A supplier's contribution can include:
- *Solution* (technology and/or functionalities). The supplier provides a working technology, tools, standard application or infrastructure.
- *Expertise or skills.* The supplier has the (additional) necessary knowledge in a particular field.
- *Capacity and manpower.* The supplier has the capacity and the manpower, and this is attractive from the point of view of scope or costs (e.g. offshoring).
- *Image or perception.* When a supplier is involved, the solution will be supplied on a certain level, which will indicate to the market that the application management organization cannot supply it, or at least not by itself.

```
┌─────────────────────────┐         ┌─────────────────────────┐
│ Why?                    │         │ What?                   │
│ • Solution/technology?  │────────▶│ • Customer?             │
│ • Expertise or skills?  │         │ • Buyer (contractor)?   │
│ • Image                 │         │ • Services or solutions?│
│                         │         │ • Partnership?          │
│                         │         │ • Prime contractor?     │
└─────────────────────────┘         └─────────────────────────┘
            ▲                                   │
            │                                   ▼
┌─────────────────────────┐         ┌─────────────────────────┐
│ How?                    │         │ When?                   │
│ • Service delivery      │         │ • ..                    │
│ • Organization          │◀────────│ • ..                    │
│ • Process               │         │                         │
│ • Communication         │         │                         │
└─────────────────────────┘         └─────────────────────────┘
```

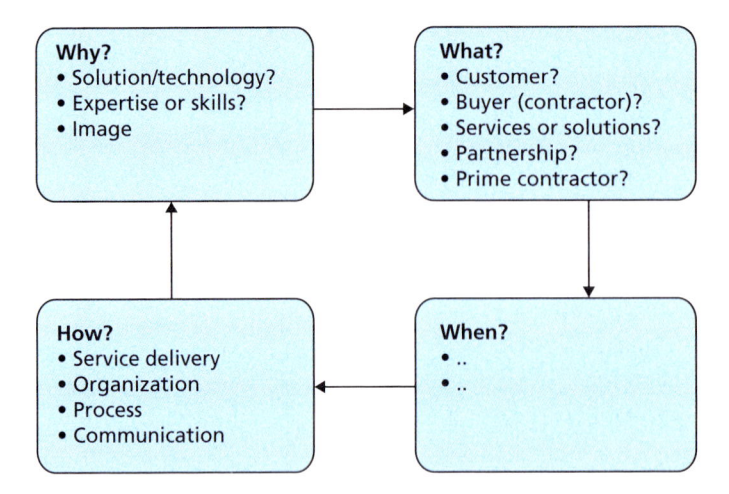

Figure 9.9 Supplier definition topics

b. What?

The second question is what exactly is introduced and in what form and what kind of management is involved. The application management organization will shape the initial ideas about cooperating with a supplier. At this point in time, it is unknown which impression any potential supplier will have, but to have a general idea right from the start will speed up the process and will in general stimulate effectiveness.

Examples of types of cooperation are:
- Customer: the organization's objective is to acquire a technology, infrastructure tools, functionality or generic functionality, which requires minimal control and administration. The organization is simply a customer or a user.
- Buyer: the organization acquires capacity (people, computers) if necessary. The application management organization decides what is to be acquired and how it will be used.
- Services or solutions (subcontractor): buying functionality, services or tools on the basis of responsibility for results, where the supplier acts as a responsible subcontractor or supplier.
- Partnership: outsourcing parts of the execution of the services, by outsourcing the functionality: where the supplier has a large amount of freedom to decide on the shape of the solution and the integration.
- Prime contractor: the selection of a contractor, who will, generally speaking, be the integrator, main contractor, etc.

These types may overlap.

c. Who and when?

The third question is about which suppliers to engage with - the selection process. The process for each situation and each circumstance can differ. Sometimes the solution is obvious (contacts, existing relationships), at other times there will be a need for a brief selection process, and sometimes even a more extensive selection process will be necessary.

As well as the 'who' question, there is also the 'when' question:
- In which situations will there be collaboration, and in which situations not?
- Is the commitment exclusive, or simply incidental or situational? What are the obligations?

d. How?
The final question is how the process is organized, how it is set in motion, and how the cooperation with the suppliers is embedded in the organization or in the applications to be delivered. The steps to be followed are:
- The design of the process, including focusing on the way decisions are made, selection, the negotiations, and where appropriate, using a proof-of-concept.
- Working out how it is integrated into the existing services.
- The design of the internal organization.
- Setting up the guidelines for the layout and agreements processes.

9.5.3 Supplier definition activities

Inventory of the suppliers:
- Identify the internal requirements and translate them to potential suppliers, and determine possible opportunities.
- Identify the requirements for existing suppliers and the services provided.
- Determine the real requirements (the 'why' question).
- Determine the desired nature and interpretation (the 'how' question).
- Identify the opportunities and options in respect of customers/services.
- Select interested parties/suppliers.

Definition of suppliers' opportunities and determination of impact and alternatives:
- Answer the 'who' and 'when' questions.
- Determine the impact on the organization, service, skills, quality control system, etc.
- Consider and determine alternatives.

Definition of the suppliers' market:
- Deciding on the required suppliers, the type of design and the scope for margins and negotiations.
- Deciding on supplementary measures, for example in respect of the internal skills, the current quality control system, market trends, etc.
- Design of the selection project.

Setting up the suppliers' strategy:
- Preparation of the selection project (determining the selection criteria, pre-selection and negotiation process).
- Determining the selection criteria.
- Selecting and negotiating.
- Design of the relationships in application management's own organization.

9.5.4 Supplier definition results

Supplier portfolio:
- Suppliers.
- Services delivered.
- Nature of contracts and services.

Findings of supplier inventory:
- Current suppliers and contribution to services.
- Developments and (changing) needs for suppliers or new suppliers.
- Required need and required shape.
- Possible collaborations and proposed frameworks.
- Alternative scenarios.
- Impact as to the market, skills and competences, technology, etc.

Supplier strategy:
- Strategy with regard to suppliers.
- Plan/process for selecting suppliers.
- Measures regarding own organization.

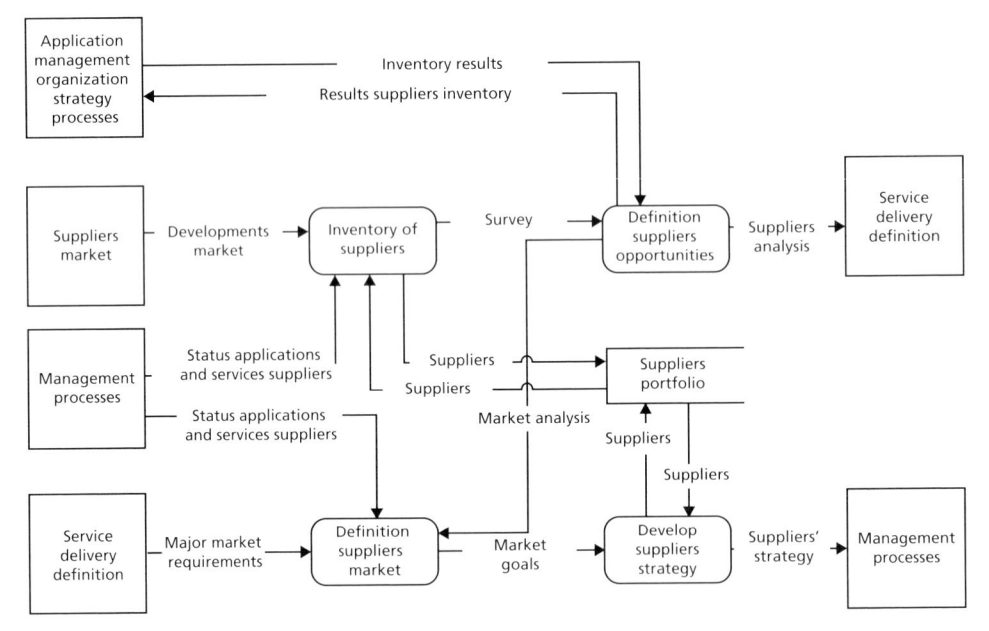

Figure 9.10 Supplier definition diagram

9.5.5 Supplier definition relationships

Supplier market (input):
- Market developments.

Application management organization strategy processes (input):
- Service delivery definition: main features of supplier policy.
- Account and market definition: findings from market and accounts inventory (impact on technology and customers' standards).
- Capabilities definition: findings from capabilities inventory.
- Technology definition: findings from technology inventory.

Application management organization strategy processes (output):
- Service delivery definition: supplier analysis.
- Capabilities definition: findings from supplier inventory.
- Supplier definition: findings from supplier inventory.
- Technology definition: findings from supplier inventory.
- Service delivery definition: findings from supplier inventory.
- Account and market definition: findings from supplier inventory.

Management processes *(input)*:
- Financial management: status of financial costs relating to suppliers.
- Contract management: status of volume and development of contracts.
- Planning and control: status of capacity volume.
- Quality management: status of quality management system.

9.6 Service delivery definition

9.6.1 Goal of service delivery definition
Service delivery definition is the process that focuses on the demand side and the supply side of the application management organization, translated into a concrete working strategy aimed at the future.

The goal of this process is to design the required service for a period of two or three years. This is done by translating the options and limitations from the current situation, from the market, the accounts, the capabilities, and the technology into a coherent policy. This will then be processed further in the general application management organization strategy processes.

9.6.2 Service delivery definition topics
Central to the service delivery definition are the product and service catalogue (PSC) and the product-market combinations (PMC) over a period of three years. The service delivery definition includes the development of a vision and the integral assessments in respect of the entire market, customers, skills and technology. This is the picture we get:
- *What* is the service to be supplied?
- To *whom*?
- In *which way* will this be carried out? (for instance, make-or-buy).
- With which *methods/development tools* or suppliers?
- Which *capabilities* are needed (main outline) for this purpose?

The approach is primarily top-down: alongside developments and opportunities from the market, capabilities or technology, there needs to be coherence in the PSC and PMC. This is where it all starts with a mission. One way of phasing this trajectory is:
- The stating of a mission. This mission provides a very brief idea of which services from which area of expertise will be offered for a two to three year period, and to which customer groups.
- The formulation of goals that will translate the mission into units that can be measured.
- The definition of one or more strategies that will result in these goals.
- Recognizing the critical success factors (CSFs) for the success of the strategy.
- The assessment and allocation of the resources required for the realization.
- Planning of the realization goals.

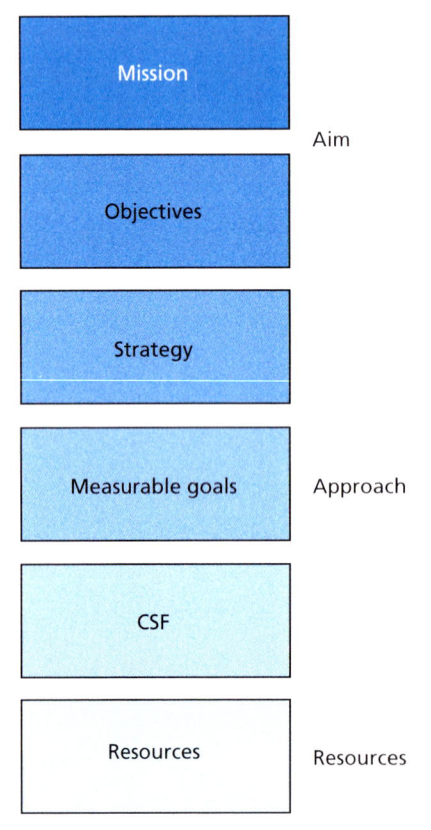

Figure 9.11 Topics of service delivery definition

9.6.3 Service delivery definition activities

Defining the mission and goals:
- Identifying the services/service catalogue required for the next two to three years.
- Identifying the customers in relation to services for the next two to three years.
- Identifying the skills and expertise (capabilities) in relation to the services and customers for the next two to three years.

Defining the strategy and direction:
- Defining the main outline of the strategy to achieve this.
- Setting up measurable goals.
- Deciding on the management structure.

Defining the resources:
- Defining the availability of the resources.
- Identifying which resources are required.
- Attributing and allocating resources.

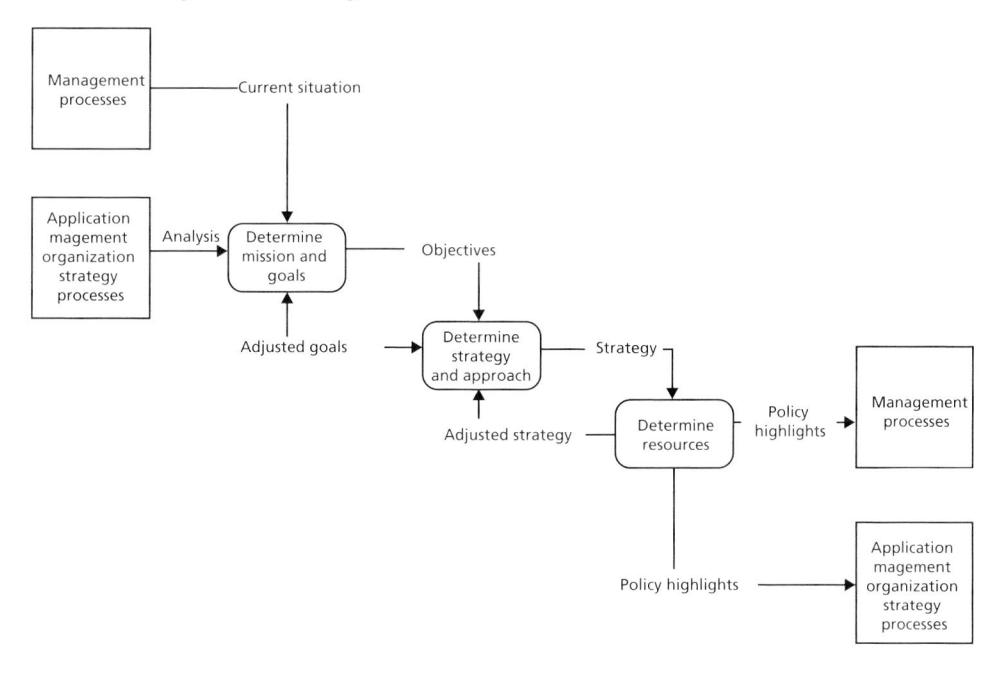

Figure 9.12 Service delivery definition diagram

9.6.4 Service delivery definition results
Policy outlines
- Mission;
- Goals;
- Strategy;

- Measurable objectives;
- Critical success factors;
- Resources.

9.6.5 Service delivery definition relationships
Application management organization strategy processes:
The relationship between service delivery definition and the other application management organization strategy processes is covered in paragraph 9.1.2. There are two streams:
- Analysis (input): the analyses acquired from the various application management organization strategy processes, the different needs regarding change and impact constitute input.
- Outlines and cohesion of policy (output): the outlines and cohesion in their turn constitute the input for the next steps in the general application management organization strategy processes.

Management processes:
- Current status of the services (input).
- Outline policy (output): further results for the management processes will be delivered by the general application management organization strategy processes.

10 Using ASL

10.1 Introduction

A small survey
I asked many people from several (and large) companies what their opinion is of the incident handling and implementation of the incident processes within their organization. These people are experienced in implementing processes and managing them. They can see beyond the details.

It appears that 90 percent of the people questioned are basically dissatisfied. Nearly everyone indicated that primarily, they attempt to resolve the incident themselves or try to find answers with colleagues. Occasionally they call the helpdesk because they need a call number, with the use of which something might be arranged or acquired. No one takes it seriously.

The question is, does the helpdesk realize that people look at it in this way? More so, does the measured customer satisfaction reflect the actual situation correctly? Finally, if you indicate that you are not satisfied, you need to elaborate a bit further. And besides, you do not want to offend this person, who is only trying to resolve the issue as best he can with the limited capabilities and knowledge at his disposal.

But the majority still uses this strategy: no more questions and trying to create a workaround. The result is that many people are spending their time inventing their own solutions and getting things working, or they ask their immediate colleagues. Unfortunately nobody feels the need to do something to change this: despondency is the word here.

Relevant questions are:
- Why is this happening?
- Is the helpdesk aware of this and do they even want to know?
- Is the manager of the helpdesk aware of this and does he even want to know?
- Are the people who designed it this way aware of this?
- Are those people going to repeat their actions when it happens again?

Note/afterthought
There are of course enough helpdesks where it does work, and where users do feel supported. And the helpdesk itself should not feel they are being targeted by what is written here. It is not about the people of the helpdesk. This is about principles often being more important than the actual results.

A popular topic is the use of ASL and the design of the application management organization. This theme has already been specifically discussed in various sections of this book, and the same goes for the various design and implementation factors.

But in this book on the ASL framework it would be too much of a leap to discuss this topic in depth. Yet there is a small section specifically regarding its use.

First, it examines the principles in the usage of ASL. Therefore, Section 10.2 addresses the role of ASL, the role and importance of processes and the role of the designer.

This chapter discusses:
- The pitfalls and lessons learned.
- Generic design and implementation factors and strategies.
- NEN 3434.
- Other resources.

10.2 Pitfalls

10.2.1 The role of ASL within application management

ASL is a framework. A framework is a structure that can be used for multiple purposes:
- *Structuring tool*: ASL describes the activities within application management. ASL can be used to identify which activities are being carried out where, and which activities are not carried out, or not explicitly carried out.
- *Communication tool*: ASL provides a clear conceptual framework and provides a definition of concepts and activities. It can also be used as a communication tool.
- *Design and implementation tool*: ASL shows the operational relationships. ASL provides the tools for implementation, and provides experience on what is working correctly. This is why it is an instrument used in the design of application management organizations and processes.
- *Best practice tool*: in addition to structures and concepts ASL contains hundreds of best practices used in the interpretation, implementation and support processes. These best practices can apply to the specific situation and provide a strong starting point in the actual design of the processes.

ASL is not prescriptive; it does not dictate that something should be designed or executed in a certain way. Therefore, 'According to ASL, this must be done' is an invalid argument.

10.2.2 The role of processes

There are quite a few views regarding the usage of processes in an organization. Hence the following four statements:
- The process does not exist.
- Processes are not fully independent from the organization.
- A process is only a resource.
- Without concrete goals there is no working process.

The process does not exist
A process does not exist. A process is a theoretical term/concept in a booklet, in a theoretical model. It is abstract. Only implementations of processes exist. An implementation of a process is realistic and exists.

> ASL recognizes the change management process. This ASL process does not exist in the organization. But there is a change management process implemented, for which the paragraph from this book was the starting point. It has several steps and the purpose is similar to the one in the book. The book has been translated into the organization.
>
> Within an organization there are often many types of services and different situations: the organization will recognize multiple deployments that differ from each other.

Processes are not fully independent from the organization.
It is often said that (the implementation of) processes are organization-independent. This means that the processes are independent of the organization's structure, the chain of responsibility, and (occasionally) independent of the tasks. Here is where we find the great value of the process, because these elements regularly change (reorganization happens frequently).

However, processes are never completely separated from the organization:
- The execution can never be dissociated from the overall responsibility of the organization for which the process has been designed.
- A process cannot be separated from the services of the organization, its starting points and end points.
- Ultimately a process cannot be dissociated from how the whole is controlled and what is important when giving direction.

Therefore, processes are not completely organization-independent.

A process is merely a means to a goal.
Often a process is designed because it is mandatory. The work should be professionalized and this is why processes need to be designed. A project is started with the objective to define and design the processes, and this is translated to the recording and describing of processes. Because of this, ends and means are easily interchanged. With the implementation of a process, a goal must be achieved. Processes can sometimes be the means to achieve this goal.

Without concrete goals there is no working process.
Frequently a process is initiated without clear and specific goals. Or there are goals, but they are highly abstract ('higher customer satisfaction').

> Certain supermarket chains establish processes to keep the prices as low as possible. A lot of the work is done by the customers themselves and the queues at the check-outs are allowed to become longer. The process shows that if only four customers are in line at the checkouts, then one checkout must close.
>
> Other supermarkets want to regard the customer as the focal point. The implementation of the process in that situation will look different.

Or there are targets, but no choices have been made between the targets.

If the targets are not formulated clearly or when no choices have been made, this means that during implementation the control capabilities become the specific target for the process. It creates a process that yields a lot of control information, which offers all the opportunities to see how the process proceeds. This is a different objective from optimum service, cost efficient service, flexible service, reliable service, etc.

10.2.3 The role of the designer

The designer needs to be skilled
This is probably the biggest pitfall. Without having extensive knowledge of the subject matter (in the case of ASL, this is application management), the designing of the process as a whole becomes risky. There are a few reasons:
- Knowledge of the subject matter fields and terminology. Application management is a profession with many specific terms and interpretations. Words such as information model, data model, functional system design, use-case are inevitable. Without knowledge there is no communication possible with the people who have to do the work.
- During implementation, the question of where boundaries should be placed is a continuous concern: at which point is something still useful, and when not.

The pitfall is that processes are being set up without the designer knowing the subject matter.

> Application management and infrastructure management are different forms of IT services. Their core qualities, their structure and their operations are different.
>
> For business information management, very different processes play a part even if they seem the same. Some good KPIs (key performance indicators) in infrastructure management are catastrophic for business information management. Defining one KPI within infrastructure management for change management, called 'speed of processing and implementation of a change' is often a good move. For business information management it is not: in various situations the KPI 'rejecting a change request in a polite way' is a good KPI. The goal in business information management is to only really make meaningful changes at a time that works best.

Use the knowledge and experience of the employees
Application management is a profession that requires a high level of training. Almost without exception all employees have strong analytical skills. The majority of them usually know exactly what needs to be done. Not making use of these skills suggests that their knowledge and experience is not very highly regarded.

Establishing a well-functioning and permanent process is difficult
Designing a process is complicated. It is relatively easy to fall into the trap of describing a process and then declaring it to be operational. One obvious consequence is that the process is a procedure, preventing something from happening or forcing something to happen in a certain way. A process then simply becomes a new way of saying no. The quality of the processes is therefore an important issue within quality management. Within quality management, one must constantly question whether the process still

complies: whether it is still consistent with the agreements. And, as the example at the beginning of the chapter pointed out, the seemingly objective measurements do not always give an accurate picture of the way in which it is experienced.

10.3 Design and implementation factors and strategies

In the previous section several pitfalls in the application of ASL were discussed. What has not been discussed is how a translation can be made from the framework into the actual implementation in practice.

There is too much material to address this issue in-depth in this framework book. There are several other books (such as *Strategic management of information in ASL and BISL*), articles and best practice methods that will offer support when designing. And in the future there will be much more documentation available.

However, many design and implementation factors taken from actual practice were already listed during the introduction of various chapters. It is known that these factors have significant impact on the implementation and completion of the process. Of course there are more and there are also a number of generic factors. Examples of generic factors are:
- The necessity (or need) to implement processes. In some cases there is a necessity or compulsion to work according to processes. In other cases that necessity is less, and there is less time available to invest in defining the processes. This has an impact on the scope and depth with which processes are implemented.
- External restrictions. Often demands are made from the environment, such as the customer or the government, or a certain maturity level is demanded of a cluster, for example.
- The organization's skills and expertise in this field. Broadly stated: to what extent can they design by themselves, to what extent does one need external expertise, to what extent is a fresh pair of eyes necessary?
- The timelines, the available and budgeted capacity. How large is the available budget, how much time is available, when should something be achieved and what impact will it have on the expected outcome? The question of whether there is a growth approach (one step each year), or if there should be a predefined outcome at a specified time (for example all items at maturity level 3), has an impact on the direction of process improvement and its results.
- Demands from the environment regarding internal processes. Obviously the environment (customers or suppliers) will impose requirements as to how an internal process should be designed.

Due to all these factors the implementation, organization and change of processes is difficult. However, this is inherent to day-to-day practice. Actual day-to-day practice is rarely simple: designing a process is not something you learn from a booklet. There are no booklets that contain all the information and steps that automatically lead to the correct solution for every situation.

> A top chef simply cannot work in a food products factory. The business process has a profound impact. In a top restaurant the meals are served directly and prepared one at a time. In a factory they are not served directly, people work in large numbers, one deals with complex logistic processes, both at the front and in the back.
>
> Similarly, an industrial bakery will have a different process implementation from a small artisan bakery.

10.4 NEN 3434 and the maturity levels

10.4.1 Improve the approach and maturity levels

Identifying the maturity level when designing a process is a commonly used tool. These maturity levels indicate to what extent processes are described, monitored, controlled and improved. The maturity levels relate to (the implementation of) the process itself, how the process itself has been defined, implemented, designed and developed.

The main advantage of maturity levels is that a controllable improvement project may arise, with which one could make decisions regarding the degree of design, and one can also set goals and improvement goals.

10.4.2 Standard NEN 3434

Additionally, for application management the Dutch NEN 3434 standard has been developed. The standard is partially based on the ASL framework and the ASL philosophy. This standard enables the certification of application management processes. NEN 3434 recognizes five maturity levels per process, where the certification has four levels[1] (levels 2, 3, 4, 5). The recognized standard is summarized as follows:

- Level 2: structured.
  - Basic activities take place in a structured and evident way, by application management teams or in project teams.

- Level 3: standardized.
  - All activities take place in a structured way, are evident, documented and standardized.

- Level 4: optimizing.
  - The process is continuously improved based on qualitative and quantitative indicators.

---

[1] The requirements at level 1, described in the appendix of the standard, are not of substantive enough to base a certification upon them.

- Level 5: chain-oriented.
  - The process is designed, executed and improved in alignment with chain partners within the organization itself, as well as the chain partners of the user organization.

10.4.3 Determining ambitions

When designing a process one is quickly inclined to think: the higher, the better. It also creates the impression that organizations with higher levels of maturity provide a better service. That is not necessarily the case. There are additional considerations:
- Designing and implementing processes comes at a price. When an organization performs its service well, in general this means a higher maturity level, but it also means higher costs.
- Unless it is explicitly taken into account when designing the process, the organization will become less flexible: it is more difficult to deviate from defined processes. If there is a lot of friction between the actual desired method and the described method, a sense of bureaucracy will quickly arise.
- People need to understand the process and the nature of the process and act in the appropriate way. Otherwise one runs the risk of turning it into a procedure.
- Good outcomes can be delivered without explicit processes. A requirement is that there are only a few control options and checks. But top programmers can make top applications without explicitly defined processes.

This is why it is extremely important to know why and for what purpose a process needs to be designed. Even more, it is important that it fits in with the culture of the organization and the 'maturity level' of the employees.

The trick is choosing a maturity level that is not too high but rather one which is too low: the minimum level needed to be able to act without taking too many risks.

Often there are external objectives that demand a certain maturity level. When this is the case it is important to make sure the organization can keep up with the pace.

For this, certain empirical rules apply (though, not in every design and improvement situation):
- It is logical that the maturity levels of the processes within a cluster are similar (equally high).
- It is logical that the maturity levels of the processes within a cluster vary. Not all clusters are equally important in every situation.
- For many companies it is logical to start with the operational clusters. The thought behind this is that it is not very effective to formulate a policy if the execution is not controllable. However, this rule does not always apply: if there are not any problems with the business processes, then it is often illogical to start from there.

10.5 Additional tools

10.5.1 Introduction

The NEN 3434 has already been covered; it describes a number of requirements placed on the execution of application management. The translation between ASL and NEN 3434 is easy because ASL played a part in the development of the NEN 3434. As a result, the NEN 3434 can be used as a certification tool for ASL.

10.5.2 Self-assessments

Besides NEN 3434 there is also the ASL self-assessment tool. A self-assessment is a tool that enables an organization to independently determine the maturity level of its processes. Unlike an audit or certification, here the organization itself is responsible for the outcome. This does not mean that one can always perform a self-assessment. As with an audit, in-depth knowledge of ASL is required, and also the quality of the results and the evaluation process can be improved by the use of supervisors, who understand the criteria, the underlying goals of the criteria and the cross-connections between the criteria.

A self-assessment is less extensive than an audit; it requires little burden of proof, therefore it is less factual. It is about one's own experience, not the factual situation. As a result the self-assessment can be performed more quickly than an audit.

The ultimate objective of a self-assessment is not to determine at what level the organization is operating: it is rather a means to determine what measures will be taken and which actions need to be initiated to improve the situation.

10.5.3 Best practices and templates

On the ASL BiSL Foundation website there are many best practices freely available for downloading. Best practices are provided as template documents, checklists, questionnaires, sample descriptions, etc.

These form the core of ASL and they also form the largest part of ASL's added value. With this, a comprehensive toolbox of concrete products is available, which is rapidly deployable in any application management organization. The experience of many organizations is incorporated into it.

The underlying idea is that these best practices can be downloaded, used, and tailored to the specific situation. Given the 80-20 rule there is no need to consider how it should look and what should happen. It is sufficient to identify the adjustments required from the organization and apply them to the best practices.

This method is recommended. Fine-tune it to the organization's specific situation in order for employees to identify with it, and also for the specific points to be concluded. Obviously there are not best practices available for every specific situation.

10.5.4 Additional literature

There are other books on the market[2]. In the literature several are listed (Appendix E) these include:
- *ASL: a management guide*: a short introductory book on ASL.
- *Strategic management of information provisioning in ASL*: a textbook for ASL.
- *New information provisioning*: a book that provides further interpretation for the Application strategy cluster.

Another useful book and a good introduction for management is the book *Manage IT! Organizing IT demand and IT supply* by Thiadens.

In addition, many articles and best practices are available on the ASL BiSL Foundation website, as we have already stated. In these articles and best practices different perspectives of application management are discussed and explained. There is a separate book in preparation which further discusses the design of application management. Even then, the following still applies in every situation: an application management organization must organize itself.

10.6 Integration of services and connection between the models

To conclude this book, a brief roadmap will be outlined for designing processes. The task initiation, the determination of the demand, the underlying cause and the objectives will be skipped. Also, the major impact of contracts and contract settlements will not be discussed. This step-by-step plan starts after these activities have taken place.

1. *Determine the environmental factors*

The first step is identifying the positioning of the application management organization and services in the environment. To support this, implementation parameters have been given in various chapters. The different ways of management are the second group of key environmental factors (as described in paragraph 2.2.4), as are the explicit and implicit requirements of the services. The latter means the expected core values of the services, such as reliability, flexibility, the degree of pro-activity or the way in which the customer should be addressed. The internal quality requirements regarding the services are factors that should be included too.

These environmental factors are leading when designing the process.

2. *Determine the interfaces*

The second step is determining the interfaces between the customer and the application management organization. Examples of interfaces could be: a specification from the

---

2   Of course, these will not be fully adapted to ASL 2 immediately.

customer, reports, service levels to be achieved and the reporting of these levels, application strategy, etc.

The interfaces with the suppliers need to be determined. These interfaces are usually settled in the contract, although not always in detail. This is why it is logical for the process design to be in keeping with the contract management process.

The interfaces are the starting point and the destination of the process: the process starts with the interfaces and will end with the interfaces. The requirements for the interfaces are ultimately the results that should be realized by the design of the process.

3. *Start with the interfaces (input and output)*
The next step is to translate the interfaces to principal steps in the process. The output should be realized from the process inputs or from the inputs and outputs from other processes. The same applies to other processes, which in their turn should use the output of this process. This 'design stage' may lead to the conclusion that the input or output is not complete. In that case, the interfaces from the previous step need to be adjusted.

4. *Translating from requirements to the process*
The fourth step is to recognize how the quality requirements, service standards and core values are translated and controlled during the execution of the service. This does not mean that these requirements always lead to (concrete) control indicators. Certain core values and requirements are not easily translated into indicators, or it may be undesirable to do so. To attain these values other resources are needed, such as communication with the employees (including expectations, reviewing, mentoring or coaching, etc.).

5. *Recognizing the control information*
The fifth step determes the control information, the indicators which will be explicitly reported and/or controlled. The question to be asked in this step is to determine on the basis of which information control will take place. The underlying questions include:
- How do these indicators become concrete?
- How is this information collected?
- How is it administered?
- How reliable and detailed should the information be?

Choosing the right set of indicators is important: a set that is too large and/or an incorrect set will soon lead to incorrect forms of control and/or the sense of a bureaucratic organization. A credo that often applies is "in limitation, one recognizes the master".

6. *Design the process*
Eventually the processes are designed. The simplest starting point is to use a best practice, determine how well this fits and then to adapt this practice to the specific

situation. This could be a best practice from the ASL BiSL Foundation website, but an existing best practice from within the organization would also suffice.

7. *Validate the design*
The second to last step is validating the design of the process. In this step the translation from input to output and back are validated, and it is also checked whether the requirements are realized as a result of this. However, it is more important to see if the requirements regarding the process and the intentions of the services (from step 1) are realized. And it is perhaps even more important to recognize whether the process design is blocking the requirements and intentions. Too strict a control may lead to less flexibility in services.

8. *Fitting the process into the environment*
The last step is embedding the processes into the environment. In step 3 the interfaces and the mutual agreements are distinguished. An explicit step is required to validate if everything is correct and fits together. Experience indicates that very often adjustments are still needed.

There is a further step 9, which follows after the design and implementation of the processes. Often one will still identify the need for a couple of changes, or spot some weaknesses. As a result of this, a rapid extra 'release' after implementation is recommended. Also, one will observe that the environment is continually changing, that the requirements change, and as a result shortcomings will arise. Therefore, adjustment will continually be necessary. Quality management has the responsibility to ensure that these adjustments take place continuously. Therefore step 9 is not included in this description: step 9 is part of the daily work and steps 1 through 8 can be summarized as 'creating the next improved version'.

Appendices

A Frequently asked questions (FAQs)

This appendix contains some of the most frequently asked questions (FAQs). There are more of course, and you will find these at the ASL BiSL Foundation website.

Why does this book talk so much about customers instead of customers?
A customer is almost always a customer. A customer is not always a business enterprise; it can also be another application management organization.
The term 'customer' might also imply that this party would be entitled to make decisions about functionalities and costs, etc., and that the supplier (which in this book is synonymous with application management and sometimes infrastructure management) should conform to this. But this is not always the case.

Sometimes, the customer and supplier don't know each other at all: in the huge open source world the unambiguous and well known relationship between application management and the software user is totally unclear. This is why we use the term 'customer' so often.

However, in the majority of cases, it will be a paying customer, with a contractual relationship with the application management organization.

Why is there no incident management process?
There is a (sub)process that corresponds to incident management (call handling), but we have included this in use support. We decided to use a different term in order to place more emphasis on pro-active communication, in order to cut down on the number of incidents.

In practice, there is much attention for handling incidents (whether or not mechanically), but less attention is paid to ways to promote the correct use of the application. This is partly due to the fact that completely intuitive and fully robust information systems will never be developed (partly as a result of balancing costs and benefits).

The link between the sub-processes call handling and pro-active communication within use support has been established to translate incident-related lessons learned quickly and effectively into pro-active communication. The questions and complaints make it possible to act and communicate quickly.

What about problem management?
Problem management is a separate process within ITIL, but it is not recognized by ASL. The 'functionality' of problem management is included in quality management.

There are several reasons for not having a problem management process linked to incident management:
- The first reason is that there does not have to be an incident in order to identify a problem. Such a link is very reactive, and many problems are easily identified without an incident having occurred. It would be wrong if problems could only exist after the occurrence of incidents. The goal should be to prevent incidents.
- A problem is an underlying (structural) shortcoming in the product (i.e. application), the production process, the organization or the quality system (the supporting infrastructure, including methods and techniques). These subjects are a responsibility of quality management. As a consequence, problems result in proposals for improvement of these subjects and are the principal input for quality management.
- If problem management was a separate process, a process like quality management would be very minimalistic.

So, problem management is quite a reactive way of solving problems.

Where is security management?
There is no security management process within ASL. There are a number of reasons for this:
- First of all there is a continuity management process. This examines the continuity and vulnerability of the information systems. Security is an integral part of this process.
- Security is not a goal in itself. Rather, it is a part of the measures that are intended to protect the organization's continuity, by ensuring the continuity of the application and infrastructure, and their usage.
- In actual practice, security forms part of the solution's functionality; in other words, it is a part of the specifications and service levels.

Are ASL, ITIL and BiSL compatible, and if so, how?
The first answer to this is that they are compatible and aligned. You can see how by looking at the process diagrams, which show arrows pointing to the other service management domains, such as business information management. These arrows reoccur in the BiSL diagrams as input flows. Similar diagrams are not found in ITIL, and therefore cannot be shown.

The processes are quite often employed in organizations that use all three models. So, practice shows this is possible.

Secondly, the arrows and the directions of the arrows cannot be transferred just like that. Sometimes, the arrows point inwards, but in some circumstances they will point outwards; it will depend on the situation. This is where integration will be an issue.

Why have capacity management and availability management been combined?
Within ITIL, availability management and capacity management are separate processes.

ASL makes no distinction between the two for several reasons:
- The first reason is that the ASL approach is outside-in. This means that it is less relevant whether the issues that occur are reliability, availability, or capacity related. The difference between these characteristics is of minor importance for the environment and for the internal organization.
- The second reason is that the various features also have mutual relationships. Insufficient capacity can lead to bottlenecks in availability and reliability, and vice versa.
- The third reason is that the control towards the infrastructure works in a similar way. This makes it unnecessary to implement an extra process, which makes the implementation and execution cheaper.

Why is continuity management not combined with IT operation management?
This process does not have as much of an operational character as that of IT management. The character of dependency and quality analyses is not just operational. This certainly applies to IT operation management, and even more so to continuity management.

Why is there a supplier management process?
Making use of suppliers is a logical consequence of the described developments. It has become the norm for an organization to provide a service together with others.

Where contract management answers the question "Does the service we supply conform to the agreements, and which internal measures should be taken in order to make sure this is the case?" supplier management should ask the question "Has something been supplied and what should it have been?".
Contract management looks at it from the supply side.

So, the content is exactly the opposite.

Why are master contracts handled within contract management?
At the strategic level, the goal is to create a policy and a strategy in respect of the markets and customers. This means that it is pro-active.

The customers usually decide for themselves which suppliers they will do business with. This cannot be forced, and thus the handling of a master contract by the supplier is reactive in character.

Besides this, closing a master contract follows more or less the same procedure as closing a regular contract. This results in a difference in level between BiSL and ASL regarding this subject. Within BiSL, master contracts are placed at the strategic level, while in ASL they are positioned at management level. The reasoning behind this is that application management cannot force master contracts to be closed, but when it comes to a tender this has to be handled in a controlled way.

B ASL 2 modifications to ASL 1

This appendix provides a brief description of the differences between the previous ASL version (now known as ASL 1) and ASL 2.

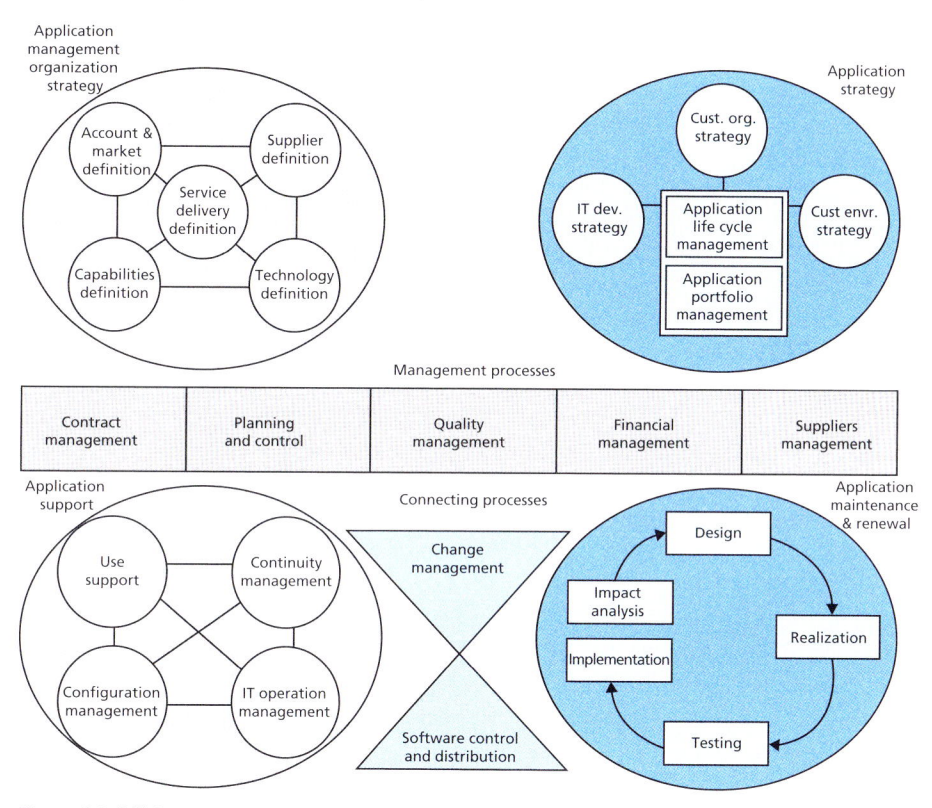

Figure B.1 ASL2

Main structure

The main features within the ASL framework structure are unchanged. There are still six clusters: analysis has shown that this division works well in practice, and is recognizable. But some of the names of some clusters have been changed, there have been changes within the clusters themselves, and also the structure of some clusters has been altered. On top of that there are a number of other structural changes in the book.

For all process clusters, the implementation variables have been named and made explicit. By means of these parameters, the influence of the environment on the processes is explicitly named. A great deal of attention is paid to these factors, either in the introductory paragraphs within a process cluster, or in the introductory paragraphs for a process.

The descriptions at the end of the process paragraphs have also been changed. People involved expressed their wish to maintain these descriptions, but more structured and more informative.

Cluster names

Four cluster names have been changed with the intention of clarifying the content and aligning them with corresponding cluster in the Business information Service Library (BiSL).

a. Maintenance ⇨ Application support
The ASL 1 cluster name Maintenance was misleading. Seeing as the primary goal of this cluster is to support the operational phase of applications, Application support has been chosen. Although there are also some activities that are more directing and monitoring than supporting, for instance translating service levels for availability and performance into requirements to which Infrastructure management should conform, the cluster name has been kept short.

b. Enhancement and renovation ⇨ Application maintenance and renewal
While 'maintenance' (corrective, preventive, perfective, adaptive) is broad enough to cover most changes to application code and/or parameters, and other artifacts such as documentation, 'renewal' has been added to emphasize that structural renovation and even replacement of an application is covered by this process cluster.

c. Organization Cycle Management ⇨ Application management organization strategy
This process cluster has been aligned with the corresponding cluster in BiSL: I-organization strategy.

d. Applications Cycle Management ⇨ Application strategy
This process cluster has been aligned with the corresponding cluster in BiSL: Information strategy.

Application support processes

a. Merging of availability management and capacity management
The availability management and capacity management processes have been merged into a new process: IT Operation Management. This merge represents a middle road between BiSL and ITIL. The reasoning behind this merge is as follows:
- In production, these processes have more points of contact than before. Nowadays a lack of computer capacity in combination with a poor system set-up may lead to availability problems.
- The way both of these processes are managed, is comparable. The merge can result in increased efficiency. The management methods and the parameters used for control and report are comparable. For a customer, the difference between the

parameters for availability, reliability and capacity are not very relevant: these are figures that have to be controlled and can be included in the same report.

However, continuity management has not been merged. In practice, continuity management has more of a tactical nature than availability management and capacity management. Maybe someday in the future, continuity will have a similar natural feel as the other topics: that is when it would be logical for it to be included.

b. Configuration management
A limited number of substantial changes have been included in configuration management. Subjects such as name-giving conventions are outdated. Ambiguity has been removed from the text, for instance the goal of configuration management regarding the registration of where which versions are running. Therefore, the separation from and the difference with software control and distribution is clearer. Or to put it in technical terms: the executable and the software versions are named, not the sources from which they originate.

The service items remain the same. It is true that in practice they are not much used, but because of the continued growth of distributed systems (and SOA concepts) their importance is growing.

c. Continuity management
There is no change here. Explicit attention is paid to the topic 'security'.

d. Use support
Incident management has been renamed: it is now called *use support*. The interpretation and the aims remain relatively comparable. The main reason for the new name is the proactive aspect of the process. The new name emphasizes the proactive character as well as the reactive character. The old name, incident management, suggests a predominantly reactive character, and also in practice, the word 'incidents' is often used as a synonym for 'breakdowns'.

Application maintenance and renewal

The Application maintenance and renewal cluster involved the smallest number of modifications. Very little has changed in respect of content and structure, but there are some additions such as implementation parameters. Special attention is paid to working in service chains or in information chains.

a. Impact analysis and designs
There are no fundamental changes, just some necessary internal changes. The word 'specification' has been reserved for business information management. Specifications represent input for the processes. The product of designing is a design.

The process is also embedded in the broader context of information chains and service chains.

b. Realization and testing
The same point applies to the realization and testing processes. The diagrams have been adjusted accordingly.

c. Implementation
The interpretation of the process has been somewhat broadened and updated. The outline has remained relatively unchanged. The rollout theme has been added and some adjustments have been made in order to stay in line with BiSL.

One suggestion was to replace the name 'implementation' by 'implementation support' or 'implementation preparation'. However, the name remains the same because the name is now pretty current, and changing it would suggest a bigger change than it actually is. So for the sake of upward compatibility, the name stays the same.

Connecting processes

a. Change management
The text has been completely re-written. Accents have changed but the intention of the process itself remains the same. The cohesion and consistency with BiSL was difficult. This has been adjusted and corrected. The diagrams are consistent once again.

b. Software control and distribution
There are relatively few changes; the impact in the outside world has been added. Other names were considered but there was really little justification: again, it would suggest a greater change than it actually was.

Management processes

This is where we find the biggest changes. The majority of the processes have different designs and different content. The continuous dynamic and options to change the control structures have become part of the processes.

In short, this means that all of the processes have been rewritten from scratch. The process diagrams have been changed, but the main structure remained quite the same. The content, subjects, the streams and the text for the processes are almost totally different.

a. Contract management instead of service level management.
The scope and content of the old service level management process are too limited and too operational. Commercialization has increased and for the larger organizations, an SLA is no longer the tool on which the relationship is based.

So, the name has been changed and the scope considerably widened. Therefore the content is new. Its place in the illustration is at the left-hand side of the management processes (towards the customer).

b. Supplier management
Supplier management is a new process, and did not exist in ASL 1.

The aim is to make and monitor the agreement with the suppliers (which includes the subcontractors). Its provisional name was subcontractor management. The final name is *supplier management*. As a result of this the 'suppliers' definition' would be a more suitable name for the 'suppliers' management' process within BiSL in the strategic cluster.

c. Quality management
The scope of the process has been broadened: as well as internal quality (together with its increased importance), the quality and the integration of the subcontractors' services also falls within its responsibility. The text is new.

d. Financial management instead of cost management
The name has changed because in the new setting, the supplier now needs to support and monitor their own business case. This creates two business cases; the one belonging to the organization itself and that of the customer. A great deal of attention is focused on the internal business case and the billing and cost charging structures that are inevitable in the current setting. The paragraph is totally new.

e. Planning and control
The scope of this process remains the same. As a result of the approach the content has been explicitly broadened to include the cooperation between customer, organization and possible subcontractors. Extra attention has been paid to project versus line. The text is completely new.

Application strategy

a. Customer organizations strategy
The 's' after the name 'organization' is new. The scope and content now depend on the market and implementation. Since shared solutions (packages, standard components) have become the market standard, in many cases there is not just one single customer organization, but there are various customer organizations.

b. Application life cycle management
Application life cycle management used to be called *life cycle management*. The model has not changed very much, but the text has been renewed and lengthened, partly as a result of the issue log.

c. Application portfolio management.
Application portfolio management used to be called *IT portfolio management*. The model has not changed very much, but now the scope and interpretation depend on the implementation. Here the same thing applies, i.e., the scoping has explicitly been added, also as a result of the issue log.

Application management strategy

Application management organization strategy has also changed substantially. The impact of this is substantial too.

a. Account and market definition
This process is new and is composed of market definition and account definition. The two processes have been combined because there was a considerable overlap. The observation that this process sometimes seemed rather theoretical also played a role here. The content and text are new.

b. Supplier definition
This is a new process.

c. Technology definition
The interpretation is altered. Content is altered and expanded. The text is new.

d. Capabilities definition
This has a new name; it used to be called 'Skills definition'. The new process takes 'skills' to a higher level, that is, the organizational level. The organization's skills are called *core competences* or *capabilities*. The name and large parts of the text are new; the intention and content have also changed.

e. Service delivery definition
There are few substantial changes.

C Diagram techniques

Process model

For the theorists among you, in this appendix we will explain the process diagrams. In the descriptions of the processes, process diagrams were added. The process diagrams are a theoretical illustration of the information streams between the processes. This means there is a (theoretical) process model underpinning the ASL framework.

Symbols

The process diagrams are stored in data-flow diagrams (DFDs).These process diagrams contain various symbols. DFDs recognize four types of objects.

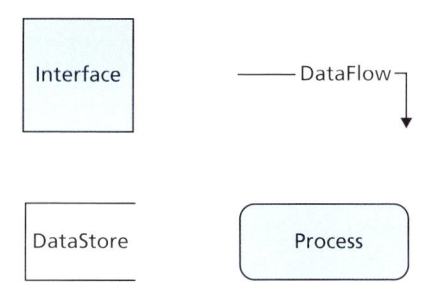

Figure C.1 Symbols used in process diagrams

Data stores can be seen as media, in which information is stored.

Processes can be seen as activities in which information processes take place. A process can be further specified by decomposition: underlying processes.

Interfaces (external entities) are external information recipients and producers.

Data flows are information streams between processes, data stores and external entities.

Explanation of process diagrams

If you look more closely, the different process diagrams may appear to be mutually inconsistent. Most of the time this is not the case. Various processes such as configuration management, software control and distribution, and change management deliver information to a great many processes. For the sake of legibility, these information streams have not been included. The same applies to the 'control processes' within the business processes.

Furthermore, some of the streams within the processes have been generically modeled.

One example of this is software control and distribution. Within software control and distribution, application objects are checked in and checked out. In the design process, this checking in is crystallized in the information stream of the agreed design.

The control processes are generic across the business processes, just like the strategic processes are generic across the management processes. This means that these processes have information streams leading to and coming from almost all the underlying processes.

The output of all the management processes to the business processes for instance, has been collated into data flows such as planning (planning, service levels, quality criteria, etc.). In its turn, the output of these processes acts as input for the control processes, and has also been generically modeled.

D Consistency between ASL and BiSL

I = input, O = output.

BiSL-process	Input/output	ASL-process	Input/output
End user support	I 2nd line call	Use support:	I New call
	O answer/status	Use support:	O Call handling
	Not in BiSL	Use support:	O 2nd line call
	Not in BiSL	Use support:	I Call handling
Operational supplier management	O Questions and change requests	Use support:	I New call
	I Runs etc.	IT operation management	O Processing info
	I Various plans and measures	Use support:	O Communication
	I Various plans and measures	IT operation management	O Supplementary measures, O Operations plan
	I Various plans and measures	Continuity management	O Continuity plan
	O Various Information	Use support:	I Developments
	O Feasibility	IT operation management	I Feasibility
	O Feasibility	Continuity management	I Feasibility
Specify information requirements	O Modification functionality processing	Impact analysis, design	I Functionality modifications
	O Results	Design	I Processing/specifications
	I Consequences usage	Impact analysis	O Consequences usage
	O Verification (IA)	Impact analysis	I Verification
	O Verification	Design	I Verification
	I Concept design	Design	O Concept design
	I Accepted specifications	Design	O Accepted design
	O Acceptance	Design	I Verification
Review and testing	I Acceptance test support	Implementation	O Support acceptance test
	I IT New release	Software control and distribution	O Shipments
	O Acceptance results	Implementation	I Acceptance result
	O State of agreement	Implementation	I Agreement declaration

BiSL-process	Input/output	ASL-process	Input/output
Change management	I Required changes	Change management	O Change request
	O Feedback		I Feedback
Transition management	O Assignment	Implementation	I Assignment
	O Changed assignment		O Changed assignment
	I Feedback execution of assignment		O Feedback support O Support modifications data definitions etc. O Support adaption of production environment
Financial management	I Invoicing	--- (financial administration)	---
Contract management	O Requirements and demands	Contract management	O Requirements and demands
	O Assignment, contract, SLA	Contract management	O Contract, assignment
	I Concept SLA	Contract management	I Concept contract
	I Service level report	Contract management	O Contract realization
(missing within Contract management)	IO Measures	Contract management	IO Measures
Establish information chain developments	O Developments	Customer environment strategy	I Developments
Establish business process developments	O Developments	Customer organizations strategy	I Developments
Establish technological developments	I Developments	Application life cycle management	O Application strategy
	I Developments	Application portfolio management	O Application portfolio strategy
Information life cycle management	O Developments	Application life cycle management	I Developments
	O Strategic plans	Application life cycle management	I Management plans or strategy
	I Strategy	Application life cycle management	O Application Strategy (sometimes)
	O Choice from scenarios	Application life cycle management	I Reaction to scenarios
	I Scenarios	Application life cycle management	O Scenarios (from
Information portfolio management	I Scenarios and Strategies	Application portfolio management	O Scenarios and Strategies
	O Developments	Application portfolio management	I Developments
	O Selection from scenarios	Application portfolio management	I Selection from developments or strategy

BiSL-process	Input/output	ASL-process	Input/output
Strategic supplier management	O New requirements or tenders	Contract management	I Requirements and demands
	I New contract or new agreements	Contract management	O Concept contract
Missing within Strategic supplier management	O Contract	Contract management	I Contract, assignment

E Literature and further reading

ASL, a management guide
Remko van der Pols en Yvette Backer
A short summary of ASL for managers. The book contains an illustrative case for each process.
Van Haren Publishing, 2006.
[the ASL 2 version published at the end of 2009]

NEN 3434:2007
Standard for application management. Organizations can be certified, based on NEN 3434
NEN.

Strategisch beheer van Informatievoorziening met ASL en BiSL
Remko van der Pols
Application management textbook, with ASL and BiSL as starting points.
Academic Service, 2005.

Nieuwe Informatievoorziening: informatieplanning en IT in de 21e eeuw
Remko van der Pols
Approach and tooling for creating an information strategy and information planning based on replacement and renewal.
Academic Service, 2003.

ASL Self-assessment
Kees Deurloo, Remko van der Pols en René Sieders.
A booklet containing propositions that organizations can use to initiate an analysis based on the ASL framework and maturity levels as a basis for process improvement. The self-assessment follows the NEN 3434 maturity levels.
Academic Service, 2004.

BiSL, a framework for Business Information Management
Remko van der Pols, Ralph Donatz en Frank van Outvorst
Description of the BiSL-framework.
Van Haren Publishing, 2005.

BiSL, a management guide
Remko van der Pols en Yvette Backer
A management summary of ASL.
Van Haren Publishing, 2006.

De kleine ITIL V3
Louk Peters, Maarten Bordewijk, Jeroen Ermers.
Not actually little, as the title suggests, but a very thorough book about ITIL, version 3.
Academic Service, 2008.

Manage! Organizing IT demand and IT supply
Theo Thiadens
A manual for organizing IT and information management etc.
Van Haren Publishing, 2008.

www.aslbislfoundation.org
The official website of the ASL BiSL Foundation. Here you will find the best practices, as well as a great many publications and a glossary.

Index

A

acceptation test 87, 91
access path analysis 55
account & market definition 180
a change proposal 100
ACM 149
adjusting 115
agreements 142
analyzing 115
application lifecycle management . . .163
application maintenance 6
Application maintenance 7
application management 6
application objects 104
application-oriented 33
application policy 170
application portfolio management . . .168
association arrangement 119
availability management 216

B

business case .137
buyer 194

C

calamities 60
capabilities 185
capabilities definition 176, 184
capacity 124
capacity management 53, 216
chain 158
change 98
change management 98
change package 82, 107
change set .82, 106
character 116
cleanup 55
CMDB 48
commercial apparatus 180
comparability 18
complaints 43
configuration management 47
Configuration Management Database 48
connecting processes 30
Connectivity 18
consumer 41, 116
consumer organizations strategy 155
contact tools 180
continuity 59
continuity management 59
contract 120
contract management 116
contractor 215
Controllability .18
control processes 34
cost pass-on structure 138
cost structure .138
critical success factors 198

D

denormalization 55
dependability 52
dependency analyses 60
design 75
development method 77
development methods 66
development tools 152
directive 34

E

emergency fallback 60
emergency procedure 99
evaluating 115
executable 48
executive processes 34
expertise .184, 185
external business case 22
external quality 20
external suppliers 193

F

failure 42
features 152
financial management 136

Flexibility. 18
framework agreements 120
framework contract 217
fraud. 60
functional design 75
functionality 118
Functional maintenance 7
functional system test. 86
function points 127

G
goals 198

I
implementation. 90
improper use 60
incident control. 27
incident management. 27
incident management processes 41
instructions 43
interfaces 118
internal business case. 23
ISPL 142

L
logical design. .75
logistic process 104
logistics chain 156

M
main contractor. 194
maintenance 30
manageability .53
management criteria 132
management processes 111
management resources 152
maturity levels. 206
means. 55, 198
mission 198
modernization. .30
modification portfolio 171
monitoring. 115
MTTR 53

N
necessity to set up processes 205
NEN 3434 206

O
OCM 32, 175
operational change portfolio. 112
operational ICT management. 51
operational level 30
operation assignment. 92
operations realization 56
operation test .87
organization. .131

P
partial use 8
partners 176
partnership 194
patches 43
performance in operational situations. 51
performance management. 55
planning. 115
planning and control 124
proactive communication 41
problem 43
process 131
processing 52
product. 131
Product Breakdown Structure 127
production test 87
productivity factors 127
product-market combination 180
proof-of-concept. 195
prototyping 76

Q
quality management. 131
quality monitoring 133
quality plan 134
quality planning 133
quality review 133
quality system 131

R

realization 81
release 98
reliability 52
Reliability 18
renewal. 25
resource management 54
Reuse 8
rollout. 132

S

scope ACM 151
SDDB. 49
security. 60
security management 216
service 119
service delivery database. 49
service delivery definition 197
service-oriented 33
sharing of information 28
shipment. 107
software documentation 81
software management and distribution
104
sources 48
specification. 75
standardisation .8
strategic 34
strategic change portfolio 112
strategies 198

subcontractor .194
suitability. 53
supplier definition. 176
suppliers. 193
supplier's contract management 141

T

tactical change portfolio 112
target group. 41
Technical maintenance 7
technical system test. 86
technology definition 188
test 85
test cases 86
tuning. 55

U

ublic domain 28
Understandability. 18
unit test 86
use-cases 77
user support. 40

V

vulnerability studies. 60

W

wishes. 43
workload 54
workload management. 54